THE CUSTOM BODY ERA

THE CUSTOM BODY ERA

Hugo Pfau

SOUTH BRUNSWICK AND NEW YORK: A. S. BARNES AND COMPANY
LONDON: THOMAS YOSELOFF LTD

A. S. Barnes and Co., Inc.
Cranbury, New Jersey 08512

Thomas Yoseloff Ltd
108 New Bond Street
London W1Y OQX, England

SBN 498 06767 X

Printed in the United States of America

To my wife,
Irene,
who not only encouraged me
but read the manuscript.

Contents

THE CUSTOM BODY ERA

PART IV

PART V

PART VI

Foreword

The idea of writing this book came to me a couple of years ago when I realized both that there was a considerable interest in the period and in the automobiles it spawned, and in the people responsible for them, and that very little authentic information was readily available.

Having discussed the project with several people, and absorbed the response to some magazine articles I wrote on the subject, I have finally sat down to work on it.

A small part of the material has previously appeared in *Motor Trend* magazine, and I thank the Petersen Publishing Company for permission to use it, in somewhat revised form.

Acknowledgments

I said in my introduction that I was compiling this history while some of the people who participated in it were still alive. I must start my list of acknowledgments with the names of those who died while the manuscript was in progress—Bob Bohaty, John B. Judkins, Max Kade, Fred Moskovics and "Barney" Roos.

While much of the material comes from my memory and from my own files, I have been given access to the archives of the Amesbury Public Library, The New York Public Library, The Automotive Collection of the Free Library of Philadelphia, The Automotive History Collection of the Detroit Public Library, the library of the Automobile Manufacturers Association, and the Research Library of Harrah's Automobile Collection. To all of these my thanks.

Some former associates have also been consulted, Tom Hibbard, Ralph Roberts and R. L. Stickney of LeBaron; Rudy Creteur of Rollson; Enos Derham; and John Dobben of John B. Judkins Company.

I also wish to thank the many individuals who have helped with information or comments. Alvin Arnheim, Jim Bradley, Mary Cattie, Bill Gibson, Herb Lozier, Mike Lamm, Al Michaelian, Ed Robinson and Ray Wolff come to mind, as well as Floyd Marshall and George Moffitt, who supplied some of my illustrations. I should really thank all the membership of the Classic Car Club, the Antique Car Club, the Pierce-Arrow Society, and similar groups, but most especially Bob Turnquist.

THE CUSTOM BODY ERA

PART I

PART 1

1
The Background

THE finest automobiles the world has ever seen were produced during the 1920s and early 1930s. Perhaps I am influenced in this opinion by the fact that I contributed somewhat to the period, as a member of the staff of LeBaron, but I honestly feel that in many respects they have not been surpassed.

For one thing, the choice of truly fine cars was much greater than at any time since. There were a dozen fine chassis being built in America, and those who wished could select from at least another dozen from abroad. The best of these were fitted with coachwork from a number of fine body builders here or in Europe. Competition led not only to improvement in design but to the development of quality to the highest standards.

There were a number of small to medium sized manufacturers of both chassis and bodies, staffed by master craftsmen, who were dedicated to the ideal of building the best rather than simply the most.

At the same time prices (and also income taxes) were far lower than they are today. The cheapest cars on the market cost less than a quarter of the price of the cheapest American car today. By the same measurement a car custom built to the standards of, say, a Hispano-Suiza town car of 1929, worth somewhat over $20,000 at the time, would cost three to four times as much today. Not many of even our leading citizens would consider spending $60,000 or $75,000 for a new car.

Most of the establishments engaged in custom building have long since gone out of business, and their records have been lost or destroyed. I have decided to compile this history while some of my friends who had a hand in the achievements of the time are still alive.

2
The Beginning

CUSTOM body building was not a new idea of the twenties. Many of the earliest automobiles were custom built—one of a kind—simply because there was not yet enough demand nor sufficient technology to support quantity production. It is a matter of record that Gottlieb Daimler's first automobile was a gasoline engine and drive gear that he installed in a coach he had ordered for this purpose, but without revealing his plans to the coach builder. He merely specified that the vehicle be built for maximum strength and durability.

During the ensuing years, many coach builders became automobile manufacturers. Their talents for building attractive and luxurious vehicles were simply transferred from horse-drawn to motor-powered ones. Brewster, Cunningham, and McFarlan, among others, were names which began as carriage builders and continued as important makers of luxury motor cars.

Other carriage builders became the body builders of the automobile age. Some who had mass-produced wagons and carriages became production body-builders. Studebaker entered the automobile field building bodies for electric cars, and only later built complete automobiles, first electric and then gasoline powered.

Northern Indiana had a number of other wagon and carriage firms, and many of them became automobile manufacturers. In the mid-twenties, this area boasted quite a few plants that assembled chassis out of various available components and fitted them with bodies of their own make. They hadn't supplied the horses for their wagons, and now they bought their engines from Lycoming, Continental, and others.

Amesbury, Massachusetts, was for many years a center of the coachbuilding industry in the East. In fact, one section of town became known as "Carriage Hill" because so many of the factories were established there. Currier & Cameron in Amesbury built the body for the first Stanley Steamer in 1894, and many of the subsequent ones for the cars as-

1899 Locomobile Steam Car. Photograph by the author at First Annual Swap Meet, Reno, Nevada, 1965.

sembled in the nearby city of Lawrence.

The cars which Colonel Pope of Hartford showed at the Horseless Carriage Show in Boston in 1898, possibly America's first automobile show, also had bodies from Currier & Cameron. The early Locomobile steam cars, built in Boston from the Stanley brothers' designs, were fitted with bodies from the Briggs Carriage Company, also in Amesbury.

Biddle & Smart, Walker and Hume all started in Amesbury, and over the years the first of these absorbed many of the smaller factories there. Judkins began in what was then called West Amesbury and later renamed Merrimac. There will be more on these fine names in later chapters.

Charles Duryea built the first car in America in 1892, in Massachusetts, followed a year later by the Apperson Brothers, who built a car designed by Elwood Haynes in their factory in Kokomo, Indiana. I can recall being taught in school as a boy that Haynes invented the automobile, but since then it has been established that Duryea preceded him, and of course both Daimler and Benz built their first cars in Germany even earlier, in 1886.

Charles B. King is credited with driving a four-cylinder car in Detroit in 1894, possibly the first with that many cylinders. Alexander Winton built his first car in Cleveland in 1896, and is reputed to have made the first sale of an automobile in this country, in 1898.

By this time, both Daimler and Benz were producing cars in Germany, and Daimler had licensed Panhard & Levassor to use his patents in France. Panhard in turn licensed Peugeot to build automobiles under these patents in 1890, and these proved so successful they began to make their own a year later.

In England, the Daimler Motor Company was formed in 1896, and one of the first problems was to encourage repeal of the archaic "locomotive laws." These had required that any self-propelled vehicle on a public road must be preceded by a man on foot with a red flag. The success of the campaign for repeal is still celebrated with the annual London-to-Brighton Run.

William Steinway, the piano manufacturer, was much interested and acquired the American rights to Daimler's patents. Through his efforts, Daimler exhibited his cars at the Chicago World's Fair in 1893. Later some were built here by the American Mercedes Company, in which the Steinway family had a substantial interest. The works were not far from their piano factory, on Steinway Street in Long Island City, New York.

DeDion-Bouton was another early car maker in France. Starting with rather large steam cars in the 1890s, they switched to gasoline soon after, and developed the unique rear axle construction which has recently found favor again.

The early automobile bodies were much like the carriages which the same firms were still building. Frames of wood were paneled in plywood. Most of the early cars were similar to the buggies of the period, with an engine attached somewhere, often in the rear or under the seat. A few closed cars were

An early closed automobile, built by Judkins on Columbia Electric chassis. Note driver's seat as on a horse-drawn hansom cab. From catalog of John B. Judkins & Co.

built, and these looked much like the closed horse-drawn carriages of the time.

When Wilhelm Maybach developed a new design for Daimler in 1901, which became known as the Mercedes, he incorporated for the first time many of the basic ideas that have continued to this day. The engine was in front, with a radiator and a metal cover, which we call a hood and our English friends call a bonnet.

With this change, more metal panelling came into use. E. R. Thomas has been credited with introducing the metal-covered body to America in 1903. By 1905, Pierce-Arrow was using cast aluminum body sections. However, wood frames were still being used to form the basic structure of the body, and these were retained for many years.

Recently I saw a Victor steam car in my late friend Robert Bohaty's garage. It had an all-metal body which Bob, who was considered rather an expert in these matters, felt sure was original. The car had been built in 1901, and a little research in Floyd Clymer's book on steam automobiles revealed that this company, formed in 1900, had indeed offered all-metal—and therefore fireproof—vehicles from the start.

The first all-steel closed bodies were developed by the Budd Manufacturing Company in Philadelphia, based on their experience with railroad cars, and introduced on the Dodge of the early twenties. Over the next few years, this type of construction became

"Luxury attained new heights in the brougham of 1890," says the caption from catalog of John B. Judkins & Co.

the standard for production models. Although safety was stressed in the early advertising for all-steel bodies, I believe their general adoption was based more on their lower cost in volume production.

Wood remained the principal material for the frames of custom bodies and those for the more limited volume expensive cars. Here again, cost was a factor. In limited production or for an individually built body, wood could be shaped more cheaply than steel. The cost of expensive dies is nominal when spread over hundreds of thousands of cars, but prohibitive on a single unit or even a few hundred.

Later on, in the mid-to-late thirties, many so-called custom bodies were, of necessity, merely modifications of standard bodies. The need for lower prices dictated that the steel framework be retained as far as possible, with perhaps a new superstructure added. Town cars and convertibles were frequently made out of sedan bodies with some or all of the upper section removed, and a new wood framework built up over the remainder.

Since the last World War, even less custom building has been done, and much of this has been confined to less drastic modifications. Often only the interior has differed from the standard bodies.

The cost of building a completely individual body from scratch would be prohibitive today. Conversations with the few people still engaged in related activities lead to a quick guess of a price somewhere in excess of $30,000. Anyone who has attempted a thorough restoration in recent years will be aware of the expense involved.

3
My Start

JUST about every designer I have ever known started drawing automobiles at a relatively early age, and became sufficiently proficient to earn a living at it.

I had, perhaps, a slight advantage in that my family had a car at a fairly early stage of the industry—1915. My father felt it would be useful to his business, and since owning a car involved some hazards in those days, he sent my brother to a special course being given at the West Side Y.M.C.A. in New York. This included classes not only in driving but in automobile repair, a necessary complement since service stations were few and far between.

Having successfully passed the examination for his chauffeur's license, my brother set out to find a suitable car within our limited budget. It turned up in the shape of a 1913 Pope-Hartford with various ailments. My brother spent several weeks repairing it, after which it did regular service for a few years. It was quite reliable and large enough to serve as a delivery vehicle. It was a big seven-passenger touring

1912 Pope-Hartford Touring Car. The author's family's first car was similar, but with a longer body to accommodate seven passengers. Photograph from the owner, Harrah's Automobile Collection.

car, with Westinghouse Air Springs that gave a comfortable ride.

An unbroken succession of other cars followed, including an Overland, a Willys-Knight V-8, and a Hudson Super Six among others. It did not take me long to realize that some of our neighbors had more attractive cars—one had a Mercer touring car and another a Kissel Speedster. Soon I decided that I could draw an even better looking one, and by the time I was 11 or 12 much of my spare time was spent at this task.

One of my sisters was engaged to a chap who had just graduated from Stuyvesant High School, the first technical high school in New York, and suggested that I go there. It offered a variety of courses in both freehand and mechanical drawing and was an ideal training ground for my planned career.

Incidentally, this brother-in-law, Herbert Wiertz, had a step-father who had been a locomotive engineer on the New York Central. His first car was a Locomobile steamer, followed by what he always called his "One-Lung" Cadillac. Later he had a 1909 Cadillac with copper water jackets on its four cylinders.

1909 Cadillac Touring Car, owned by Mr. William Chamberlain, photographed about 1912. Photograph from Mr. Herbert Wiertz, shown at the wheel.

I was still drawing cars, and found particularly useful a course in Ship Design, which I believe was the only one ever offered in an American High School. It lasted as long as its instructor, A. H. Brenzinger, was available. Besides learning how to develop the lines of a ship's hull, which was later helpful in working out the lines of an automobile body, I also acquired the knack of reproducing a

"ship's curve," the wood or celluloid pieces we used to guide our pencils. One of them proved particularly useful for my scale drawings at LeBaron, and I still have it.

Somewhere during my early High School days, a contest was announced in connection with the New York Automobile Show, then held at Grand Central Palace. A prize was to be awarded for the best original design submitted. I went down with some drawings under my arm, but since I was only in my early teens at the time, I had some difficulty persuading anyone that I was a serious entrant. I finally did get to show my drawings to someone connected with the contest, but they were not accepted as a formal entry.

1923 Isotta-Fraschini Roadster, designed by LeBaron, Carrossiers, and built by The Clayton Company. This car was exhibited at the 1923 Show of the Foreign Automotive Association.

As you can imagine, I was haunting automobile shows at this period. When I heard that the Foreign Automotive Association was to hold one at the Astor Hotel in November 1923, I determined to see it. This show competed with the Salon for that one year, and was run in the same manner. I can remember being particularly impressed by two exhibits, that of Voisin (which included a rather racy, streamlined phaeton) and the LeBaron stand.

A week or so later, I approached a door in the building at 2 Columbus Circle, which bore the legend "LeBaron, Carrossiers," with another roll of drawings. They included one or two of those I had taken to Grand Central Palace and some more I had drawn since then. They seemed to impress Ray Dietrich, and after some discussion with him and Ralph Roberts, I was hired as a part-time office boy and apprentice.

Since I was attending school only in the mornings (there were double sessions because of overcrowding back in the early twenties, too), I would have lunch and then report to the LeBaron office for

1923 Isotta-Fraschini Sport Cabriolet, designed by
LeBaron, Carrossiers, and built by the Derham Body
Company. This car was exhibited at the 1923 New
York Salon.

1922 Lafayette Sedan-Limousine designed by LeBaron,
Carrossiers.

the rest of the afternoon. We worked Saturday mornings, too.

At this point, LeBaron was not yet building bodies in their own plant, but designing and engineering them, and then arranging to have them built by such custom shops as Clayton, Demarest, Healy or Locke in New York, or Derham in Philadelphia.

Most of the office space was taken up by two huge drafting tables, where the full size body drawings were prepared. One was used by Ray Dietrich, and the other by Frank W. Pease (later chief engineer for Hayes Body). Much of my education in body engineering came from them. Sometimes I was allowed to trace some portion of the body for which separate blueprints were needed.

In most cases, drawings were taken to the body shops by Dietrich personally, so that he could go over any details that needed explaining. Occasionally I got to deliver some detail drawings. Needless to say, these were most interesting visits, since I had the opportunity to see the actual construction in progress.

Near one of the windows overlooking 58th Street sat R. L. Stickney, who did some of the designing but spent much of his time producing the remarkably beautiful and accurate renderings which I do not

believe have ever been surpassed. I still have trouble persuading some of my friends that reproductions of these renderings are not photographs of the actual cars. Since a number of them are among the illustrations in these pages, you can judge for yourself.

A few feet away, I had a place for my own drawing board, and whenever there was free time I was encouraged to do a sketch. As I finished each one, someone on the staff would criticize it and offer suggestions for its improvement. I have one with the pencil marks Ray Dietrich made as he pointed out various features that particularly interested him.

Since light was more important for designers and draftsmen, the business portion of the office was near the door, farthest from the window. Ralph Roberts had his desk there, along with the secretary. Along a back wall stood a specially made filing cabinet with big flat drawers to hold sketches, blueprints, photographs and renderings.

That cabinet was moved to Detroit when we closed the New York office of LeBaron in 1930, and I checked on it immediately after the war. Like many similar items, the cabinet and its contents had been disposed of as scrap. A sad ending for what would now be a priceless collection.

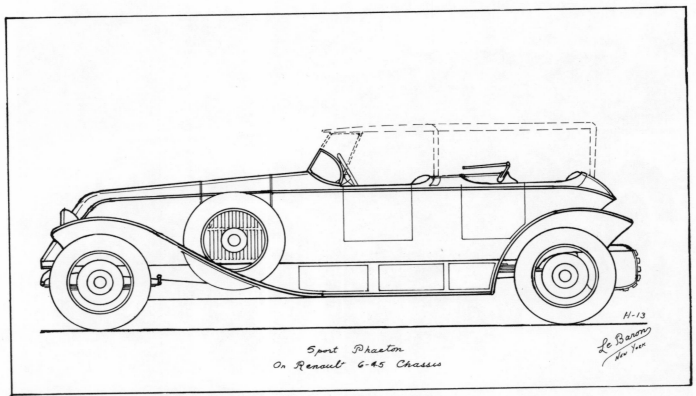

Sport Phaeton
On Renault 6-45 Chassis

H-13

Le Baron
New York

1925 Renault 45 Sport Phaeton. Original design by the author for LeBaron.

PART II

4
LeBaron

LeBaron

THE firm of LeBaron, Carrossiers, had been founded just a few years before, in the Spring of 1920.

Thomas L. Hibbard was, I believe, the leader in setting up the firm, although he had left for Paris a few months before I joined it. He had, as he wrote in a series of articles for *The Classic Car,* worked for Kimball & Co. in Chicago and for Leon Rubay in Cleveland, both early custom body builders, before entering the service in World War I. After trying unsuccessfully to obtain his discharge from the Army while still in France, in order to take a proffered job with Kellner & Cie., he returned to the United States and went to work as a draftsman with Brewster.

There he became friendly with his fellow draftsman, Raymond H. Dietrich, and together they formulated the idea of setting up a consulting firm to prepare designs and engineering drawings for bodies, in the same way an architect performs these services for a building. In some cases the drawings were sold outright, but more often they arranged to supervise the building of the body for a fee, again following the architect's practice of charging a percentage of the selling price of the body.

They chose the name LeBaron, Carrossiers, for its French flair. Carrossiers is the French word for carriage builders.

Soon after they set up the firm, they were joined by Ralph Roberts, who had met Hibbard while working at Rubay during summer vacations. He waited until he graduated from Dartmouth to become an active member of the firm.

Late in 1921, Ray Dietrich took a leave of absence from LeBaron to spend a few months as a consultant to the Smith-Springfield Body Company in Massachusetts. He spent several months there helping to design and engineer bodies for the new Rolls-Royce Corporation of America, which was just starting to build chassis in a nearby factory.

In the Spring of 1923, Tom Hibbard left for Paris to see what business could be found there and also to check on the possibility of having bodies built in Europe. He wound up in a partnership with Howard Darrin and did not return to the firm although he still had an interest in it.

A few months earlier, William C. Durant had purchased the Locomobile Company as one of the units of his challenge to General Motors (which he had assembled but lost control of during the 1921 deflation). He immediately engaged LeBaron to design a new series of bodies for it. Locomobile was at this time America's most prestigious car. Bodies were built individually or in small series, and prices for the complete car ranged from $10,000 up.

Since the Locomobile factory was in Bridgeport, Connecticut, many of the bodies were built by either of the two local concerns, the Blue Ribbon Body Company or the Bridgeport Body Company. The close contact with Locomobile brought frequent

1923 Packard Convertible Sedan, designed by LeBaron, Carrossiers, from their advertisement in catalog of the Foreign Automotive Association Show, 1923.

1924 Wills Ste. Claire Town Cabriolet, designed by LeBaron, Carrossiers. This is a photograph of a rendering by R. L. Stickney.

visits, especially by Dietrich, to these body builders. Early in 1924, a merger was proposed by the Bridgeport Body Company.

The resulting firm shortened the name to LeBaron, Inc. Its first officers were C. W. Seward, President (a post he had held with Bridgeport Body); Raymond H. Dietrich, Vice-president, Chief Engineer and Sales Manager; Ralph Roberts, Secretary; and J. H. Hinman, Treasurer and Works Manager. Now for the first time LeBaron had facilities for building the bodies they designed.

The original announcement mentioned that Thomas L. Hibbard would "continue to handle the foreign business of the company from his headquarters at 12 Rue de Berri in Paris." At this time, he had already formed his partnership with Darrin, but a friendly relationship continued over the following years.

R. L. Stickney had joined LeBaron near the end of 1922. He had worked at Locomobile under Frank deCausse, and they both left when that company went into receivership before the Durant purchase. DeCausse set up a consulting business similar to LeBaron's. Stickney went first to Locke & Co. for a few months, then moved to LeBaron.

1923 Lincoln Town Cabriolet, designed by LeBaron. The first bodies of this design, #917, were built by Demarest or Derham, but later ones at the newly acquired LeBaron plant in Bridgeport.

In the Spring of 1925, Ray Dietrich succumbed to the blandishments of Detroit and left LeBaron to set up a new firm there under his own name. It was sponsored and financed by the Murray Corporation, who were building a considerable share of the bodies for Lincoln, Packard, and other fine cars. While they had set up a design studio under the very capable direction of Amos Northup, who had just left Wills Ste. Claire to join Murray, they felt it desirable to be associated with the prestige of a custom body firm as well as to get Dietrich's services as a consultant.

During this time, I continued my part-time association with LeBaron, except for a few months early in 1925 when I resigned temporarily to devote more time to my extracurricular activities at Stuyvesant. I also wanted to decide for myself whether to continue my education or to accept the standing offer of a full-time job with LeBaron.

I can still recall Ralph Roberts's strong arguments against my going to college. He pointed out that most of his former Dartmouth classmates had become bond or insurance salesmen. I know that every week one or more of them came to see him in this connection.

My personal drawing board was still in the LeBaron office, and whenever I had time I was welcome to drop in and do some sketching. I did enter the College of Engineering of New York University in the Fall of 1925, but after a few weeks I felt I would be better off with LeBaron and I left college to return to my career there.

In the Summer of 1967, my wife and I visited Mr. and Mrs. Ralph Roberts, now living in retirement in a beautiful home in Pasadena, California. He reminded me that he had once arranged to have me awakened every morning by the telephone operator of the Biltmore Hotel. My family had gone to Europe for a month or two, and I had great difficulty getting myself up in the morning. For a few days, Roberts himself called me to make sure I was out of bed, but then a friend of his who was assistant manager of the Biltmore at the time suggested that their operator call me just as she did the hotel guests. It was arranged in some way, and the calls continued for several weeks until my family returned.

Early in 1926 I realized that there were some mysterious things going on behind the scenes. They took some time to mature, but at the end of the year it was announced that LeBaron had been purchased by the Briggs Manufacturing Company, then the largest body builders in Detroit. Soon afterwards we

1928 Lincoln All-Weather Town Cabriolet by Le-Baron. From Roslyn Motors advertisement in 1927 New York Salon catalog.

left our rather dingy quarters at 2 Columbus Circle for smaller but more luxurious space at 724 Fifth Avenue, between 56th and 57th Streets. Just recently the Columbus Circle building was finally torn down to make way for Huntington Hartford's art museum.

Ever since the merger with Bridgeport Body, the space-consuming drafting tables had been moved to the factory and our activities in New York were confined to scale drawings, specifications, and, of course, Stickney's renderings. To facilitate his work, a special north window was cut into the wall of our new office, overlooking a setback of the adjoining Heckscher Building. It is still there.

For a while, Ralph Roberts commuted between New York and Detroit, but he soon set up his permanent headquarters at the Briggs plant, under the name of LeBaron Studios. Here he collected a staff of young designers to work primarily on production designs for Briggs. They developed many of the Model A and later Fords, most Chryslers from 1930 on, as well as bodies for Stutz, Graham-Paige and other Briggs customers.

At the same time, one of the Briggs plants on Meldrum Avenue in Detroit was set aside for the building of custom and small-series bodies. A new corporation, the LeBaron-Detroit Company, was formed to operate this.

While the nameplates still being used at the Bridgeport plant read simply "LeBaron," in a stylized script, those for the Detroit plant were rectangular with the name "LeBaron-Detroit Company" engraved on them. During 1931, after the Bridgeport plant had been closed, some of the bodies built in Detroit carried the earlier style script nameplate until their supply was used up.

While I left LeBaron at the end of 1931, as part of a large-scale retrenchment at that time, I have discussed the affairs of the firm over the next few years with some of the people who remained, including Ralph Roberts, the only one of the original three partners who was still part of the firm, at least until the start of World War II.

At the end of 1931, there were still a fair number of Stutz, Pierce-Arrow and Packard bodies in process, as well as a goodly portion of the Stutz and Marmon 16 standard bodies, which had been built but not finished in the LeBaron-Detroit plant. It took several years to work these off, and at least some of them

1929 Stutz Blackhawk Town Car by LeBaron. One of the earliest individual bodies from the LeBaron-Detroit plant, shown at the 1928 Salon.

1936 Packard Town Car by LeBaron. Portions of this body were adapted from the standard Packard sedan. Photograph by the author at Classic Car Club meeting, Buck Hill Falls, Pennsylvania, January 1967. The owner of the car, Mr. Louis Gravel of Montreal, is at the wheel.

were never completed because the chassis makers went into bankruptcy.

At the same time production continued on the Lincoln Convertible Roadsters for some years, with various modifications of the design for succeeding chassis models. A few Lincoln and Packard town cars were built, as well as limousines on the same chassis. The latter were essentially their standard sedans with partitions added and more luxurious interiors installed.

About this time, Alvan Macaulay, Jr. became active in Packard styling, and a number of bodies he designed were built by the LeBaron-Detroit Company although they carried nameplates of the Packard Custom Body Division. LeBaron also designed some new Packards—town cars, phaetons and a boattail roadster—during the early thirties.

By the late thirties, completely custom bodies had almost ceased to be built, and even town cars were created by modifying production sedan bodies. With the advent of World War II, the LeBaron plant was shut down and converted to some form of war production. As mentioned, at this time all the records, designs and photographs there, including those I had moved out from New York in 1930, were disposed of. Custom body production ceased for the duration, never again to resume in the old manner.

Ralph Roberts's design studio also shut down, but rather than accept a minor position for the duration he resigned and moved to California to join Lockheed Aircraft. After the war he formed a partnership with a young engineer who was an expert on fiberglass. Much of their work was experimental, and as Roberts put it, not more profitable than the custom body business in the twenties. Soon this partnership

was dissolved as his associate moved into consulting work, and Roberts retired.

In the meantime, Alvin Pranz, who had been the interior specialist for LeBaron Studios in Detroit, took charge of their entire activity as normal business returned after the war. He was largely responsible for the development of methods of bonding wood veneer to steel which resulted in the Chrysler Town and Country models of the early post-war era.

When Walter Briggs died in the late forties, his son had no desire to continue the business. All bodybuilding activities were sold to the Chrysler Corporation. Along with these went the rights to the name "LeBaron," which had been registered as a trademark by Briggs sometime during the 1930s.

One of our neighbors at 2 Columbus Circle back in the early twenties was the Fleetwood Metal Body Company. It is rather ironic that this is just about the only other surviving name from the custom body era, although in my estimation neither the Fleetwood Cadillacs nor the LeBaron Chryslers of recent years are truly comparable with the product of either firm in its heyday.

5
Brewster & Co.

BREWSTER & CO.

DURING the 1920s, there were a number of custom body builders in New York City, many of whom had been carriage builders earlier. Brewster & Company were probably the most famous, and rightly so, for they introduced many innovations, while at the same time maintaining the highest standards of quality.

The firm was started by James Brewster in 1810 at 52 Broad Street, not far from the present site of the New York Stock Exchange. Later they moved "uptown" to Broome Street, and at the turn of the century they were located on Broadway just above Times Square, close to what was to become Automobile Row.

In 1910, when the firm was 100 years old, Brewster put up a rather sizeable factory on Queensboro Plaza in Long Island City, which still stands. Part of the building is now occupied by Andrea Radio & Television, the company started by Frank A. d'Andrea after his earlier "FADA" radio company had been sold to other interests. The bronze Brewster nameplate is still on a corner of the building.

At the beginning of 1926, the family sold out to the Rolls-Royce Company of America, and served the dual purpose of being the New York Branch of the Springfield firm and its principal source of coachwork. William Brewster, grandson of the founder, became a vice-president of Rolls-Royce.

Earlier, Brewster had been the importer of the English Lanchester, and at various times had also sold Rolls-Royce, Packard, and Marmon chassis with Brewster bodies. These ventures followed the demise of the Brewster car, which had been much admired for town use early in the century.

The Brewster automobile had a four-cylinder sleeve-valve engine of the Knight type, very smooth and quiet, mounted in a relatively short chassis with

1921 Brewster Panel Brougham on the 4-cylinder Brewster chassis.

1921 Rolls-Royce Touring Phaeton by Brewster.

a narrow turning radius. Most of those I recall were fitted with elegant town car bodies, although there were other body styles including an occasional roadster. They were distinguished by an oval radiator that contrasted nicely with the usually rather severe body lines. In the early twenties they sold for $7,900 for the roadster and somewhat over $10,000 for town cars.

After the Depression started, Brewster arranged to build a series of town cars on modified Ford V-8 chassis, with a very unusual heart-shaped radiator shell. These were not available through Ford dealers, but could be purchased only directly from Brewster. A number of these cars are still in existence, but I always feel a twinge of pain when I hear them referred to as "Brewsters." A few similar bodies were mounted on Buick and Packard chassis during the mid-thirties, and possibly some of those which had originally been built on Fords were later remounted on other chassis.

William Brewster was a hard taskmaster and kept a close eye on everything that went on in his shop. I have been told that he always carried a metal scriber in the pocket of the striped trousers that, with a morning coat, made up his regular working costume. As he walked through the paint shop, he would cast a penetrating look at each body. If he were not satisfied with the finish on any panel, he would make a big "X" with his scriber. Since this dug through several layers of paint, it meant quite a bit of extra work for the painter at fault. They rarely made the same mistake twice.

During the early twenties, the Brewster plant was being run by Henry Crecelius, who could qualify as an expert craftsman himself, having started at Locomobile. He was also a perfectionist who insisted that every detail be of the high quality that the name Brewster had always stood for. After Rolls-Royce bought Brewster, he became Chief Body Engineer for Lincoln.

In those days of nearly vertical windshields and windows, glare was quite a problem. Since many of Brewster's bodies were used extensively in town, this was a matter of some consequence to them. Reflections from street lights, shop windows and other cars could be a hazard.

Brewster did considerable research and experimenting on this subject, and came up with some widely copied solutions. The best known was generally called a "Brewster Windshield" in the trade. It was copied not only by other custom builders but on quite a few production models both here and abroad. There was a lower windshield pane that sloped slightly forward, with an upper one canted sharply to the rear. The side frames holding these were fitted with an odd-shaped piece of glass, an irregular trapezoid, and the frames themselves extended upward to support an outside visor.

Another version a bit later had a single windshield pane sloping forward toward the top. The first of these had a separate side pane, but later this was improved by using a cast pillar to hold the windshield with a matching one at the front of the door. This improved the visibility considerably, and Brewster obtained a patent on the design. Both types had been conceived with the idea that the angle of the glass would reflect unwanted light away from the driver's line of vision.

Another Brewster innovation was their oil finish, introduced in 1906. In those pre-lacquer days, the best varnish paint job did not last too long. Brewster concocted a formula that contained no varnish and did not dry out completely. It lasted much longer. It could be distinguished by the brush marks, which remained visible, but which with Brewster's craftsmanship enhanced the appearance of the car. Repeated polishing gradually smoothed them. Many

1926 Rolls-Royce Canterbury Sedan by Brewster. This shows the earlier type of Brewster windshield. Reproduction of illustration by R. L. Stickney for Rolls-Royce catalog.

PICCADILLY

1926 Rolls-Royce Silver Ghost Pall Mall Roadster. Reproduction of R. L. Stickney rendering for Rolls-Royce catalog.

1926 Rolls-Royce Silver Ghost Pickwick Sedan. Reproduction of R. L. Stickney rendering for Rolls-Royce catalog.

PICKWICK

1929 Packard Sport Phaeton by Holbrook, exhibited at 1928 New York Salon. Reproduced from Holbrook advertisement in Salon catalog.

1930 Lincoln Lady's Town Brougham, from LeBaron catalog for 1929 Salon. This was a special design for the Paris Salon.

1930 Hispano-Suiza Convertible Phaeton. This was a special design for the LeBaron Salon catalog, but is similar to the Duesenberg pictured with Chapter 22.

BUCKINGHAM

1926 Rolls-Royce Buckingham Sedan by Brewster. Windshield is later type patented by William Brewster. Another Stickney illustration from Rolls-Royce catalog.

other body builders tried to copy this finish, but I do not believe any ever succeeded completely. The formula was a closely guarded secret.

While Brewster, like their competitors, would paint a car almost any color the customer desired, one of their most popular colors was Brewster Green, a soft medium-dark shade with the added advantage of being almost glare-free. In those days the aim of a good town car was unostentatious elegance.

Many wealthy families had a distinctive color for their carriages during the nineteenth century, so they could be readily identified. Brewster had many customers for whom they had been building carriages for several generations, and when they began building town cars for the same people, often the color scheme of the family's carriages was continued on their automobiles.

After the business was sold to Rolls-Royce, most of the body work for this chassis was transferred to Springfield, and the Long Island City plant was used only for strictly custom bodies and for repair work. In 1928, however, the body-building for Rolls was moved back to the Long Island City Building, partly because many of Brewster's best craftsmen were not

happy in Springfield and wanted to return to their homes in New York.

About this time, too, the designing chores were taken over by Carl Beck and some young assistants, who produced much more advanced ideas. After 1931, production of Rolls-Royces was discontinued in this country but the body business under the Brewster name continued for some few years, largely concentrating on the relatively inexpensive town cars mentioned earlier.

Brewster was one of the very few body builders who sold complete cars almost exclusively, rather than just bodies. As mentioned, they were appointed dealers for several makes, which they sold only with Brewster bodies. Even the town cars on modified Ford chassis were available only directly from Brewster, not through Ford dealers.

Although most of the family no longer had any connection with the firm after the business was sold to Rolls-Royce, Henry Brewster returned to the body business briefly in 1927. He had been associated with other firms as a designer earlier, but in that year he formed a partnership with Harry Holbrook, who had recently sold his interest in the Holbrook Company. They took over the former Blue Ribbon body plant in Bridgeport, under the name of the Holbrook-Brewster Company. A few bodies of rather daring design were built, notably some Mercedes for the following Salon, but the venture was undercap-

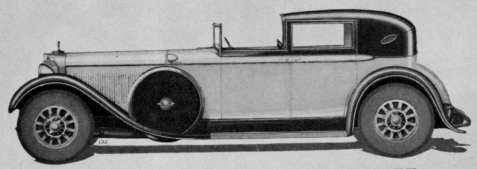

MERCEDES BENZ COMPANY
INC.
247 PARK AVENUE
AT 47TH STREET

THE FULL COLLAPSIBLE CABRIOLET
Connotative of Dignity and Discrimination

Embodying the latest and greatest achievements of MERCEDES engineers and the distinctive
detailed body appointments of THE H. F. HOLBROOK · HENRY BREWSTER CORPORATION.

italized and closed within the year.

During World War II, one of the Brewsters was building pontoons for seaplanes. The experience with forming aluminum, acquired during custom body days, was used to good advantage.

1928 Mercedes-Benz Town Cabriolet by Holbrook-Brewster. From their advertisment in 1927 New York Salon Catalog, where this car was exhibited.

6
Locke and other New York Firms

RIGHT along with Brewster as a criterion of conservative quality workmanship was Locke & Company.

J. Vinton Locke started as an apprentice with Healy just after he graduated from Hamilton College in the 1890s. Soon afterwards he moved to Demarest & Co., where within a few years he became their superintendent. In 1902 he obtained financial backing from the Fleischmann family and opened his own shop. By the mid-twenties, Locke & Co. had a modern factory at East 56th Street and York Avenue in New York City.

For a time, Locke, too, sold complete automobiles. They were the importers of the French Hotchkiss, which in the days not long after World War I was advertised as "Made by the manufacturers of the famous Hotchkiss Machine Gun."

In 1925, Locke obtained some orders for several small series of bodies for Franklin. These were followed by similar series orders for the Chrysler "80" and the Lincoln. To accommodate the increased production, a larger factory was purchased in Rochester, in January 1926.

About the same time, they obtained the services of Wellington Everett Miller, previously with Walter Murphy in California, and of John Tjaarda, a talented young Dutch designer who had also spent some time in California. Miller has since done a great deal of the work on the Floyd Clymer Scrap-

books, drawing in part on his experience not only with Locke, but with General Motors and later with Packard.

Another Locke designer, George Tasman, worked mainly in New York City until he moved to Rochester in 1928. In the thirties both he and John Tjaarda joined the LeBaron Studios in Detroit. There Tjaarda found a use for the experimental design for a proposed rear-engined car which he had worked out for Fred Duesenberg a few years before. It became the Lincoln Zephyr.

Unfortunately, Mr. Locke died suddenly at just about the time the Rochester plant went into production, and the nature of the company's business changed somewhat. A few individual bodies were still being built in New York, but most of the activity at the 56th Street shop was devoted to repainting and repair work. A properly maintained town car was repainted at least once a year, oftener if it spent the winter in Florida.

Both Locke and Brewster were experts in the application of cane panelling. In genuine French canework, paint composition was applied from a force-tube somewhat like those used by pastry chefs for cake decoration. The paint was purposely left rather thick, and applied over the lines of the pattern which had been chalked on the body. The pattern followed that of woven canework, and since the paint was quite thick it had much the same texture. This method was more durable than the use of actual woven cane, which was also available and which would be cemented to the body and sometimes loosened.

Another old carriage builder who went on to build automobile bodies was Healy & Co., where Mr. Locke had started his career.

They were especially noted for their elegant and unusual interiors. One of their favorites was a "beamed ceiling" effect, in which the framework of the roof was left exposed. Sometimes this was finished in natural wood color, but more frequently it was painted to match the headlining fabric, or even covered with the material itself wrapped closely

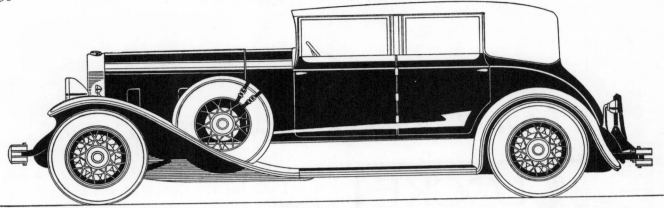

1930 Franklin Convertible Sedan by Locke. From
Franklin Custom Body Catalog, Floyd Marshall Collection.

1927 Lincoln Panel Brougham by Locke, exhibited at
1926 New York Salon. Lower half of rear portion of
body finished in painted canework.

1918 Cadillac Town Cabriolet by Healy. Photograph
courtesy Automobile Manufacturers Association.

around the wood framing.

Healy also did some excellent work with built-in vanity cases, and I can recall one of the Stevens-Duryeas at an auto show in 1921 that had diamond-shaped mirrors set into the inside quarter panels.

One of Healy's best customers was the New York Cadillac distributor, Inglis M. Uppercu. When the latter set up the Aeromarine Bus Company in the early twenties, Healy did most of the body work. These vehicles were predecessors of later airport buses. Healy gave up custom building in 1926 to concentrate on the bus business; he sold much of the equipment to Walter Murphy at the time. Unfortunately, they decided to merge with the bus company and it collapsed soon afterwards.

Demarest & Co., where Mr. Locke also worked for a time, had been carriage builders, too. Their shop was on East 72nd Street and there they built some of the early LeBaron-designed bodies, including the first Locomobile Sportif in 1923.

Demarest continued to build a few bodies well into the late twenties, but much of their work then was repairs, repainting, and remounting of bodies onto new chassis. They performed this latter service on several LeBaron bodies and I paid a number of visits to their plant in this connection. Often extensive rebuilding of the cowl and rear quarters was necessary to accommodate a differently shaped hood and a longer wheelbase. Fortunately the tendency was for chassis to grow longer each year, which made the

1922 Roamer Town Cabriolet by H. R. Chupurdy.

modifications to the doors and rear body panels a simpler operation.

The Clayton Company in the West 40s, Chupurdy & Co. on West 53rd Street, and F. R. Wood & Sons in Brooklyn were somewhat smaller but similar firms. Clayton also built some of the early LeBaron designs.

Wood had as their designer for a time young Henry Crecelius, Jr., who had learned his trade under his father at Brewster. Wood had built some of the early delivery trucks for John Wanamaker, probably the most attractive commercial vehicles on the streets of New York in the early part of the century. Later they concentrated on truck and bus bodies.

The Brooks-Ostruk Company was a bit further uptown, on West 65th Street. In addition to building bodies, they became agents here for the Minerva. By the mid-twenties, they had formed a rather close association with LeBaron and we did practically all of their body building. We had an arrangement whereby these were sold as "Body by Paul Ostruk," and I can remember signing his name to quite a few design sketches. Most of the Minervas still in existence, and reputed to have a Body by Ostruk, were actually designed and built by LeBaron.

One of the few survivors of those days is the Humer-Binder Company, still in existence although in a new location at 440 East 108th Street, near the East River. Today they are the agents here for the Golde Sliding Sunroofs, imported from Germany, and also do quite a bit of repair work and an occasional restoration.

When I visited them recently, Herman Binder mentioned that he had put a partition into a sedan just a few months earlier. He had had to crawl in and do the wood work himself because he no longer could find the skilled craftsmen needed. He is past 70 but still active although his son, Matthew, now

1924 Locomobile Town Car built by Demarest to design by LeBaron, and exhibited at 1923 New York Salon.

1924 Minerva Sedan-Limousine by LeBaron, sold as with "Body by Ostruk."

manages the business.

Apparently that was the last such job he tackled, however, since while editing this manuscript I was informed that he had told our local Chrysler dealer that he could no longer undertake such jobs.

I do not recall that Humer-Binder built many complete bodies in the twenties, but they were the New York repair depot for LeBaron. Often some adjustment was needed after a car had spent a month or two on the road, and if it could not conveniently be driven back to our plant in Bridgeport, we would have Humer-Binder take care of the problem at their place on 53rd Street.

In those days, the "El" ran across there, as the Sixth Avenue line swept westward to join the one on Ninth Avenue for the rest of the run up to the Polo Grounds. I can remember often interrupting a conversation with Herman Binder or a customer while

1928 Packard Town Cabriolet by Rollston, from their advertisement in 1927 New York Salon Catalog, where the car was exhibited.

a train rumbled by outside the window.

Another firm that survives, although in somewhat different form, is Rollston (now the Rollson Company). Started about the same time as LeBaron, in a shop on West 47th Street by Harry Lowenschein, the firm was particularly known for the excellence of its workmanship.

Rollston's finish was particularly admired by G. C. Parvis, custom body manager for Packard's New York branch. Many times he called me over to show me how nicely one of their bodies was upholstered, and to point out that he did not consider our work as good. It took several years, but we finally achieved what he conceded to be a comparable level of quality.

Since much of their work was for Packard, which has become a collector's favorite, quite a few Rollston bodies survive. In their early days, most of their bodies were town cars, but in the late twenties they developed a rather attractive Convertible Victoria and this kept them in business through the thirties, being a much more saleable type in those chauffeurless days.

In the late thirties, Mr. Lowenschein retired and the firm was reorganized by Rudy Creteur, who had been his designer and general manager. At the 1967 Grand Classic in Morristown, New Jersey, I was pleasantly surprised to see Mr. Lowenschein, now in his eighties, walking around with Rudy Creteur to see the cars on display.

During World War II, Rollson began making stainless steel galley equipment for submarines, and

1932 Duesenberg Convertible Victoria by Rollston.
From Duesenberg Catalog, Floyd Marshall Collection.

this type of work continues to be their main activity in a new plant in Plainview, New York. Among the items they manufacture are custom-built yacht windows. The hardware for these comes from the Rostand Mfg. Co., who had supplied most of the windshields, auxiliary seats and other components to Rollston, LeBaron and other custom body builders.

When Rudy Creteur showed me through his plant recently, he pointed out one area he had had specially built, with an overhead door leading to the loading platform. It is just the right size to build himself a custom body some day.

1941 Packard Town Car by Rollson. From Packard
Super-Eight Catalog.

7

Derham and other Philadelphia Firms

THE DERHAM BODY CO.

1925 Packard Town Car by Derham, from their advertisement in 1924 New York Salon Catalog, where the car was exhibited.

DOWN in Philadelphia another survivor continues, the Derham Body Company of Rosemont, Pennsylvania, just down the "Main Line" from the city limits. When I started in the business, the Derham boys, sons of the founder, were running the company. Jim was the salesman while Enos did the designing and ran the factory. While I met Jim frequently when he came to New York to visit various dealers, I used to see Enos only at the annual Salon, but since we were close to the same age we became quite friendly.

I was happy to see Enos still at the old stand when I stopped by a year or two ago, and have since seen him a few more times. They survived the depression by concentrating on modifications such as making a limousine out of a sedan and with an occasional order for a convertible. During the War, they built mobile canteens for use in the shipyards in the Philadelphia area. Enos told me this was no problem since they had no priorities and had to build much of their interiors of wood, even though metal would have been better and easier to maintain. Fortunately, his workmen were quite at home with wood.

I suggested to Enos that there was a large demand for quality restoration, and I am glad to see that he has undertaken such work even though the lack of skilled craftsmen has limited the volume. When we discussed this again on a subsequent visit, he told me he had done a few restorations which averaged somewhat over $10,000 each. No firm price can be quoted beforehand, since until the work is started there is no way of telling what problems may be encountered, or what body parts may have to be handmade since duplicates of the originals are not available. Note that this refers to body and cosmetic restoration, not mechanical or engine work.

Like many others, Derham had started as a carriage-building firm in the nineteenth century. They had a reputation for quality workmanship even before they built their first automobile body, and were one of the firms selected by LeBaron to execute their designs in the days when we were just designers and engineers without our own plant.

During the late twenties and early thirties, Derham built a number of convertibles with lines closely following those Hibbard & Darrin were using in Paris. In a recent series of articles in *The Classic Car*, Tom Hibbard mentioned licensing Derham to use his designs. However, Enos Derham told me he did not recall any such arrangement, and thought he had just borrowed the ideas much as we used to borrow from each other. I'll have to let them fight that point out between them.

Shortly after World War II ended, Derham also added a Chrysler agency to their activities, since the custom body business was no longer very profitable. They continued to do a number of conversions for Chrysler and Packard especially, installing partitions in sedans and adding leather roofs to give them a town-car effect.

Sometime around 1952, R. L. Stickney and I conceived the idea of reviving the name LeBaron with a new firm. One of the people we consulted was Alan Buchanan, sales manager of Mezey Motors, Lincoln dealers in New York. He told me that he had asked Enos Derham to submit a number of designs and quotations for custom-built Lincolns from time to time, but almost invariably lost the order to Jack Inskip of Rolls-Royce. Inskip could deliver a

1926 Packard Sedan-Limousine by Derham, shown at the 1925 New York Salon, from their advertisement in the Salon Catalog.

1929 Lincoln Convertible Roadster by Derham, shown at the 1928 New York Salon, from their advertisement in the Salon Catalog.

more prestigious Rolls-Royce with an English custom body for less money than the Derham-Lincoln would cost. That was a major factor in our decision not to go ahead.

Enos Derham also told me that he had submitted a design and quotation for a Convertible Sedan to the Packard dealer in Philadelphia around that same time. The price was to be $15,000 for the body. Some months went by before an order materialized, and by then Derham had to decline it because they had in the meantime lost some of the key craftsmen essential to building this type of body. Quotations were obtained from other firms capable of handling

1930 Franklin Town Cabriolet by Derham, from Franklin Custom Body Catalog, Floyd Marshall Collection.

the work, and ranged from $30,000 to $75,000. That should explain why custom bodies are no longer being built.

Around 1928, another member of the family started a short-lived custom body firm in partnership with an imported car dealer in the Philadelphia area. It was called the Floyd-Derham Company, and did come up with some rather extreme but attractive designs. The bodies were actually built in the Wolfington shop. Unfortunately the times were not conducive to starting a new business in this field.

Alexander Wolfington's Sons, to give the full name of the shop mentioned in the preceding paragraph, was another firm that dated back to carriage days. The elder Wolfington was the son of a Halifax ship captain, who did not follow in his father's footsteps. Instead, he came to New York around 1870, and after an apprenticeship with Brewster moved to Philadelphia to establish his own firm.

Most of his initial business was repairing of carriages, but he also built a few, gradually expanding the latter phase of the business as his clientele and reputation grew. When the same customers—Stotesbury, Gimbel, Blair were some of the names—came to ask Mr. Wolfington to build bodies for their newly acquired automobiles, he did so, although probably reluctantly.

By 1910, his son Harry Wolfington had taken over the business, and was doing quite nicely building custom bodies. Since they required frequent repainting, he hit upon a "convertible" idea. He would sell his customer two bodies, an open one for the summer and a closed one for the winter. When the seasons changed, the bodies were shifted and one of them was put through a complete rehabilitation in the Wolfington shop to be ready for the following season. Some other body builders did the same thing later on, and

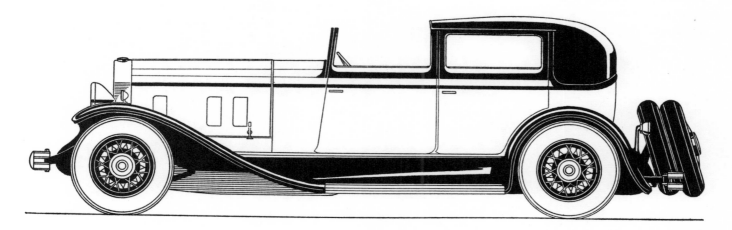

1928 Isotta-Fraschini Convertible Sedan by Floyd-Derham, shown at the 1928 New York Salon, from their advertisement in the Salon Catalog.

I recall one or two customers at LeBaron who had us building two separate bodies for the same chassis.

By the early twenties, the Wolfingtons started to build bus bodies. Among their early customers in this field were some of the leading Atlantic City hotels, for whom they designed special vehicles to pick up their guests at the railroad station.

About this time, Wolfington pretty much dropped out of the custom body business, possibly because the bus bodies were more profitable. They did a good deal of repainting and repair work still, and some of this business fortunately kept them going during the early part of the depression. Except for the brief fling with Floyd-Derham, I do not believe they built many custom bodies after 1925.

J. M. Quimby & Sons, in Newark, New Jersey, was another body builder of the early part of the century who later switched to building buses. John Dobben, for many years Chief Engineer for Judkins, worked there in his early days. He told me that Quimby's star salesman had been H. M. "Deacon" Strong, later sales manager for Wm. Wiese & Co., one of the principal sources of upholstery fabrics for the custom body industry.

Scattered throughout the New York and Philadelphia metropolitan areas were a number of smaller shops which specialized in repairs and repainting, often of high quality. A few of these did an occasional alteration, or remounted a body on a new chassis, but in general they were not considered custom body shops in the true sense.

Sometimes confusion exists because these firms, after repainting or remounting a body, added their own nameplate. This is more apt to be found on cars dating back before 1925, and except where the full history of a car is known, it would be difficult to identify the actual body builder.

8

Fleetwood and other Pennyslvania Shops

FARTHER out in Pennsylvania was the town of Fleetwood, home of the Fleetwood Metal Body Company. The firm had been founded in 1912 by H. C. Urich.

As mentioned, up to 1926 or so their New York Office was in the same building with LeBaron's, at 2 Columbus Circle. When Detroit became aware of the importance of styling in 1925, the Fisher Brothers bought Fleetwood and made it a division of the Fisher Body Company. That was the same year that they hired Harley Earl away from the Don Lee Studios in California, and the Murray Corporation lured Ray Dietrich away from LeBaron. Mr. Urich retired at this point, but Ernst Schebera, their Sales Manager who had run the New York office, continued with the company for some years.

Soon afterwards, Fleetwood's office was moved to Detroit into one of the General Motors buildings, and in 1929 a new plant was set up in Detroit and the one in Fleetwood was closed. I have since been told that for several years thereafter the population of Fleetwood refused to buy any General Motors cars, even though the only dealer in town handled Chevrolets. The local residents went twenty miles away or more to buy other makes.

Actually, as independent manufacturers, much of Fleetwood's work had been on Lincoln, Packard, Stutz, and such imported cars as Isotta-Fraschini. They also built a number of Rolls-Royces. Even after they became a subsidiary of Fisher Body, they continued to build quite a few bodies for Stutz and Isotta.

One Isotta-Fraschini that was quite striking was a town car with polished aluminum for the top of the hood and cowl, continuing back to form the tops of the front doors and sweeping up the front pillars of the rear compartment. The car was shown at the 1925 New York Salon and purchased by Rudolph Valentino. When he died, it remained as part of his estate, complete with the Cobra mascot which was his trademark.

The idea for this design came from a Hispano-Suiza that had been built in Paris. Elmo diPaoli, sales manager for Isotta, approached both Fleetwood and LeBaron to copy it. He showed us photographs of the original car, which had massive windshield wings with an intricate attachment to the front doors, so they would open and close with them. We felt that this was not a practical idea and tried to convince diPaoli that he should let us build it with regular windows in the front doors, an idea that we were just beginning to use on open front town cars. He turned down our suggestion and ordered the body from Fleetwood, who were willing to use the windshield wings.

We later built a Lincoln town car at LeBaron with the same windshield wings for a customer who insisted on them despite my best efforts to persuade him that our All-weather construction, as we called it, was superior. I finally agreed to make the elaborate windshield wings only when he flatly refused to give me the order on any other basis.

Fleetwood in turn built two or three more town cars of the same design for Isotta, and also a few on other chassis such as Packard and Rolls-Royce. Since duplicates of the Valentino Cobra mascot are now available, I imagine each of the similar Isottas surviving now has a Cobra, and is being described as the "original" Valentino car.

This Isotta and quite a number of other Fleetwood bodies had rather intricate wood panelling in the interior. Often the entire partition behind the chauffeur, below the window, was one large section of inlaid

1925 Isotta-Fraschini Town Brougham by Fleetwood,
exhibited at 1924 New York Salon and purchased by
Rudolph Valentino.

1926 Packard Town Brougham by Fleetwood, shown
at 1925 New York Salon. Patterned after the Valentino
Isotta, this is one of the last Packards built by Fleetwood. Photograph by John Adams Davis, courtesy
Automobile Manufacturers Association.

1928 Cadillac Transformable Town Car by Fleetwood, exhibited at 1927 New York Salon.

1928 Stutz Prince of Wales Sedan by Fleetwood, exhibited at 1927 New York Salon.

1939 Cadillac 75 Town Car by Fleetwood, from Fleetwood-Cadillac Catalog.

marquetry. The source of this paneling was the Linden Mfg. Co. of New York, who made similar wood panels for other body builders as well. Some are illustrated in Chapter 46.

During the early twenties, the Daniels V-8 was one of America's prestige cars. The chassis were built in nearby Reading, and Fleetwood supplied the bodies for quite a few of them. I remember several Daniels town cars running about New York then whose bodies came from Fleetwood.

Even after Fisher bought Fleetwood, they continued to show bodies on chassis other than Cadillac and LaSalle at the Salons. Since Fleetwood had only one space, with room for four cars, and at the 1925 Salon these already included a Lincoln, a Packard and a Duesenberg in addition to a Cadillac, they also showed at least one body each on the stands of Isotta-Fraschini, Maybach, Mercedes and Rolls-Royce.

As this was only a few months after the Fishers bought the firm, the arrangements had undoubtedly been made earlier. However, in subsequent Salons they showed Stutzes, Isottas and Rolls-Royces regularly up until 1929. I do not recall that they exhibited anything but Cadillacs after the Detroit plant went into operation late that year.

Another body builder in that part of the country was the Charles Schuette Body Company in Lancaster. They had a tendency toward rather boxy lines, but they built quite a few town car and limousine bodies up to the early twenties, as well as a number of taxicabs. Later they concentrated on bus bodies, but were out of business by 1927.

Kline in York built a rather massive car in the early part of the century, and supplied most of their own bodies. I am not sure whether they made bodies for anyone else.

Further West, the E. J. Thompson Company in Pittsburgh had started with carriages. In the 1921 Body Builders' Show they exhibited a Talbot-Darracq Phaeton among others. A few years later they turned out some fabric-covered bodies on the Childs system, which I shall describe more fully in connection with Merrimack. I do not believe they built many truly custom bodies beyond the early twenties, although they did produce one or two series of special bodies for the Dodge chassis, which they sold directly to Dodge dealers. Like many similar firms, they switched largely to bus bodies in the mid-twenties.

9

Brunn, Willoughby, Holbrook, etc.

UPPER New York State had several good custom body shops, in addition to the one Locke set up in Rochester. The largest was probably Brunn & Company in Buffalo. I have an idea that during the 1920s Brunn built more custom bodies, and small series, than any other manufacturer.

Herman Brunn started as an apprentice in his uncle's carriage shop in Buffalo. He later worked for the New Haven Carriage Company, who made bodies for the Columbia Electric Car built by Colonel Pope in Hartford, Connecticut. From there he went to Bab-

cock in Watertown, New York, ran the Andrew J. Joyce Carriage Company in Washington, D.C., for a while, and finally returned to Buffalo to set up his own company.

Mr. Brunn was quite friendly with the elder Henry Ford and built some of his personal cars. Naturally he built quite a few Lincolns as a result, but he worked on many other chassis as well. For a time he did a considerable business with Pierce-Arrow, who were his neighbors in Buffalo.

One of his finest Pierce-Arrows was a town car for the Shah of Iran, which I had the opportunity to inspect when it was at Pierce's New York City branch prior to shipment abroad. It was painted pure white, with gold striping and the Shah's crest on each rear door. All of the exterior brightwork—radiator shell, door handles, windshield frame, etc.—was gold

1922 Lincoln Phaeton by Brunn.

1929 Pierce-Arrow Town Brougham by Brunn, built for the Shah of Iran. Note his crest on rear doors. Photograph courtesy of Automobile Manufacturers Association.

1928 Lincoln Convertible Victoria by Brunn, exhibited at 1927 New York Salon. From their advertisement in Salon Catalog.

1930 Cord L-29 French Panel Brougham by LeBaron, built especially for the 1929 Salon. Reproduced from LeBaron Salon catalog.

1930 Stutz Blackhawk Convertible Roadster by LeBaron. This was another special design for the LeBaron Salon catalog.

1930 Lincoln Convertible Roadster by LeBaron. Although part of the Lincoln line, all bodies of this type were built by LeBaron. This one was shown at the 1929 New York Salon, and is reproduced from LeBaron Salon catalog.

1930 Rolls-Royce Phantom I Gentleman's Sport Sedan. A special design for the LeBaron Salon catalog.

1935 Lincoln Town Cabriolet by Brunn.

plated. The interior was done in a specially woven white brocade with a laurel leaf motif, and the interior hardware was solid 18-karat gold. Not many cars even in those lush days were so elaborately appointed, yet the effect was one of simple luxury, rather than ostentation.

One reason Brunn got this particular order may have been that they had a reputation for exceptionally solid construction. They often used bronze castings for body braces instead of the more usual wrought iron. These were heavier, but also less flexible.

While Brunn's reputation was largely based on impressive town cars and limousines, they early mastered the art of building a sound convertible and produced quite a few bodies of this type for various cars. Many were built in small series, but their most striking designs were individually done, sometimes especially for the Salons. While their town cars were quite conservative, I can recall many Salons where the Brunn stand featured a convertible in striking, eye-catching colors.

Brunn continued along much the same lines through the 1930's, getting a large share of the town car business from Lincoln during this period. While the volume was reduced it was still appreciable.

I was pleasantly surprised recently to learn that Herman C. Brunn, son of the founder of the company, is now associated with the Ford Motor Company and had a hand in the development of the Lincoln Continental Mark III.

Farther East, in Utica, were Willoughby & Company, headed by a charming gentleman named Francis Willoughby. Their styling was conservative but they were noted for the quality of their workmanship, especially their upholstering. They leaned to deeply tufted cushions with exceptionally soft, comfortable padding.

While many of their bodies were for Lincoln and Packard, Willoughby also built several attractive town cars on the Wills Ste. Claire. In the very early twenties, when it was still a prestige car, they also built several series of bodies on the Cole V-8.

1925 Wills Ste. Claire Town Car by Willoughby, exhibited at 1924 New York Salon. From their advertisement in Salon Catalog.

1928 Lincoln Enclosed-drive Limousine by Willoughby, exhibited at 1927 New York Salon. From their advertisement in Salon Catalog.

Since they concentrated to a considerable extent on chauffeur-driven styles on which demand dropped rather sharply after the 1929 crash, Willoughby unfortunately did not survive that by long.

North of them, in Watertown, was the H. H. Babcock Company, where Herman Brunn worked for a time. They were the source of some Dodge town cars on a special long wheelbase chassis in the early twenties, one or more of which were owned by J. P. Morgan. For a time they also built some Franklin bodies and a few for the Duesenberg Model A. However, they were simultaneously building commercial bodies for light delivery trucks and eventually concentrated on this business.

Down the river at Hudson, New York, was the plant of the Holbrook Company. This was another old firm that had started with carriages, and in the early twenties I recall them particularly for their limousine bodies on Lincoln, Packard and similar chassis.

Bob Bohaty for some years had a tow truck that had been fashioned out of a Holbrook Packard limousine, cut off at the chauffeur's partition. It is mounted on a 645 chassis, but from the lines I believe it was originally built around 1925 and later remounted on the newer chassis. Bob came to my

rescue several times in that truck, and in fact made a service call with it just minutes before his death.

By 1927 Holbrook had developed a flair for striking sport phaetons and their Salon exhibit that year included one on a Packard with a polished aluminum hood and moldings. The next year they had another one with a polished panel several inches wide running completely around the car. They also had a town car and a sport sedan on the new Duesenberg introduced at that Salon.

Unfortunately, they ran into financial difficulties right after the 1929 crash. Harry Holbrook had left the firm earlier to found the short-lived Holbrook-

1922 Dodge Town Brougham by H. H. Babcock, on special long-wheelbase chassis.

1916 Crane-Simplex chassis with Holbrook Limousine body fitted about 1921. Yes, it is a Crane-Simplex, identifiable by certain chassis details, although it has been disguised with a Rolls-Royce radiator and hood. Photograph courtesy Automobile Manufacturers Association.

1926 Lincoln Town Cabriolet by Holbrook, shown at 1925 New York Salon. From their advertisement in Salon Catalog.

Brewster Company. Rollston at the time acted as the New York repair depot for Holbrook, and much of the Holbrook staff joined Rollston.

Rudy Creteur told me an interesting story about that Duesenberg sedan for the 1928 Salon. It seems that the hydraulic breakes had not been properly connected on this, one of the first Model J chassis, but this was not discovered until the car was on its way to the Hudson River Day Line pier, to be loaded on one of their boats for the trip to New York. The car was somewhat damaged during the loading proc-

ess, but fortunately did not go overboard.

Holbrook immediately called Rollston to arrange to have the necessary repairs made as soon as the car reached New York City. Fortunately, Rollston's shop was only a few blocks from the Day Line pier at this end, and the car was towed over without incident. By a superhuman effort the repairs were completed in time to move the car to the Commodore Hotel the next day and get it into its place before the opening of the Salon.

10
Judkins and the New England Coach Builders

BOSTON was also a good market for fine carriages in the days of the horse. It is well known that horses were popular there even in the days of Paul Revere.

Naturally a number of old carriage builders became custom body makers when the automobile arrived. As mentioned earlier, many of them had settled in the Merrimac River valley, around Amesbury, north of Boston. One of the finest firms there was the J. B. Judkins Company.

Judkins & Goodwin was founded in West Amesbury, later called Merrimac, in 1857. The partnership changed several times in the next few years, but soon settled down to John B. Judkins & Son. The grandson of the founder, also named John B. Judkins, lived until recently and I have been in correspondence with him. He had run the firm in the 1920s and 1930s.

While they built other types as well, Judkins were particularly well known in the twenties for their Coupes and Berlines, all rather similar in style, on Lincoln, Pierce-Arrow and other chassis. These were built in series in what was considered good quantity by custom builders of the time, 100 or more of a style.

Judkins also built some very elegant town cars, including a nice panel brougham on a Lincoln for the 1924 Salon. As can be seen from the color rendering reproduced herein, it was painted maroon and black, with brass radiator and accessories, nostalgic even for that day.

Another striking vehicle was the Coaching Brougham they showed at the 1926 Salon, recently restored by Harrah and on display at his museum in

Reno. Actually this was first referred to as a replica of a Concord Coach. John Dobben, then chief engineer aand designer for Judkins, recently told me the idea had come from either a Concord Coach in a New England museum or from a similar private vehicle at Henry Ford's Wayside Inn. At any rate, he drew up several pencil sketches and Henry and Edsel Ford selected one of them.

Even the interior trim was patterned after the older vehicle, with tufted upholstery and little hammocks of fishnet to hold the passengers' odds and ends. It is quite possible that some of the craftsmen who did this work had earlier done the same for the horse-drawn coaches. When I visited Harrah's just after this restoration had been completed, I complimented them on the close reproduction they had achieved of the original color scheme of Coaching Yellow and Black, with red striping. I learned that they had done this with nothing more to go on than a verbal description of the original paint job.

After the New York Office of LeBaron was closed in October 1930, R. L. Stickney refused an offer to go to Detroit, and instead joined Judkins. Custom bodies were in declining demand then, but they continued on for a few years building special trailers for sales and demonstration exhibits. Stickney illustrated at least one catalog for them, including sketches of early carriages, a Columbia Electric Taxicab, and a more current Lincoln town car, all of which are reproduced in this chapter or earlier ones.

In the same town was the Merrimack Body Company. They built some custom bodies but were perhaps better known at the time for the production bodies they built for various small automobile manufacturers and the limited series for some of the larger ones such as Packard. In the mid-twenties, they built some fabric-covered bodies on the Childs system. Like the Weymann bodies, they were lighter than the conventional construction with aluminum paneling,

1926 Lincoln Coupelet by Judkins, exhibited at 1925 New York Salon. The drawing shows how the top folds.

1925 models from Judkins advertisement in Salon catalog. A Lincoln Berline Landaulet, Pierce-Arrow Series 80 Coupe, and Marmon Sedan.

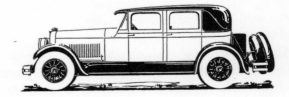

1927 Lincoln Coaching Brougham by Judkins, as shown at 1926 New York Salon. This is reproduction of our rendering for *Lincoln Magazine*. The restored car is in Harrah's Automobile Collection.

1929 Lincoln Coupe by Judkins, shown at 1928 New York Salon. Judkins built hundreds of such Lincoln coupes, with minor variations from year to year. From their advertisement in Salon Catalog.

1934 Lincoln Town Brougham by Judkins. Note special fenders with integral headlights. Design by R. L. Stickney for Judkins.

although they were not really flexible like Weymann's patented construction.

Merrimack built some bodies for the early duPont cars, but I have found a reference in a trade magazine of the period that Waterhouse & Company was founded in 1928 to "make bodies for duPont." I have tried unsuccessfully to trace this further and learned only, from my friend Bill Gibson of Boston, that all the records of the Merrimack Body Company were destroyed just a few years ago following the death of the last of its former owners.

It is quite possible that the personnel of Waterhouse came from Merrimack and took the duPont business with them. Waterhouse set up shop in Webster, Massachusetts, somewhat to the West of Boston.

While they built other types as well, Waterhouse were best known for their Convertible Victorias. They were one of the first to introduce this body style, which had originated in Europe, to the United States. For several years they built quite a few of them on various chassis, with almost identical lines. The body had one great advantage in being rather compact, so that it could be adapted to almost any car with a minimum of design or structural changes.

Gradually others became equally adept at building this body type, and there are many extant with the nameplates of Dietrich, LeBaron, Rollston and others. With the increasing competition, and the onset of the depression, Waterhouse disappeared from the scene.

Another carriage builder who started in Amesbury, in the 1850s, was Hume. Various members of the Hume and Walker families seem to have had a sort of revolving partnership at this time, according to some old records I found in the Amesbury Public Library. In 1909 they moved to Boston, to a shop on

1930 duPont Town Car by Merrimack. Photograph courtesy of owner, Harrah's Automobile Collection.

Commonwealth Avenue near the Fenway, which became Boston's Automobile Row.

When I went to Boston on business for LeBaron in the twenties, I usually took the Owl, the New Haven's midnight train. It arrived in Boston quite early in the morning, and since most dealers did not open until 9 A.M. or so, I would have breakfast at the South Station and then walk up past the Common and the couple of miles out Commonwealth Avenue. It made a very pleasant constitutional.

Hume originated a rather striking design for a sedan with a very rounded rear roof line which was quite distinctive, and was especially admired by Marmon. Hume's designer of the time, W. E. Pierce, became styling consultant to Marmon in the mid-twenties. To get Pierce's services full time, Marmon eventually took over Hume, but did not continue the business very long.

Farnham & Nelson were in Roslindale and turned out some very interesting bodies in the early twenties, including Locomobiles and some rather streamlined double-cowl phaetons on various chassis. In 1924 they turned to building bus bodies, which were more profitable at the time.

Several smaller firms in Amesbury, such as Hollander & Morrill, were building custom bodies into the mid-twenties. A number of these smaller plants were absorbed by Biddle & Smart around 1925 as

they sought to expand their production of bodies for Hudson.

Springfield, a hundred or so miles west of Boston, was the home of the Smith-Springfield Corporation, later reorganized as the Springfield Body Company. They had been building custom bodies and small series for some time before Ray Dietrich took a leave of absence from LeBaron for a few months late in 1921, to become a consultant to Springfield.

1923 Marmon Sedan by Hume, exhibited at Foreign Automotive Association Show.

1923 Lafayette Town Car by Springfield Body Corporation, from their advertisement in a Salon Catalog.

It developed that he had gone to Springfield to help design and engineer bodies for the new American Rolls-Royce, whose chassis plant was nearby. Information is scarce, but I believe the original Smith-Springfield plant was taken over by Rolls-Royce, and the principals of the company bought the former Stevens-Duryea factory, also in Springfield, and turned to making bus bodies. Their Sales Manager was Newton H. Manning, who later became Assistant Manager of the Rolls-Royce body plant until this phase of their work was returned to Brewster in 1928. At that time Mr. Manning became General Manager of the new LeBaron-Detroit Company.

Early in the 1900s, several quality chassis were being manufactured in Connecticut, which served as the foundation for bodies from the New Haven Carriage Company. They had many distinguished body builders on their staff at various times, who later went on to found their own companies. Both this

firm and the Blue Ribbon Body Company in Bridgeport were largely dependent on the Locomobile Company for their business in the early twenties, and with the decline of that excellent car neither firm seemed to be able to drum up enough orders elsewhere. New Haven Carriage liquidated in 1924, and Blue Ribbon followed soon after. As I have mentioned, the Blue Ribbon plant was briefly occupied by Holbrook-Brewster in 1927–1928.

The Bridgeport Body Company merged with LeBaron as noted. Its original owners did not move to Detroit when the plant was closed at the end of 1930, and a few years later they set up a new business under the old name. They built mainly wooden station wagon bodies for various more expensive chassis such as Packard, which did not have such a model in their regular line. The firm closed again in the middle or late thirties.

1923 Rolls-Royce Limousine by New Haven Carriage Company. Photograph courtesy Automobile Manufacturers Association.

11

Dietrich and other Western Firms

Dietrich Inc.

THERE were a few coachbuilders in the Middle West early in the century, but most of them were in other fields or out of business by the 1920s. Kimball & Company in Chicago was the home of Tom Hibbard just before the "Kaiser War," as some of my friends who were in it still call it, but they never resumed production after the war. Graff was another Chicago body builder who later concentrated on buses, although they did have a Rolls-Royce in the Chicago Salon as late as 1924.

Detroit probably had some similar firms, but I know of none who were active there in the early twenties. It was therefore to fill a void that Ray Dietrich was lured away from LeBaron in the Spring of 1925. He has since reported that Edsel Ford was a prime factor in the move, but I was not privy to the arrangements at the time. I do know that the firm of Dietrich, Inc., was established with its principal financial backing coming from the Murray Corporation, who at the time were building a large share of the Lincoln production bodies as well as those for other quality cars.

The new firm did build a number of individually designed bodies, but concentrated mainly on small series with their first Salon exhibit consisting of a Lincoln, a Marmon and a pair of Packards. In the next few years they did a substantial business with Chrysler and Franklin as well. Several of Ray Dietrich's designs, originally built in small series at his own plant, were lated adapted to production by some of these customers.

One of the most famous was the Franklin Pirate, which was the first American car with doors running down to the running boards, a style which eventually led to the complete elimination of the running boards. Actually the first bodies with this feature had appeared in France in 1925, on Bugatti chassis, and credited to the "Bureau d'Etudes E. Bunau-Varilla." Several similar cars were shown at the 1927 Paris Salon.

Late in 1930 it was obvious that the volume of custom body business had been sharply reduced, and Dietrich withdrew from the company. He continued in the field of body design and engineering, however, being associated with Graham-Paige the following year—one that I also spent in Detroit.

The Murray Corporation took over full ownership of Dietrich, Inc., and with it the right to use his name. For a time they continued to turn out small series, which Ray had designed before he left the company. Quite a few of these were for Packard, including Convertible Sedans and Convertible Victorias. By 1933, these were being produced in the Murray plant, some being finished as Packard production models and others, with a more luxurious interior, carrying the Dietrich nameplate. A year or two later, the Dietrich name disappeared entirely.

Down in Cleveland, Leon Rubay had built up a sizeable custom body business before World War I, and also built small production runs for some of the higher-priced cars from that city. Tom Hibbard worked for him for a time, and there met Ralph Roberts, a native of Cleveland, who spent his summer vacations also working for Rubay. As I have related, they later became partners in LeBaron, along with Ray Dietrich.

In 1922, Rubay started to build complete cars, patterned more or less after the popular French models of the time. They were not large, but of excellent quality. Unfortunately, this enterprise was started just as the 1921 deflation reached its peak, and it proved to be the death of the firm. Some of the bodies designed for this new car had included such innovations as one with a fixed roof and windows that folded together and could be concealed behind a hinged panel in the side of the body.

The Bender Body Company was also in Cleveland, and built bodies for some of the more ad-

1928 Packard Convertible Sedan by Dietrich, exhibited at 1927 New York Salon. The small window between doors was a Dietrich idea he used on convertible bodies on various chassis. From their advertisement in Salon Catalog.

1930 Franklin Pirate Phaeton. Production model based on earlier Dietrich body. From Franklin Catalog, Floyd Marshall Collection.

1932 Packard Convertible Victoria by Murray, designed by Dietrich. Photograph by the author of car now owned by Mr. and Mrs. David Steinman of Elkins Park, Pennsylvania.

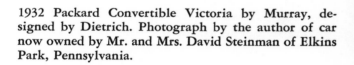

1923 Rubay Transformable Sedan with windows folding into compartment in body side. One predecessor of the modern hardtop. From *Motor Magazine,* December, 1922.

1928 Packard Clear-vision Sedan by Walter M. Murphy, exhibited at 1927 New York Salon. A step closer to today's hardtops. From their advertisement in Salon Catalog.

vanced cars of the early twenties. At the Body Builders' Show, held in conjunction with the 1921 New York Auto Show, they exhibited a Franklin Coupe and also a Kurtz Automatic Sedan. I have been unable to get any reliable information on the latter. Bender later became a leading manufacturer of bus bodies.

Several carriage builders in Indiana turned to making automobile bodies, and some made complete automobiles. McFarlan was one of these, as noted in Alvin Arnheim's book on this massive make. While they also built some bodies for the largest Auburn at one time, they had earlier turned out custom bodies on other chassis such as Locomobile in their plant in Connersville. I do not recall that they built custom bodies for any other chassis to any extent once their own car was in production.

On the West Coast, the most important body builder of the late twenties was the Walter M. Murphy Company of Pasadena. Mr. Murphy was a relative of Henry Leland, and started in business with the advent of the Lincoln car in 1921, having the agency for this as well as his body business. He soon built up a nucleus of customers in the newly blooming movie industry. As mentioned, after a while he absorbed the machinery and much of the staff of Healy from New York.

Murphy's bodies were naturally geared to California tastes and weather. I believe they built the first prototype of the modern hardtop, a Packard which they showed at the 1927 New York Salon and called a "Clear Vision Sedan." It had metal-framed windows as on a convertible and a complete absence of body-pillars above the belt. The following year they showed an improved version on a Rolls-Royce.

They also built a number of rather attractive Duesenbergs, especially convertibles, and quite a few Packards. They developed a construction using cast aluminum door posts, which suited the convertible sedan bodies very well. These were worked out so that the same castings could be adapted for bodies on various chassis, and they were also used for the "hard tops" I have described.

Bohman & Schwartz did not enter the picture until later. The principals had worked for Walter Murphy, and when he went out of business in the thirties, they set up their own shop.

Of course, in the early twenties there was another well-known custom builder in Los Angeles, the Don Lee Studios. Lee was the Cadillac dealer there, but his body shop turned out a number of outstanding models on various makes of chassis, especially for movie stars. I especially recall one huge phaeton for Roscoe "Fatty" Arbuckle on a massive Pierce-Arrow "66," which had been disguised with a completely different hood and radiator as well as special fenders.

Lee's designer was Harley Earl, and when Alfred P. Sloan hired him away in 1926 to set up the Art &

Color Section for General Motors, Lee was so upset that he cancelled his Cadillac franchise and took on the Lincoln instead. The body shop was closed except for repair work. Later on the breach was healed and Lee again became a Cadillac dealer. Some of Earl's designs were quite a bit like the more elaborate McFarlans of the same period.

Larkins & Co. in San Francisco were an old carriage building firm which turned out a few custom bodies in the early part of the century. However, by the 1920s they were engaged primarily in repainting and reupholstering. One body I have seen which carries a Larkins nameplate is, I believe, actually a Murphy body. It has the distinctive cast aluminum door posts that were characteristic of many Murphy Convertible Sedans. It is possible that Murphy built the body for Larkins, who then completed it, but more likely Larkins refinished the body at some time

and applied their nameplate to it then.

While in California recently, I was reminded that one of the Studebaker family had set up a carriage building business in the hills near Sacramento during the gold rush days. It did not survive into the automobile era.

Actually, the principal market for custom bodies during the 1930s shifted from New York to Hollywood. There were a few people there who could still afford them. I am reminded of J. P. Morgan's oft quoted reply to the associate who asked whether he could afford a yacht. Morgan's reply is reported to have been that if you had to wonder about it, you could not afford one. Much the same was true of custom-bodied automobiles. Certainly, with one or two exceptions, none of our customers at LeBaron had less than several million dollars.

1929 Duesenberg Model J Disappearing Top Coupe by Walter M. Murphy, exhibited at 1928 New York Salon. From their advertisement in Salon Catalogue.

12
Small Production Body Builders

IN addition to the firms that I consider custom body builders, there were some who may have carried out this function early in the century, but who by the twenties were supplying production bodies for small and medium sized automobile manufacturers.

Among these, I have already mentioned the two old Amesbury firms, the Walker Body Company and Biddle & Smart. The latter built some very smart-looking bodies on the Hudson Super Six which were called Suburbans, but which were sedan-limousines rather than the station wagons to which this name was applied later.

Biddle & Smart earlier had worked on various chassis, but in the twenties they were working mostly for Hudson, building all of their closed bodies except the Coach. The latter was the first really inexpensive closed body and had been developed by Briggs. Biddle & Smart also built a few more or less individual Hudsons, mostly for company executives.

While Biddle & Smart expanded considerably with Hudson's prosperity in the twenties, absorbing most of the smaller body shops in Amesbury, they came to an abrupt end in 1930, when Hudson found it necessary to switch their business to less expensive sources nearer home.

Walker had a more varied existence, but formed a fairly close association with Franklin, even to the extent of setting up a branch plant in a suburb of Syracuse. In their early days, as I have mentioned, they had been closely affiliated with the Hume family, and had built carriages before working on automobile bodies.

Part of that Syracuse plant was devoted for a time in the mid-twenties to building bodies designed by Frank deCausse, which were sold as products of the Franklin Custom Body Division. Most of these had the very square window lines which had been typical of deCausse's styling for Locomobile earlier.

There were quite a few firms in the Middle West that supplied bodies for some of the low-production,

medium-priced cars of the period. A few of these, as discussed earlier, even built complete automobiles by assembling chassis out of readily available components and fitting their own bodies to them.

Baker, Rauch & Lang in Cleveland were somewhat more ambitious. Besides building one of the most popular electric cars of the early part of the century, as has been noted in recent articles on this subject, they also manufactured the Owen-Magnetic in the teens and early twenties. More on this later.

The trademark "Body by Raulang" was considered a definite asset, and this company built the bodies for some of the better car manufacturers such as Stearns-Knight and Peerless. One of their advertisements of the late twenties lists them as a source of "distinctive bodies in lots of 100 to 10,000."

They occasionally turned out a special body, but their business was largely devoted to production runs. They also made other components. During the twenties they expanded considerably, taking over some other plants in Cleveland, including the Rubay establishment after it went into bankruptcy. As their major customers went out of business during the depression, they ceased building complete bodies but supplied parts to some major manufacturers and also turned to making electronic equipment.

The Phillips Body Company in Warren, Ohio, developed a flair for convertibles and supplied production bodies of this type to several manufacturers including Stutz and Pierce-Arrow. They were absorbed by Briggs in 1928, and some of their executives took over the direction of much of LeBaron's production soon after.

E. P. Carter was one of these, and he became general manager of LeBaron's Bridgeport plant. He and I had the sad duty of liquidating that plant late in 1930. Later he took charge of production at the Le-Baron-Detroit Company.

There were two Indianapolis firms that occasionally showed cars at the Chicago Salon, although I never considered them truly custom builders. One was Millspaugh & Irish, which built most of the bodies for the Duesenberg Model A. They were out of business by early 1929 and never had a hand in the more prestigious Model J.

The other was the Robbins Body Company, who built a number of bodies for Marmon and Stutz, including some of the Stutz Blackhawks and Speedsters, which had been designed by LeBaron. Robbins later was absorbed by Briggs.

Another firm set up in Indianapolis in 1926 was the Weymann American Body Company, which manufactured bodies under the patented Weymann system, with flexible frames and fabric covering. Weymann was a European firm that had licensed a number of the leading body builders on the Continent and in England to use their system. The Indianapolis operation, however, was a subsidiary of the parent company with some financial participation from Stutz, their principal customer.

Weymann showed one or two Stutzes in the Salons of 1927 and later, but they were really production rather than custom bodies. Of course, one must consider what the term "production" means. They were built in hundreds, not millions.

The Weymann Company did build a few individual bodies on various chassis, but these were really experimental models rather than custom bodies in the usual sense. Their system of construction made possible a body several hundred pounds lighter than conventional types, with a corresponding increase in performance.

On the outskirts of Indianapolis, there was a subsidiary of the Auburn-Cord-Duesenberg combine called the Union City Body Company. They built the bodies for the early L–29 Cords and also a number of Duesenbergs. During the later years of the Duesenberg J, a number of these cars were produced that bore a striking resemblance to earlier custom bodies built on the same chassis by LeBaron and others. We called them "factory bodies" at the time, but in the last Salon in 1931 one was exhibited under the name of LeGrande as the body builder. They have even been referred to in some articles I have seen as "the poor man's LeBaron." We were unhappy to have not only our designs pirated, but even our name adapted with only a minor change and not a word of thanks or apology.

Oddly enough, to present day minds, there were quite a few special bodies built for the Model T Ford. These were usually not really custom bodies, but something a bit different and more luxurious than

1922 Hudson Suburban Limousine by Biddle & Smart, exhibited at 1921 Closed Car Show in New York.

1925 Franklin Victoria Coupe by Walker, designed by Frank deCausse. From Franklin advertisement in Salon Catalog.

1927 Stutz Convertible Coupe by Phillips Custom Body Company.

the then limited standard Ford line. Mostly they were built in reasonable quantities to keep the cost down. Several firms built rather dashing roadster bodies for the Model T, but there were also a few real custom bodies by Brewster, Derham and others.

Needless to say, nearly every production body builder and many automobile manufacturers had what were called "experimental shops" in which prototypes for future production were built. These shops also served as the source of special vehicles for company executives and a few favored customers, usually large stockholders.

Their quality was frequently quite up to the standards of the custom builders, since the craftsmen who could produce such work had often been lured away from the custom shops by higher pay and other incentives. It is very difficult in many cases to identify the source of any such bodies that survive.

At the time they were built, nobody was thinking about posterity and they were simply a convenient way to work out new ideas, or to satisfy some V.I.P.

1930 Stutz Speedster by Robbins, designed by LeBaron Studios in Detroit. From Stutz catalog, Floyd Marshall Collection.

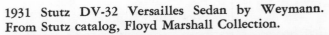

1931 Stutz DV-32 Versailles Sedan by Weymann. From Stutz catalog, Floyd Marshall Collection.

1925 Pierce-Arrow Series 33 advertisement from New
York Salon catalog.

1925 Lincoln Town Brougham by LeBaron, exhibited
at 1924 New York Salon. Reproduction of R. L. Stickney rendering for Salon issue of *The Lincoln Magazine*.

1925 Lincoln Panel Brougham by Judkins, exhibited at 1924 New York Salon. Reproduction of R. L. Stickney rendering for Salon issue of *The Lincoln Magazine*.

1928 Minerva Sport Sedan by LeBaron, exhibited at 1928 New York Salon. Reproduced from LeBaron advertisement in Salon catalog.

Framework of a Weymann body, showing flexible connection of frame members. From Stutz catalog, Floyd Marshall Collection.

1932 Duesenberg Phaeton by LeGrande. This is a copy of the LeBaron Phaeton exhibited at the 1928 New York Salon. From Duesenberg catalog, Floyd Marshall Collection.

13
European Coach Builders

THERE were a number of excellent body builders in Europe, often also with a long tradition as constructors of fine carriages. In fact, the word "Carossiers" in the original name of the LeBaron firm is the French for "coachbuilders." I have sometimes been asked if it was not a misspelling of "Carosserie," which it is not. The latter is the word for the establishment doing the coachbuilding, as distinct from the people involved.

Possibly the best known in this country were the two Americans in Paris, Hibbard & Darrin. Tom Hibbard had, as mentioned, left for Paris a few months before I joined LeBaron, to investigate the possibility of having bodies built in Europe. There he formed a partnership with Howard Darrin much along the lines of LeBaron—that is, they did the designing and engineering in Paris, and had the bodies built by Van den Plas and others. Later they set up their own factory in a Paris suburb.

Hibbard came up with a "rolled belt" design which suited especially well the Minerva, for which they had become distributors in Paris. He also developed a unique convertible sedan in which a triangular section of the top came down between the door windows. Both ideas were copied extensively both in Europe and in this country.

Many of their customers were American, since they could often buy a Minerva from Hibbard & Darrin with one of their bodies for considerably less than a similar car would cost them in the United States. Quite a few factors entered into this, including the fluctuating rates of exchange. Often Belgian merchandise was very much cheaper in France, and this worked to the advantage of people who traveled a good deal. There was an International Set then as now, except that they traveled by luxury liner instead of by jet.

At one point, Hibbard located a firm which could make very thin aluminum castings, and some of Hibbard's later bodies used these for door frames and panels. Hibbard worked out his designs so that the

1927 Minerva Enclosed-drive by Hibbard & Darrin, exhibited at 1927 Chicago Salon.

same castings could be used on a variety of bodies for different chassis.

When Hibbard left the firm in the early thirties to return to this country, Darrin formed a new partnership with another manufacturer named Fernandez. Some of their styling during the next few years was quite rakish.

Also in Paris were two very well known firms, Kellner & Cie. and J. Rothschild et Fils, who sent quite a few bodies to this country during the twenties. Many were imported by the local distributors for Renault, Voisin and other French cars, while others had been bought in Europe and shipped over by their owners.

Most of the bodies from Kellner that came here in the twenties were either convertibles or town cars and limousines. Quite a few were Renaults, since they had an active factory branch here; and there was generally a pair of Kellner-bodied cars in their showroom. One convertible coupe design was bought from LeBaron by Renault in 1924 and the bodies were built at the Kellner plant. The Rothschild bodies I remember were mainly elegant town cars with exquisite interiors.

Carosserie Henri Labourdette was another much admired French firm. I believe they built aeroplanes during World War I, with fuselages built up out of strips of laminated mahogany. Soon afterwards they were turning out some very attractive open cars with boat-tail styling—quite streamlined. Many had the

Hibbard & Darrin Town Cars on Pierce-Arrow and Packard chassis, about 1931. Courtesy of Automobile Manufacturers Association.

1923 Renault 40 Town Car by Kellner, exhibited at Foreign Automotive Association Show. This photograph was taken in Paris and used in their advertisement in the Show catalog.

same type of wood panelling as on their planes; it was copper-riveted, which reminded one of a speedboat.

Henri Chapron came up with some rather dashing designs for four-passenger closed and convertible bodies in the thirties, and in fact had been building them even earlier. However, my recollection is that these were usually built in small series for the various limited-production cars being manufactured in France at the time. He is still doing the same type of business with the convertible coupe for the current Citroen.

There were other French body builders whose work did not reach these shores to any extent in the twenties, but some of their designs found their way here recently as restored classics. Among these are Belvalette, Driguet, Figoni & Falaschi, Gaborit, Gangloff, Leturneur & Marchand, Million-Guiet and Henri Binder. Bugatti also maintained their own body shop, as also did Voisin, where everything was custom built. Both of the latter were frequent prize-winners at the Concours d'Elegance which were popular in Europe and where they competed against the best private carossiers.

A bit to the North, Van den Plas was the largest custom body firm in Belgium. Besides the bodies they built for Hibbard & Darrin, they built many of their own design. For several years their designer was the late Count Alexis de Sakhnoffsky who had quite a flair for sweeping curves and rarely used a straight line if he could avoid it. I recall that he visited us at LeBaron around the end of 1926, when he came to this country to explore the possibility of accepting a post with General Motors. We advised him against it, and a year or so later he became chief designer for the Hayes Body Company in Grand Rapids. Still later he had an active career as an independent consultant and illustrator.

Another member of the Van den Plas family had a small shop in Paris and also opened a plant in England. This was later absorbed by B.M.C. and accounts for the Van den Plas nameplate on the bodies of recent Princess cars.

D'Ieteren Freres were another Belgian firm who produced bodies of high quality, especially luxurious town cars. Most of their bodies were mounted on Minerva or Excelsior chassis, both built in Belgium.

Germany also had its coachbuilders, but the one name that stands out in my mind in the twenties is Saoutchik. They built some rather striking Mercedes, including many SS convertibles. Since this was the only German car being imported to any considerable extent at the time, quite a few of Saoutchik's creations were to be seen here.

Other German body builders were also active in the period between the World Wars, but not many of their products came to this country. Their styling tended to be stolid and massive, which satisfied German tastes but not those of Americans. Spohn is

1922 Hispano-Suiza Phaeton by Million-Guiet. Photograph courtesy Automotive History Collection, Detroit Public Library.

1930 Minerva Limousine de Ville by Van den Plas. From Minerva Catalog, Floyd Marshall Collection.

among these, and most Maybachs had bodies from this firm. Another was Heinrich Glaeser of Dresden. Except for open cars and a few limousines, most German chassis had bodies fitted here by various of our custom builders.

Probably more bodies by Barker found their way here in the twenties than those of any other English body builder, for the very simple reason that their styling appealed most to Americans. Quite a few of these were Rolls-Royces, and many had been bought in England and shipped here after their owners toured the Continent.

Barker also built the body of Sir Malcolm Campbell's Napier-engined "Bluebird," which set a new land speed record in 1928.

Hooper & Company bodies were also to be seen here occasionally, but they tended to be rather large and ungainly although comfortable. Later they began to look more like Barker's and became more popular here. Hooper and Thrupp & Maberly built most of the Daimler limousines favored by the British Royal Family.

H. J. Mulliner had founded a carriage-building firm in the 1890s and continued with automobile bodies. While he had lost control of his firm in the thirties, he died only recently at a very ripe age.

James Young and Park-Ward were other good firms that often built on Rolls-Royce chassis. During the depression they ran into difficulties, and these two firms as well as Barker and Mulliner were taken over

1928 Mercedes-Benz SSK Convertible Coupe by Saoutchik, from an advertisement in Salon catalog.

by Jack Barclay, the Rolls-Royce distributor in London, and later by Rolls themselves.

I am not sure whether Gurney Nutting became part of this same combine, but they built some rather sporting bodies during the twenties as well as more conservative types. Windovers may also have wound up in one of the mergers that took place in England. Their specialty was fairly conservative limousine bodies of good quality, but of a somewhat lower price than the firms mentioned previously.

Some British body builders specialized in small series for imported chassis (imported to England, that is) or on one of the then-numerous medium-priced English chassis. Alford & Adlers, Mathorn, Connaught and Cunard were in this category, and

1929 Hispano-Suiza Town Car by Barker. From Hispano-Suiza Catalog, Floyd Marshall Collection.

1922 Rolls-Royce Cabriolet by Cunard, built for the
Maharajah of Patiala. From *Motor Magazine,* December, 1922.

1930 Lanchester 8 Limousine by Hooper. From Lanchester Catalog, Floyd Marshall Collection.

1928 Isotta-Fraschini Limousine by Castagna, exhibited
at the New York Salon. From Isotta advertisement in
Salon Catalog.

occasionally turned out an individual custom body as well.

Another firm that in fact turned out some production bodies in good quantity as well as small series was the Swallow Coachworks. They were often in better financial position than the chassis manufacturers, and sold complete cars as Austin-Swallows, etc. This finally culminated in the Standard-Swallow in several models, the largest of which was called the Standard-Swallow Jaguar. It was such a success that it became a separate company—Jaguar Cars, Ltd.

Finally, in Italy, there was Castagna in Milan, which built a considerable number of Isotta-Fraschinis for the American market, as well as some Mercedes and others. A few more Isottas came from Sala and Carrozzeria Touring, also in Milan. The latter firm has also produced some of the experimental bodies for various American manufacturers in recent years.

Pinin Farina started in business around 1926 or 1927, and was not yet known in this country to any extent. Ghia and Vignale also both came along later, and while all three of these firms had a pronounced effect on styling throughout the world, they did not participate in the period in which substantial numbers of custom bodies were being purchased in this country.

I have not, in this brief summary, included anywhere near all of the European body builders, but have tried to cover the ones whose work was especially prominent in the American market during the classic period. There are others whose names have become known here recently as desirable classic and vintage cars have been brought over from Europe.

One point I must mention, however, is that many of the innovations in styling during the 1920s and 1930s originated in Europe, often on custom bodies. Most heads of American automobile manufacturers as well as the custom body builders themselves traveled to Europe regularly, usually in time for the Auto Shows in the Fall and especially the Paris Salon. They always brought back new ideas, with the most unusual coming from France at that time.

14
Nomenclature

JUST as the methods of construction derived from the carriage trade, so did the terminology used by the custom body builders. Many of the names they used have since been stripped of their meaning by the practice by which automobile manufacturers applied the old names to vehicles having no connection with them.

I have in my possession a copy of Webster's Collegiate Dictionary, Third Edition, 1918, which for some years reposed in the New York office of LeBaron. While we often consulted it in other matters, we relied on our own personal knowledge of the various body styles in our work. It does, however, include some definitions carried over from an earlier day, which are significant.

This dictionary defines a *Brougham* as a form of light, closed carriage, named after Lord Brougham. It has an illustration showing a horse-drawn vehicle rather like the Panel Broughams, which many custom body builders executed during the 1920s, with square-cornered, closed rear quarters. Most custom builders used the term Brougham to apply to any town car with a solid roof over the tonneau, metal paneled, with or without windows in the rear quarters.

Cabriolet is defined as a light, one-horse carriage with two seats and often with a canopy. In the twenties, we used this term for a town car with leather or fabric roof. Sometimes this could be folded down, in which case we called it a Full-collapsible Cabriolet. Almost all of these cars, whether or not the roof folded, were fitted with landau irons. These were considered an attractive decoration, and were a necessity with a folding roof. There has also been some confusion over the name of these irons—some people called them landau joints or prop joints. The latter derives from their function of propping up the top mechanism.

Coupe, according to Webster, was a four-wheeled closed carriage for two persons inside, with an outside seat for the driver. This would seem closer to the definition of a town car, and indeed in France

Coupé de Ville was the generic term for a town car, introduced here later by Cadillac. However, in this country, coupe was generally used to mean a closed car with two doors and seating two, three or four people.

A *Victoria Coupe* was originally a body with room for four people in a sort of clover-leaf arrangement. As convertible bodies increased in popularity in the late twenties, the term *Convertible Victoria* was used by Waterhouse and later adopted generally for a two-door model with individual front seats and a full-width rear seat.

Limousine is defined as an automobile with permanent enclosed top "like a coupe." In America, the term was generally used for a town car with permanent roof over the chauffeur. The early ones had no windows in the front compartment, using side-curtains instead, but later models which were completely closed but had a partition behind the driver were usually called *Enclosed-drive Limousines*. On the Continent, *Limousine* denoted rather a sedan type body. The French for a time referred to this as a *"Conduite Interieur"* or Inside Drive, while the English called it a *Saloon*, as they still do.

One variation of this type was one that we at LeBaron, and some other body builders as well, called a *Sedan-Limousine*. Our own distinction was that a Sedan-limousine was intended to be driven at least occasionally by the owner. The front compartment was therefore more luxurious than one on a strictly chauffeur-driven car, generally upholstered in the same material used in the rear. We also went to great lengths to make the dividing partition as inconspicuous as possible when the glass was lowered. No customer of ours would admit that he couldn't afford a completely separate car for those occasions when he drove himself.

Terms like *Berline* or *Imperial Limousine* were used by some firms to designate what we called an Enclosed-drive Limousine, but I believe this was done more by production builders except for Judkins whose Berlines were part of the Lincoln line for

1928 Renault Coupe de Ville, which we would call a Panel Brougham. From Renault catalog, Floyd Marshall Collection.

1926 Rolls-Royce Sudbury Sedan-Limousine. From Rolls-Royce catalog illustrated by LeBaron.

some years. Quite a few manufacturers of medium-priced cars in the twenties offered such a model. It was usually the regular sedan with a partition added behind the driver.

Webster says a *Landau* is a four-wheeled covered vehicle with the top divided so that the vehicle can be used open or closed. A *Landaulet* was a small Landau. By the time I entered the business, a Landaulet was any body on which the portion of the top behind the doors could be folded. In the early twenties there were some Coupe-Landaulets built by Judkins, LeBaron and others. Judkins called them *Coupelets.* They were two- or three-passenger coupes with only the small section of roof behind the doors folding. However, most Landaulets were town cars or limousines with the rear section of the roof made to open. Sometimes there was a blind-quarter, all of which folded, but often there was a quarter window. In that case, frequently the section of the roof over this window could also be opened.

Open cars were somewhat less confusing. A *Roadster* seated two people (sometimes a rumble seat allowed for two more), and if it was an especially sporting version it was often called a *Speedster, Runabout* or *Raceabout.* At one time Stutz called all their open cars Speedsters, regardless of capacity. They even had a seven-passenger Speedster.

A *Touring Car* was an open car designed for four or more passengers. This was the most prevalent style of the early part of the century, until it lost ground to the less expensive closed bodies that appeared in the early twenties. A *Phaeton* was a light, sporting Touring Car, which borrowed its name from the horse-drawn vehicles of the same general type. *Torpedo* is included in that 1918 Dictionary as "an automobile body built so that its side surfaces are flush." I would say that it was generally used for a Phaeton of rather slim, streamlined shape. In fact, there was occasional use of the term "Torpedo Phaeton."

1925 Lincoln Convertible Roadster by LeBaron, exhibited at 1924 New York Salon. From *Lincoln Magazine,* Salon issue.

1927 Lincoln Sport Phaeton by Dietrich, exhibited at 1926 New York Salon.

Another expression used up to the mid-twenties was "Victoria Top." This was a canopy-type top over just the rear seat of a Phaeton or Touring Car. It derived from the type of folding top used on horse-drawn Victorias. In bad weather, an extension could be added to reach up to the windshield.

There has been some confusion over the terms *Convertible Coupe, Convertible Roadster* and *Cabriolet,* all of which have been applied to 2/3 passenger cars with windows in the doors and folding roofs. The earliest of these was Convertible Coupe, which is still in use. LeBaron introduced the name Convertible Roadster as early as 1924, and from 1928 on used it to signify a car whose top folded very flat, or even into the body. It was closer to an open roadster in appearance, although fitted with disappearing side windows.

Some owners of these cars—especially the Lincolns, of which we built several hundred—have apologized to me for using the original designation, assuming that Lincoln had concocted the name. When I explain that LeBaron devised it, and the reason for it, they are usually quite surprised. Finally,

Ford called the convertible Model A *Cabriolet,* and this name soon spread to general use.

Since designers are all highly individualistic, there were other names coined from time to time to describe a particular variation of a body style. LeBaron used the term *Prince of Wales Sedan* for a body which looked somewhat like a Convertible Sedan, with leather roof, rear quarters dropping below the belt line, and a coupe molding running down from the windshield. Its name derived from the fact that the Prince, now the Duke of Windsor, had a Barker Rolls-Royce of similar style.

There was no restriction on the use of his title in this country, and since he was very popular among the polo set on Long Island, the name had good snob appeal there. I do not recall any objection from the Duke, and I know that he was often a guest of one or another of our customers who had a "Prince of Wales" model.

Sportif was coined, I believe, by Daniels for an open car that was a cross between a Phaeton and a Roadster. The name was later applied to the Phaeton that LeBaron designed for Locomobile in 1923. *Salamanca* was used for years by Rolls-Royce for a Cabriolet type of Town Car, on the grounds that their first such vehicle had been built for the Count of Salamanca.

In this chapter, I have tried to give the interpretation of the name of the various body styles as we used them at LeBaron, along with something of their background from carriage days. Most of our contemporaries followed the same usage, although there were some variations. Perhaps the only definitive answer for any particular body is to find out, if possible, what its builder called it in the first place. That does not include any of the censorable comments he may have made during its construction.

1923 Rolls-Royce Convertible Sedan by Barker & Co., built for the then Prince of Wales, now the Duke of Windsor. Bodies of similar lines by various American custom body builders were known as "Prince of Wales Sedans." Photograph courtesy of the Montagu Motor Museum.

1926 Rolls-Royce Salamanca. From Rolls-Royce catalog illustrated by LeBaron.

Cover of 1928 New York Salon Catalogue.

15

The Automobile Salon

THE showplace for the custom bodies and fine cars of the twenties and early thirties was the annual Automobile Salon. Since *Motor Trend* did me the honor of publishing an article I wrote on this subject, in their February 1965, issue, I am taking the liberty of including this with a few interpolations:

It was early Sunday afternoon, December 2, 1928. A uniformed guard removed a velvet rope across the Ballroom entrance in the Hotel Commodore in New York. The latest, most fashionable Automobile Salon had begun.

It would be shown here for a week, then repeated at the Drake in Chicago in January, and finally move to the Los Angeles Biltmore in February. It was, as usual, the most exclusive and impressive automobile show in the world.

Admission was by invitation only. The engraved cards were divided among the exhibitors who, in turn, sent them to the elite of New York, to people who liked fine cars and didn't care what they cost, and to the top Detroit executives.

To quote from the Salon catalogue: "It is dedicated to the display, amid appropriate surroundings, of all that is fashionable and really meritorious in high-grade motor car chassis and custom coachwork." These were florid words, but not when you consider the list of exhibitors:

EXHIBITING

Cunningham	Mercedes
Isotta-Fraschini	Minerva
Lancia	Renault
Rolls-Royce	

EXHIBITED BY COACHMAKERS

Cadillac	Franklin	Packard
Chrysler 80	LaSalle	Pierce-Arrow
Duesenberg	Lincoln	Stearns-Knight
	Stutz	

COACHWORK EXHIBITED BY

Brewster	Fisher	Locke
Brunn	Fleetwood	Murphy
Castagna	Hibbard & Darrin	Rollston
Derham	Holbrook	Weymann
Dietrich	Judkins	Willoughby
	LeBaron	

If this arrangement of names seems a bit odd, it's because it reflects a basic rule of the Salon throughout its existence. It had originally been conceived as a showplace for imported cars and fine coachwork. American chassis could be shown only by the custom body builders. The only exceptions were Cunningham, who maintained their own custom body shop, and Rolls-Royce. The Rolls exhibited in 1928 came from the American factory at Springfield, Massachusetts, but in earlier years they had come from England.

Having attended every Salon from 1924 to the last in 1931, I can still picture them quite clearly. The main exhibits were in the Grand Ballroom, with a few smaller ones in the foyer and another group in the East Ballroom. Occasionally there was an overflow of exhibits into the lobby of the hotel—perhaps half a dozen additional cars.

A special elevator was built into the Commodore Hotel so the cars could be taken from the trucks of the P. J. Brady Trucking Company right to the Ballroom. All gasoline and oil had to be drained from them before they were permitted into the building. The cars shown in the lobby were rolled down the stairs at the West end, held back by heavy ropes and winches on the trucks.

LeBaron was the only exhibitor with two stands—one under the name of *LeBaron* directly opposite the main entrance to the Grand Ballroom, and a second in the East Ballroom under the name of *Ralph Roberts of LeBaron.* Since each stand could hold four cars, this meant a total of eight on our own stands, with usually a few more sprinkled among the exhibits on European chassis—always some Minervas

A view of the 1926 New York Salon. Fleetwood's stand is in the foreground, with a Rolls-Royce Brougham centered. The Minerva stand is just beyond, with a LeBaron-Ostruk Town Cabriolet partly visible. Photograph by Nathan Lazarnick, courtesy Automobile Manufacturers Association.

and frequently an Isotta-Fraschini or a Rolls-Royce.

At the 1928 Salon, the *piece de resistance,* standing in the front center of the main LeBaron stand, was a Lincoln Aero-Phaeton. Finished in brushed aluminum with bright green fenders and upholstery, it stood out sharply from its more subdued neighbors. The boat-tail, with a fin shaped like an airplane rudder, was far advanced for its day, and the radiator cap boasted a specially sculptured ornament in the shape of an airplane. (After original publication of this article, I learned the car is still in existence in the hands of Ray Radford of Vancouver, Washington, in whose garage I visited it in the Summer of 1967.)

Another conspicuous car by LeBaron was a huge Duesenberg Model J Phaeton at the center of the second LeBaron stand. This was the show that introduced the Model J to the world. The same car, restored and repainted, was shown at the Coliseum in New York in April 1963.

On the Isotta-Fraschini stand, one of the raciest vehicles was a four-passenger Sport Sedan, also by LeBaron. Finished in bright yellow and black, with roof lines simulating a convertible and covered with gleaming black patent leather, it made quite an eye-catcher.

From the standpoint of present-day enthusiasts, the Stutz Roadster-Phaeton on LeBaron's East Ballroom stand would also seem quite desirable. On the long 145-inch wheelbase, it boasted a folding rumble seat with full doors, and a tonneau windshield that rolled down into the body.

1929 Lincoln Aero-Phaeton by LeBaron, which was featured at the 1928 New York Salon and then at the following Chicago, Los Angeles and San Francisco Salons. A recent photograph by its present owner, Mr. Ray Radford of Vancouver, Washington.

1929 Stutz Roadster-Phaeton by LeBaron, shown at 1928 New York Salon. Reproduction of R. L. Stickney rendering for LeBaron Salon Catalog.

On the Minerva stand was a "Gentleman's Sport Sedan" by LeBaron, with a built-in bar. There was a silver maple cabinet across the front seat-back, fitted with a zinc-lined icebox and a set of silver tumblers and cut-glass decanters. Several similar cars were built, and at least one seems to belong to the Hollywood genius who rents cars to the movie studios. I keep seeing it on the "Late Show."

The remaining cars on the LeBaron stands might seem stodgy today, but they represented the real bread-and-butter of the custom body business of the time: a Packard Limousine and a Packard Town Car, a Lincoln Town Car with broadcloth upholstery in the rear embroidered in needlepoint, and a small Town Car on the Stutz Blackhawk chassis that was also introduced at this show.

Other builders also had outstanding cars in the Salon. One of the most revolutionary was the Convertible Coupe with disappearing top by Walter Murphy, which helped to introduce the Duesenberg J. There were also other Convertibles by Dietrich, Brunn and Derham. Walter Murphy had a Rolls-Royce Sedan that might be the forerunner of the modern hardtop. It had four doors with very narrow posts between, as on a Convertible, and the windows

rolled down in their frames. Some of the most unusual bodies in the show were the Weymann Stutzes, with their fabric-covered flexible construction.

Naturally, we had some last-minute problems in completing the cars for the Salon. That Lincoln Aero-Phaeton, for instance, was to have aluminum wheel covers which we had ordered from Hibbard & Darrin in Paris. The covers arrived on the French Line two days before the Salon opened. I arranged with Ford to get them through customs and rush them to their service building in Long Island City, where the car was getting final attention.

Late in the afternoon, the wheel-discs arrived, neatly packed in wooden cases and surrounded by mounds of excelsior. There was only one thing missing—instructions on how to attach them. We unpacked everything and found an assortment of nuts, bolts and clamps. The mechanics threw up their hands, but, with a little ingenuity, I got the first set on under their watchful eyes, and they did the rest.

The doormen for the Salon were the same Pinkerton men who took tickets at Belmont Park race track. They knew most millionaires by sight. Even with the carefully controlled distribution of invitations, it was felt desirable to have them do a bit of extra screening. After all, many of our distinguished citizens were on more than one mailing list—they might have given their extra tickets to the cook.

One day, I was told that Henry Ford was arriving for his usual tour of the Salon. After making sure that our main stand was in order, I went to the East Ballroom to check on the other, where I carefully opened the rear door of the Lincoln Town Car to show off its interior. Very soon, Ford came striding through in his quick way, hurrying along but not missing a thing. He was accompanied by Walter

1929 Packard Convertible Sedan by Dietrich, exhibited at 1928 New York Salon. From their advertisement in Salon catalog.

Briggs, who was building most Ford bodies and had recently bought LeBaron.

A few minutes behind them, a rather plainly dressed, middle-aged woman strolled along leisurely, looking around with considerable interest. I heard the town car door slam, and looked around to see a Lincoln salesman obviously trying to protect his treasure from the common people. I opened the door again so that Mrs. Ford, too, could get a good look at the needlepoint upholstery. Incidentally, she admired it very much.

Interior of Lincoln Town Brougham by LeBaron, with needlepoint upholstery. The pattern is a copy of that used in a sedan chair built for Marie Antoinette by the Adam brothers in the Seventeenth Century. From rendering by R. L. Stickney for the *Lincoln Magazine*.

At a later Salon, in 1930, there occurred what we called "The Battle of the Marmon." The Marmon V-16 engine was introduced here. While the bodies were built at the LeBaron-Detroit plant, they'd been designed by Walter Teague with very angular lines and we weren't too proud of them. The Marmon was relegated to the back of the East Ballroom stand, behind a Lincoln Convertible Roadster. Some of the Marmon executives complained, but we convinced them that we controlled the space and had sole decision on the placement of the cars. Or so we thought.

When the Salon was about to open the second day, the Marmon stood in front and the Lincoln at the back. Not only that, but every door was locked and the brakes tightened so that the cars couldn't be budged. I still haven't found out who switched them during the night. At any rate, we got the cars back to their proper places before too many visitors arrived.

Next morning, guess where the Marmon was! This time, we got a top-level conference to settle matters for good, and even some Marmon mechanics to help move the cars.

The Salon was one of the social events of the season. Many customers dropped in between dinner and the theater, or perhaps on their way to a party. So many of them were in evening clothes that it became mandatory for all exhibitors and their staffs to wear tuxedos after six.

Since the Salon was always held more than a month ahead of the New York Auto Show, it served as the place to introduce most of the chassis that make up today's Classics. Besides the Duesenberg J and the Marmon 16, the Cadillac 12 and 16, the Lincoln and Packard 12s, the Stutz SV-16 and DV-32, the "small" Pierce-Arrow "80" and the later 8- and 12-cylinder Pierces, the Chrysler Imperial, and many others made their debuts at the Salon. It would be nice to have a display of equal magnificence today.

The above was based mainly on the 1928 Salon because I had available not only LeBaron's 1928 Salon catalogue, but the official catalogue of the Salon itself. Actually, the 1921 Salon had a greater number of exhibitors:

BODY BUILDERS EXHIBITING:

Brewster	Fleetwood	New Haven
Brooks-Ostruk	Healy	Pease
deCausse	Holbrook	Rochambeau
Derham	Locke	Springfield
	Murphy	

CHASSIS EXHIBITED

Benz	Fergus	Minerva
Biddle	Fiat	Packard
Brewster	Hispano-Suiza	Pierce-Arrow
Cadillac	Isotta-Fraschini	Rauch & Lang
Cunningham	Lafayette	Richelieu
Daniels	Lanchester	Rolls-Royce
Delage	Lincoln	S.P.A.
Dorris	Locomobile	Stevens-Duryea
Duesenberg	McFarlan	Sunbeam
Falcon	Mercedes	Winton

Trade magazine comment at the time mentioned that interest would center on the new 8-in-line engines and four-wheel brakes. They did not predict that a dozen fine cars shown at the 1921 Salon would be off the market within a year or two.

1929 Duesenberg Model J Phaeton built for Mr. W. F. Ryan, and used as an illustration in LeBaron catalog for 1929 Salon.

1930 Packard All-Weather Cabriolet, from LeBaron catalog for the 1929 New York Salon. This body was ordered specially for the Salon, but produced orders for several duplicates.

1930 Stutz SV-16 Sedan-Limousine by LeBaron, built specially for the 1929 Salon. A few more of the same design were built. Reproduced from LeBaron Salon catalog.

1931 Pierce-Arrow Cabriolet by LeBaron, built for an aunt of racing driver Phil Hill and now part of his collection. Photograph by the author at Concours d'Elegance, Pebble Beach, California, 1967.

PART III

16
The Lincoln

NATURALLY most custom bodies were built on relatively expensive chassis. Probably the favorite in this country during the 1920s was the Lincoln. It was generally considered to be the finest American chassis of the time. Its prestige was further enhanced by Edsel Ford's encouragement of the custom body industry.

When Henry Leland developed the Lincoln, he had in mind to make it the finest automobile he could produce. He succeeded so well that his basic chassis with the V-8 engine with a 60-degree angle betweeen banks was continued almost unchanged, mechanically, for ten years after its introduction in 1921.

The quality that Leland built into the car, coupled with the 1921 deflation which made itself felt just after he got the Lincoln on the market, put him in financial difficulties. It has been widely rumored that Henry Ford put up the $3 million to buy the assets of the Lincoln Motor Car Company in order to keep Edsel occupied with running this subsidiary and thus keep him from wanting to share in the management of the main company. Whether this is true or not, Edsel Ford did concentrate on the Lincoln and was given a fairly free hand, although his father kept in close touch with everything going on at Lincoln, and also insisted that the Leland standards of quality be maintained.

Edsel Ford was quite venturesome in ordering bodies for his personal use, and in 1924 LeBaron designed for him a phaeton with quite smooth lines for the period, and with a disappearing top. I had the honor of being trusted, under close supervision, to make some of the detail tracings from the full-size draft of this body.

As early as 1925, Lincoln was advertising, truthfully that "Every Lincoln body style is the creation of

a master designer," and going on to list the leading custom body builders. The usual procedure was for Edsel Ford to select a design submitted by one of the custom builders, sometimes one suggested by him, and to order from the firm that designed it a preliminary run of five bodies. If the design was for a town car or some other type on which volume could not be expected to run high, additional bodies were ordered from the same source as needed.

The more conventional types, such as sedans, were turned over to Murray or another Detroit firm for quantity production, but the original designer received an additional fee for his contribution. These bodies for several years carried nameplates reading "Designed by ——" with the name of the custom body firm in the style used on their own regular nameplates. Lincoln catalogs of the period distinguish the bodies in the same way, some models being listed as, say, "Coupe by Judkins" whereas another may read "Sedan designed by LeBaron." I mention this since there has been some confusion in recent years as to who actually built a particular body.

At LeBaron, we were responsible in 1925 for a Victoria Coupe and two- and three-window sedans, all of which became part of the Lincoln line, with the production bodies built by Murray and Wilson. The first five of the coupes and three-window sedans were built by LeBaron, however. On the two-window sedan, several additional bodies were built by LeBaron, somewhat over a dozen in all, for various individuals who preferred the additional quality or wished some changes made in the basic design.

In addition, we created a town car that was included in the Lincoln line as Model 155, but all of these bodies were built by LeBaron, perhaps twenty or so. We also built the bodies of subsequent LeBaron town cars and the Convertible Roadsters introduced in 1928. Each of these carried a regular Lincoln model number, usually changed from year to year as minor changes were introduced.

Although each small series followed the same basic design, every body was finished to the specifications of the individual purchaser with the paint and up-

1924 Lincoln Sport Phaeton by LeBaron, shown with Mr. Edsel Ford and his wife, for whom the car was specially designed. Photograph courtesy Petersen Publishing Co.

holstery they selected. The first LeBaron town car design, Model 155, was originally for a full-collapsible cabriolet, but some of the bodies were built with stationary roofs and one or two were true landaulets with only the rear quarter folding. These were relatively simple modifications made for specific orders.

Since production was never huge on any Lincoln model, other custom builders also continued making their designs in series. This was true of the Judkins Coupes and Berlines, and also the town cars and limousines from other sources such as Brunn and Willoughby.

The 1925 Victoria Coupe referred to earlier had a large bucket seat for the driver, with a two-passenger seat offset slightly to the rear and to the right of this. A folding seat went under the cowl, but could be set up to accommodate a fourth passenger. As a result, the body had rather intricate shaping, with a wide center section to fit the unusual seating, and a narrower rear deck. While we at LeBaron, accustomed to thinking in three dimensions, could readily visualize this, it was a difficult idea to convey to Lincoln management before the first bodies were actually built.

R. L. Stickney made up a clay model, using the same one-inch-to-the-foot scale we generally worked in on our designs. We didn't dare ship it, so we built a wooden box around it and I delivered it to H. J. C. Henderson, Lincoln Sales Manager at the time, so he could take it back to Detroit with him. I recall being looked at rather oddly when I walked into the Plaza Hotel with that wooden box under my arm, to take it up to his suite. Henderson left Lincoln to become an executive of Fisher Body sometime in 1927.

That was the first time, to my knowledge, that a clay model was used to present an idea to management. It was one of many "firsts" we developed at LeBaron, though we didn't claim any credit at the time. Our philosophy was simply that we could think up new ideas faster than others could copy them.

Lincoln maintained a corps of inspectors to visit

1925 Lincoln Sedan by LeBaron on stretched 144-inch wheelbase. The Jolson sedan, built a couple of years later, was similar but with a black leather roof and no landau irons.

1926 Lincoln Victoria Coupe by LeBaron, shown at 1925 Salon. The first bodies were built by LeBaron, but later production models carried the nameplate "Designed by LeBaron."

the various body builders' plants, to check the quality of any Lincoln bodies under construction. Their requirements were rather stringent in many respects, especially after Henry Crecelius left Brewster to become Chief Body Engineer for Lincoln. They even specified that monel metal screws be used to attach hinges and other body hardware.

Often Lincoln's specifications conflicted with some experimental idea we wanted to try out. When this happened, we would arrange to have the purchaser order the body directly from us, and buy only the chassis from his Lincoln dealer. Technically, Lincoln

1929 Lincoln Town Sedan, designed by Willoughby. The first bodies of this type were built by Willoughby, with later production models coming from Murray.

was not then involved in the body order and their inspector had no jurisdiction. However, he usually kept his eye on what was being done, and so far as possible we followed their requirements even when we thought our own were as good or better.

Sometimes we felt it desirable to alter the wheelbase to achieve the effect we wanted, especially on a 4/5 passenger body where we liked to place the rear seat ahead of the rear axle, both to improve the ride and to get it down lower. I'm quite sure this concept originated at LeBaron, although others came up with it about the same time.

The standard Lincoln chassis had a 136-inch wheelbase from its original design by Henry Leland until 1931. This was just a bit short of what we wanted. There was a 150-inch wheelbase "ambulance" chassis that we thought too long for good proportions, although we did build a few bodies on it. We favored a 144-inch wheelbase, but were not able to persuade Ford of its advantages until 1931. As a result, we built several Lincolns including one for Al Jolson on chassis that we had stretched to our desired length.

Jolson's sedan was probably the lowest Lincoln closed car built up to that time, standing 68 inches tall when most cars were over six feet. He still wasn't happy about it when I delivered it, and told me he had wanted it "so low I'd have to crawl in." With that, he handed me his check for the body, and the Lincoln salesman one for the chassis, the two adding to about $10,000. Then he turned to the Lincoln salesman and told him to sell the car for whatever it would bring. Jolson and his chauffeur left in his "old" car, a Dietrich Packard Convertible Sedan disguised with a Hispano-Suiza radiator and hood.

The town cars from various custom builders included in the Lincoln line listed in the neighborhood of $7,000 for the complete car. These were built in small series of five or ten at a time. The Judkins Coupes and Berlines, as well as the LeBaron Convertible Roadsters, ran to somewhat larger volume. Several hundred of each were built, and the prices were correspondingly lower, around $6,000.

At the same time, quite a few individual bodies were built on Lincoln chassis by all the leading custom body firms, for which the prices ranged from $8,000 up, often $10,000 or slightly more. One such was the town brougham with needlepoint upholstery which was in one of our Salon exhibits. The needlepoint was done in France by Gobelins, duplicating the pattern of a sedan chair built by the Adam Brothers for Marie Antoinette. The fabric alone for that interior cost over $1,500.

In the thirties, Lincoln started building their less expensive Zephyrs. The design of this was based on a rear-engined car originally conceived by Fred Duesenberg with the styling done by John Tjaarda in his

spare time while he was at Locke's Rochester plant. Nothing came of the idea, and when Tjaarda moved to the LeBaron Studios in 1933, Briggs built an experimental car to this design. With various modifications, including the more conventional placement of the engine in front, it became the Zephyr.

A few years later, when Edsel Ford decided on a special car for his own use, although the styling was done by Bob Gregorie of the Ford staff, the body was built at the LeBaron-Detroit plant. That became the first Lincoln Continental.

Lincoln had some very excellent dealers, one of the best being Park Central Motors whose showroom for many years occupied the corner of 247 Park Avenue at 46th Street, in New York. It was owned by Dutee W. Flint, who had started as a Ford dealer in Providence and went on to take over not only the best Lincoln agency in Manhattan but also one in West Palm Beach.

Another source of much custom body business was the North Shore of Long Island, then consisting principally of large estates which were the summer homes of New York's wealthy families. Great Neck Motors and Roslyn Motors contributed many orders for individually custom-built Lincolns. Roslyn Motors' ads always read "At the sign of the Clock Tower," and that tower is still there.

Some custom body business came from other parts of the country, and I especially remember the Lowe Motor Company in San Francisco. We obtained orders for a number of special Lincolns through them for

1939 Lincoln Continental Convertible Coupe, from Lincoln Catalog.

the Crocker family as well as other prominent Californians.

Henry Ford always kept a Lincoln in New York for use on his visits here, generally a Brunn town car. He always stayed at the Hotel Gotham, which was right around the corner from LeBaron's office. I al-ways knew when he was in town because I'd see his car outside the hotel with his personal chauffeur, Izzy Levine, at the wheel. Izzy was a lifetime Ford employee and later moved into various executive positions in the New York branch.

1922 Lincoln Town Brougham by Brunn, built for Mr. Henry Ford and used by him in New York City.

17
Packard

PROBABLY the next most popular chassis for custom bodies was the Packard. They had a long history in this field, having built fine cars since early in the century, and many handsome bodies had been mounted on the Twin-Sixes of the period just after World War I.

By the time I entered the business, the Twin-Six had given way to the Packard Eight. There was only one eight-cylinder Packard then, which continued on as the Super eight with various modifications right up to 1942. The smaller chassis was a Six, although a small Eight replaced this in the mid-twenties. The Twin-Six designation was revived for the new twelve introduced for 1932 and built for several years. Some aficionados describe this as the finest Packard ever built. Bob Turnquist has some interesting comments about this in *The Packard Story.*

Much of Packard's custom body business was handled through their New York factory branch, where this phase was under the direction of G. C. Parvis. His personal standards were quite high, especially as to details of workmanship and finish.

During the time I had considerable contact with Mr. Parvis, he had a very capable young secretary named Mary Burns. She remained with Packard through the merger with Studebaker and the distributorship of Mercedes-Benz. I saw her again while she was with the latter subsidiary, and we spent some pleasant hours reminiscing. She told me how valuable the training under Mr. Parvis had been when she became associated with another fine car.

Packard also instituted a custom body section at its headquarters in Detroit, under the direction of Horace Potter, in 1926. They arranged for the purchase of small series of bodies from various custom builders. The organization underwent changes from time to time, and I believe more business was actually placed by Grover Parvis in New York, who worked closely with dealers and branches in other parts of the country.

Among the bodies that Potter ordered from Le-Baron for the Packard 443 were two similar sedan-limousines, one with a closed rear quarter and the other with a window. The initial order was for ten of the first type and four with the extra window, but before that model year ended we had delivered a total of 26 of the first type, and six more of the second.

In the next few years, LeBaron built a number of other Packards in small series, mostly sedan-limousines and various types of town cars. There were also a number of individually designed bodies, usually worked out to suit some well-known purchaser. However, we would occasionally get an order from Mr. Parvis for perhaps a special town car for display in his showroom. Often these would lead to additional orders for duplicates or slight modifications of the first body.

At the 1929 Salon, one of the most interesting bodies was a Convertible Roadster by Murphy on the Duesenberg. It had very smooth lines and a disappearing top covered by a hinged metal lid in the deck. Parvis felt this body style had considerable possibilities and asked me if we could duplicate it.

I pointed out that the metal lid could be a source of rattles, and suggested instead a well with canvas

1922 Packard Limousine by Holbrook, exhibited at 1921 Closed Car Show in New York.

1929 Packard Sedan-Limousine by LeBaron, photograph by John Adams Davis just after the car was
exhibited at the 1928 New York Salon. Courtesy of
Automobile Manufacturers Association.

cover as on our Lincoln Convertible Roadster introduced a year earlier. Parvis was not satisfied with this
idea, and my next suggestion was a compromise: a
top folding into the body as on the Murphy design,
but covered with a small canvas boot.

I worked out the design, and our engineering department in Bridgeport, then consisting of two people, developed the mechanism from my suggestions.
They not only got the top to fold into the very compact space available, but made it much simpler to
operate. In fact, Packard put it into production two
years later with only minor changes to fit the shorter
chassis. Like many other ideas borrowed from Le-
Baron, it was taken without any thanks or even a request for permission to use it. It had not been patented. In the meantime, we had built at least 50 of
these bodies, not bad for a custom body run in 1930
and 1931 when business was very sharply off.

Since the Wall Street crash had already taken
place, there was some question whether Parvis would
be allowed to order any of these bodies. Fortunately,
Mr. Briggs was willing to take part in the gamble,
and arrangements were made whereby Packard would
supply a chassis for each body we built, but we would
not be paid until the cars were actually sold to dealers. In practice, that meant that most of them were

actually sold at retail before the dealer's order was
placed.

Some years later, while visiting Enos Derham, I
learned that he had also been asked to develop such
a body, and was very unhappy when I took the order
away from him. At the time, he had not been told the
full circumstances, which were simply that there
would have been no order for either of us if we had
not had the financial backing of Briggs. As it was
Enos did get several orders for his design over the
next few years.

Another design developed by the LeBaron Studios
in Detroit, a convertible sedan, was included in the

1930 Packard Convertible Roadster by LeBaron. Reproductions of Stickney renderings of design by the
author, showing top raised and folded.

1941 Packard Convertible Victoria by Darrin. This model was mounted on a special short-wheelbase chassis. From Packard Super-eight Catalog.

deal with Packard. These were built at the Detroit plant. Some partly completed convertible roadster bodies were at the Bridgeport plant when it was decided to close this facility toward the end of 1930. Except for the few we could complete there, these were sent to the LeBaron-Detroit plant for finishing. During those last days at Bridgeport, I went through the paint stockroom with E. P. Carter, our general manager there. We selected some paints of which there was enough to do a whole car, and two or three of those Packards were finished with these. It is about the only instance I know of where a custom body was painted with "left-overs."

The New York branch of Packard also housed their Export Department, and we built several bodies for them. Unlike those for use in this country, which were always on the largest chassis, many of these for abroad were on the long-wheelbase model of the smaller chassis. This was due to the fact that they were intended mostly for town use in countries with high gasoline prices and tax rates based on engine size.

Up to 1928 this was no problem, since Packard was then building six and eight cylinder models which were almost identical from the hood back, the difference being nearly all in the engine length. A body built in small series for the largest eight could be mounted on the long six with only minor changes. When the small eight was introduced, there was con-

siderable difference between the two chassis. Any body for the smaller car had to be individually designed and built.

One of the finest I can remember was a full-collapsible All-weather Cabriolet, or town car, for a prominent Argentine family. It was one of the most expensive bodies we ever built (actually we lost quite a bit of money on it), but was mounted on the smaller 733 chassis.

The chauffeur's compartment could be open or closed, depending on the weather, and on a really fine day the entire top could be folded down. It was designed so the disappearing partition behind the chauffeur could be left up, if desired, to form a tonneau windshield for the passengers.

Even on the small chassis, this particular car would have cost nearly $10,000 in New York. If it had reflected its actual cost of construction, it would have run some $2,000 higher. Most custom-built Packards sold in the same price range as Lincolns, or around $7,000 for those built in small series, and somewhat more for individual designs.

You will note I have mentioned the price of this export town car as what it would have been in New York. The actual cost in Argentina, including shipping and customs duties, was somewhat over $15,-000. We felt quite proud at LeBaron that a number of our bodies were purchased abroad, where the cost of a custom-built Packard or similar car was sometimes higher than that of an individually built European car of the best quality.

18
Cadillac

ANOTHER name that has continued since the early days of the industry is Cadillac. The company was organized in 1902, and introduced their first model, a one-cylinder vehicle, in 1903 and continued production of it until 1908. In the meantime, they added a four-cylinder model in 1905, which continued with modifications until 1914.

For 1915, Cadillac introduced the first production V-8 in America, on a very fine vehicle designed by Henry Leland. Except for a change from platform-type to semi-elliptic springs in the rear, this car was continued with only minor modifications, mechanically, well into the 1930s. Even after the Sixteen and Twelve were introduced, the Eights were still the bread and butter of the Cadillac line.

No mention of Cadillac could be complete without some reference to their role in World War I. General Pershing and many other high officers used Cadillacs in France as their official cars. When this country began to experiment with that new invention, the tank, the first ones were powered by Cadillac V-8 engines.

The V-16 introduced for 1930 and the V-12 added the following year were both excellent cars, and quite a few of them have been preserved. All of the Sixteens and most of the Twelves carried Fleetwood bodies, built in the new plant set up in Detroit shortly before these models were introduced. Although the Sixteen was the more expensive of the two, selling in the $5,000 to $8,000 price range, it was the general opinion among knowledgeable chauffeurs at the time that the Twelve was the better vehicle. This opinion seems to be shared by many Cadillac enthusiasts to-

day. Some have told me they feel the performance of the Twelve, with its 368 cubic inch engine, is quite as good as that of the Sixteen which has 452 cubic inches.

I have often been asked why LeBaron never built a body on the Cadillac Sixteen. There are several reasons for this, and in fact why we built relatively few Cadillacs at all. The most obvious is that the Fisher Body Company bought out Fleetwood in 1925. While some Fleetwood bodies were built on chassis other than Cadillac and LaSalle after that time, no other custom body builder was encouraged to build on a Cadillac. In fact, it was almost impossible to buy a separate Cadillac chassis for this purpose.

The 1925 New York Salon had Cadillacs with bodies by Brunn, Fleetwood, Holbrook, Judkins, LeBaron and the Custom Body Division of Fisher. The latter was a new idea but was eliminated after the incorporation of Fleetwood as a division of Fisher. Since the purchase of Fleetwood took place not too long before this Salon, all arrangements with the other custom body firms had been made earlier in the year for the bodies they displayed at this Salon.

The LeBaron bodies on Cadillacs at the 1925 Salon were a Sport Phaeton and a Prince of Wales Sedan. They had special radiators and hoods, higher and less rounded than standard, and also special fenders, all created by us at the request of J. R. Mc-

1922 Cadillac Sedan by Fisher, shown at the Closed Car Show in New York. Note separate trunk at rear of body, one of the first fitted as standard equipment.

1926 Cadillac Sport Phaeton by LeBaron with special radiator, hood and fenders. Photograph by Nathan Lazarnick of LeBaron's East Ballroom stand at the 1925 New York Salon. Behind the Cadillac is the Lincoln Victoria Coupe described in a previous chapter, and to the right part of a Rolls-Royce Sport Sedan. Photograph courtesy of Automotive History Collection, Detroit Public Library.

Lauchlen, manager of the custom body department of Uppercu Cadillac, the New York distributor. The bodies had been ordered by him rather than by Cadillac in Detroit.

Three or four more of the phaetons were built subsequent to the Salon, and eight of the sedans, for various people who ordered them through Uppercu. Some of these were slight modifications of the original designs.

While the Salon bodies were being built, we were approached by Mr. McLauchlen to adapt the designs for a new, smaller Cadillac then being planned. We were given the impression that they would become production designs for this new chassis. Sketches of several body types were prepared and submitted to Cadillac in Detroit.

Several months went by, and since we had heard nothing further from Cadillac, Ralph Roberts made some inquiries while on a trip to Detroit. He was told that plans for the small Cadillac had been dropped. When the new LaSalle was announced the following year, we were quite astonished both by the fact that the dropped plan had apparently been carried out, and by the striking similarity of the LaSalle to the sketches we had submitted.

By this time, LeBaron had already been purchased by Briggs, who built the bodies for a large part of General Motors' biggest competitors. Ralph Roberts was already setting up the LeBaron Studios in Detroit and was in an awkward position to deal with Cadillac. He did call them, however, and told me he had been told that after all we had been approached to submit ideas for a new Cadillac model, and the LaSalle was an entirely different brand.

I myself applied to the Styling Section of General Motors in 1936, sending along some sketches to prove my ability. There was considerable interest in rear-engined cars at the time and I had developed some ideas in this connection. It seemed to me the logical place for the radiator in such a car was in the front edges of the rear fenders, and I included

1940 Cadillac Touring Sedan by Fleetwood. From Fleetwood-Cadillac catalog.

this feature in one of the sketches I submitted. I did not get the job and the sketches were returned to me, presumably after careful scrutiny. A couple of years later, Cadillac adopted the styling, although not the functional aspects of my idea. They used it for quite a while, but I never heard even a word of thanks.

Lest it seem that I am completely opposed to General Motors, I should point out that some of my family owned Cadillacs. Two of my sisters and their husbands have owned a string of Buicks and Oldsmobiles stretching back over thirty years.

In the late twenties, Cadillac bought some experimental bodies from Hibbard & Darrin, and made

arrangements to used the rolled-belt treatment typical of Hibbard's styling. This led to his spending a year on the Cadillac design staff after liquidating his business in Paris.

When first introduced, the LaSalle was a smaller version of the Cadillac V-8 and continued as such until 1934, when General Motors decided to use what was basically an Oldsmobile chassis with minor modifications. It was fitted, however, with very attractive bodies and a distinctive narrow radiator, all designed by Julio Andrade. These are undoubtedly among the best looking production models of that particular period.

1933 Cadillac V-16 All-Weather Phaeton by Fleetwood, built for Mr. Al Jolson. Photograph courtesy of its present owner, Harrah's Automobile Collection.

19
Chrysler

1928 Chrysler "80" Convertible Sedan by Dietrich, exhibited at 1927 New York Salon. Note fluted hood similar to the Vauxhall.

WHEN Walter Chrysler founded the company bearing his name, he was no neophyte in the automobile business. He had already been General Manager of Buick at a very substantial salary. He left there after a disagreement, and was hired by John N. Willys to rejuvenate his company.

Willys at the time had a new factory in Elizabeth, New Jersey, set up initially for war production. There was another "secret" project under way in the plant in 1921, financed by Mr. Willys. The Duesenberg brothers used some of the space, and the first Duesenberg Model "A" was built there. There were also a couple of other brilliant engineers at the plant, and it was rumored that they spent most of their time developing a very modern, relatively high compression six-cylinder engine.

Chrysler left Willys in February 1922, and spent two years working out his new car and organizing his new company, which was launched in February 1924. During this time he also served as president of the moribund Maxwell-Chalmers Company, which was later merged into the new Chrysler Corporation. The fact that those brilliant engineers from Willys's plant in Elizabeth turned up on the Chrysler staff may have been purely coincidental.

Chrysler's initial venture was in the medium-priced field, followed by a low-priced four-cylinder car which was essentially an updated Maxwell and which some years later acquired another new name, Plymouth. As soon as the new company was firmly established, Chrysler hired as a consultant the distinguished British engineer Laurence Pomeroy, who had been responsible for the Vauxhall 30/98 of the early twenties. He was largely responsible for the Chrysler "80" introduced in 1927, which even included the fluted hood that had been characteristic of the Vauxhalls.

Following the introduction of this larger model, there were a few custom bodies built on it. We built several at LeBaron, individual bodies designed for their purchasers. The Chrysler Corporation itself ordered some small series of bodies, mainly convertible sedans and limousines. The principal source was Dietrich, who by this time was well established in Detroit, but there were also some from Locke and Holbrook.

By 1930, Briggs had established themselves as the main source of bodies for the entire Chrysler line, which by now included Dodge and DeSoto. While DeSoto was a new marque introduced by Chrysler, they had purchased the Dodge firm from Dillon, Read & Company in 1928. Dillon in turn had bought it from the Dodge family in 1926 for $146 million. I recall the newspapers at the time printed huge facsimiles of the check, reputed to have been the largest single check written up to that time.

Since one of the reasons Briggs obtained this business was for redesign of the entire Chrysler line by the LeBaron Studios, it followed that a group of LeBaron bodies were built on the Imperial. One was a phaeton of rather advanced design, and the first of these was for Walter Chrysler himself.

A two-tone beige color scheme had been decided upon, and to go with this Alvin Pranz, our interior specialist, decreed the use of bleached walnut panelling. One afternoon I received a call from Carl Warren, our purchasing agent, who had discovered that I could often come up with answers when he could not locate a source for some needed item.

I walked down to his office, and learned that he could not buy bleached walnut. His sources of cabinet wood had suggested that we bleach it ourselves. This was a new idea to me, so that evening I visited the Detroit Public Library and consulted some books on furniture finishing. I was able to get some information and a formula for a bleaching solution made with oxalic acid.

The next morning, I borrowed a bucket in the paint shop and mixed up some of the solution, putting in a small section of walnut. During the day, I paid frequent visits to my bucket, turning the wood and watching its progress. It turned out quite well, and the next morning I set up a larger tank with more of the solution and went on to bleach a six-foot length of walnut for the seat back panel, and smaller sections for the other pieces needed. These were then carved and steam-bent to fit their destined places, and somewhat to my surprise they withstood this treatment.

1931 Chrysler Imperial Town Car by LeBaron, specially built for Mrs. Walter P. Chrysler. This car was purchased from the Chrysler Estate in 1968 by Mr. Phil Wichard of Huntington, New York. Photograph by the author, with Mr. Wichard barely visible at the wheel.

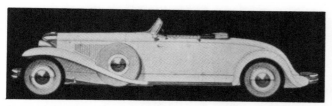

1931 Chrysler Imperial Sport Roadster by LeBaron, exhibited at 1930 New York Salon.

Another car for Mrs. Walter Chrysler, a town car, was being completed at the same time, and I shall have more to say about this in a later chapter on interiors. While engaged in the writing of this book, I learned that it had just been purchased from the Chrysler estate by Phil Wichard of Huntington, who lives only a mile or so from me. I had the pleasant experience of renewing my acquaintance with the car, which had been in storage for some twenty years and is in many respects just as it left our factory.

In September of 1930, Ralph Roberts took a trip to Europe to see what the latest trends there were, and also to visit the Paris Salon and other shows. He sent back a series of brief notes on various new ideas, one of them being long hoods extending back to the windshield. I am not sure just who pioneered this idea in France, but he did mention Willy Van den Plas in Paris as one builder using the technique.

At the Salon a few months later, Rolls-Royce showed a very novel design by Brewster, which became known as the "Windblown Coupe." It is cur-

rently being restored by Thomas Kilbane of Charleston, West Virginia. One of its features was such a long hood extending all the way back to the windshield.

Roberts felt we should incorporate this idea in an experimental Lincoln, as he was sure Edsel Ford would like it. I had moved to Detroit shortly after this Salon, and after some discussion we decided on a Club Sedan. An order was set up in the name of a Briggs executive, George Wilson, so as not to call attention to the experimental nature of the design.

Although I made a couple of rough sketches, the actual design was worked out full size on a regular body draft. Normally, this was where a scale drawing was enlarged to full-size working drawings. In this instance, it seemed the best place to work out the lines, since they would be quite different from anything we had built previously.

Much has been written, some by former associates, about Ralph Roberts not being a designer. It is true he had no training or skill as a draftsman, but he did have the ability to visualize an idea. We had developed our communications over the years to the point where I could interpret his descriptions. We even had our own verbal shorthand, and each of us knew precisely what the other meant by a Kellner back or a Barker pillar.

The design of the Lincoln sedan hinged on our ability to work out a smooth line from the radiator through the long hood and on into the body sides.

1931 Lincoln Club Sedan by LeBaron, with experimental long hood. Photograph courtesy Automobile Manufacturers Association.

The problem was complicated by the fact that we knew Henry as well as Edsel Ford would study it, as was usual with any radically new idea. Henry Ford would notice if we changed the radiator shell by a fraction of an inch, or moved the starter button from its position at the extreme left-hand end of the instrument panel. We had to be governed by these two immovable objects, and it took several hours of experimenting to get what we considered a satisfactory result. It would have been much simpler to start from scratch.

Several months later, the car was completed, but for some reason Edsel Ford was not impressed. The car was brought back to the Briggs plant and left temporarily in a garage reserved for cars that we did not want to leave standing around exposed to public view.

At the same time, we were building a prototype Chrysler Imperial Convertible Roadster, developed from the Packard I had designed the previous year. When the Chrysler was finished, Roberts asked me to drive it over to the main Briggs plant, as Walter Chrysler and some of his associates were to be there late in the afternoon. I can still remember tooling the Chrysler down Mack Avenue at 60 mph. It was the first chance I had had to see how it would perform. Unfortunately, I had to make a few quick stops, and it had no radiator cap. Some rusty water spilled out on the hood. When I got to the Briggs

plant, I drove immediately to our special garage to have the spots washed off.

As a result, when Chrysler, Zeder, Keller and the others came down to see the car, it was parked just a few feet from our experimental Lincoln. They liked the Convertible, but also admired the long hood on the Lincoln. We proceeded immediately to incorporate the long hood into the designs we were developing for the 1932 Chrysler.

Some magazine articles have indicated that Carl Breer was already working on the Airflow design at this time, but I am inclined to doubt it. We were working closely enough with the Chrysler Corporation to have known of it. Actually, Chenard-Walcker had shown a very similar design at the Paris Salon in October, 1928, and Bugatti had a car at the 1923 Grand Prix of LeMans with the same idea. These were, however, open sports cars. It is possible that some thought was being given to the idea at Chrysler, but I do not recall that it came up in any discussions with LeBaron.

The one outstanding feature of the Airflow that came into general use was the positioning of the engine. Since independent front suspension was introduced in this country in 1934, I suspect that also marked the beginning of serious work on the Airflow. It was no longer necessary to place the engine behind the front axle, and this made possible a shorter car with the rear seat placed ahead of the rear axle.

LeBaron had long been aware of the advantages of this position for the rear seat, and this had led us to recommend longer wheelbases for many of the manu-

1933 Chrysler Imperial Phaeton by LeBaron. A modification of the one built for Mr. Chrysler in 1931, and incorporating the new long hood. Photograph by the author of car owned by Mr. Harold Orchard of Garden Grove, California, at Pebble Beach Consours d'Elegance, 1967.

facturers who consulted us. Stutz, Packard and Chrysler had lengthened their largest chassis to about a 145-inch wheelbase during the late twenties, and Lincoln had finally followed suit in 1931.

All of the Chryslers from the first in 1924 to the introduction of overhead-valve V-8s after World War II had L-head engines with Ricardo-type heads to induce greater turbulence and permit higher compression. The first "80" was a six-cylinder model with $3\frac{5}{8}$ x 5 inch bore and stroke, but by 1930 this had been replaced with a straight-eight of $3\frac{1}{2}$ x 5 inch dimensions, the same as the Packard Super Eight. The early sixes had a 127-inch wheelbase, but a long chassis of 136-inch wheelbase was soon added to accommodate seven-passenger and custom bodies. By the time the Imperial Eight came along, LeBaron was closely involved and only one wheelbase, 146 inches, was deemed necessary.

One of the reasons for Chrysler's success in the large car field was undoubtedly the fact that their prices for standard models were only slightly above the small Packard and the LaSalle, while the cars themselves had the size, and consequently some of the prestige, of the large Packard and Pierce-Arrow. With a custom body built in small series, the Imperial sold for around $6,000, or roughly $1,000 less than their competition. For some reason, perhaps the lower price, they never seemed to draw the true custom trade. Nearly all of the completely individual Chryslers we built went to members of the family or directors of the corporation.

During the thirties, Briggs registered the name "LeBaron" as a trademark, and when the body-building portion of the Briggs Manufacturing Company was sold to Chrysler, after Walter Briggs's death, the rights to the name went with it.

20
Pierce-Arrow

S O far I have been discussing cars that are still being made, or were until recently, although perhaps with less elegance than they once possessed. There were others, which had great prestige in the classic twenties, but which unfortunately did not survive the rigors of the depression.

One such is Pierce-Arrow, a name synonymous with quality since the early days of the century. Before the first World War, and briefly afterwards, they had built some of the most massive cars in the country. Their first ones had been much smaller and lighter, patterned somewhat after Benz's vehicles. The George N. Pierce Company had been bicycle manufacturers before they built automobiles.

Three models were available in the 1910 decade, the 38, 48 and 66; these figures represented their taxable horsepower. The formula and tax system were borrowed from the English, horsepower being calculated from the bore and number of cylinders. In those early days, it was a good rough approximation. Later the fact that it completely ignored the stroke led to the development of the small-bore, long-stroke engines that dominated European engineering for many years.

The several Pierce-Arrow engines were all sixes at this time, with 4-inch, 4½-inch, and 5-inch bore. The smallest had a piston displacement of 414 cubic inches, the next 525 cubic inches, and the behemoth 825 cubic inches. Compare those with what are considered "big engines" today! Pierce-Arrow also built an excellent line of trucks, some of which used the same engines and others four-cylinder ones of similar design.

Production at Pierce was never tremendous, and one could almost say that each of their cars was custom built. During the second decade of this century,

they built some rather attractive open cars and also a variety of town cars and limousines that had cast aluminum sections for the doors and upper body panels. This made them durable, solid and quiet. In 1913, they introduced the distinctive fender-mounted headlights, which were optional on all Pierce-Arrows well into the thirties.

Like other makers of luxury products, they suffered somewhat from the 1921 deflation. The last of the mammoth 66s that I can remember was built that year. Only the smallest model, now called Series 31, and later Series 33 and Series 36, was continued. Development was started on a still smaller car, although not tiny, which was introduced for 1925 as Series 80. One of their advertisements for that year, reproduced in the color section of this book, lists prices for the Series 33 as $5,250 for open models, $7,000 for closed ones. The Series 80 started at $2,895.

At the same time, Pierce-Arrow concentrated on building sedans, limousines and open cars in their own body plant, and turned more to the custom builders for other types. Most of the bodies I can recall building on the larger Series 33 chassis were individually designed for their purchasers. They ranged from sporty phaetons to magnificent town cars.

For the Series 80 chassis, Pierce-Arrow ordered several small series of bodies from various firms. LeBaron built one group of sedans, some fitted with chauffeur's partition, and a somewhat larger number of town cars. Judkins contributed some of the excellent little coupes, similar to those they were building on other chassis. Brunn, a Buffalo neighbor, built several individual bodies and a series of town cars.

Although New York was the prime market for custom bodies at this time, Pierce-Arrow had an exceptionally strong dealership in St. Louis—the Western Automobile Company. Several of those Series 80 town cars we built went to prominent St. Louis families such as the Catlins and the Mallinckrodts.

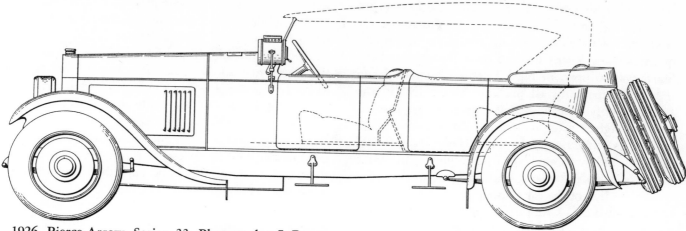

1926 Pierce-Arrow Series 33 Phaeton by LeBaron, built for Mr. Clifford Warren Smith. Note special Le-Baron spotlight, and steps in place of running boards.

The president of this dealership was Sam Breadon, who also headed the St. Louis Cardinals. It was no secret to me, however, that the real owners were the Busch family. In those days it was not generally known that they also owned the Cardinals. Actually, that was not unusual at the time—Henry Ford and Walter Briggs jointly, but secretly, owned the Detroit Tigers. It was not until after Mr. Ford's death, when Mr. Briggs acquired full control, that his ownership of the team became public knowledge. The only one of our customers who admitted ownership of a base-ball team in the twenties was Mr. Wrigley in Chi-cago.

Some years later, Marty Marion worked for one of my customers during the off season. We had lunch together one day, and I suggested some Budweiser would be an appropriate accompaniment. I got a most peculiar look. I was not supposed to know that August Busch was his employer during the baseball season. When I explained how I knew about it, we both had a good laugh, but I was cautioned not to mention it elsewhere. Of course, in the meantime, the Busch family has publicly taken over the owner-ship of the team.

Around 1928, Albert Erskine of Studebaker pur-chased a large block of Pierce-Arrow stock and be-came Chairman of their Board of Directors. Some cooperative purchasing was undertaken, and an even-tual merger was contemplated, but late in 1931 the negotiations were broken off by Studebaker because of Pierce-Arrow's declining fortunes in the depres-sion.

By the late twenties, Pierce-Arrow was almost the only manufacturer in this country still making a large six-cylinder car. Plans were already under way to replace this with straight-eights. These were intro-duced for 1929 in three series of somewhat different sizes, the largest of which was the only one on which any considerable number of custom bodies were mounted.

When I moved to Detroit in December 1930, the LeBaron-Detroit plant was completing a Pierce-Ar-row Sedan-Limousine that had been ordered for dis-play during the New York Auto Show the first week in January. Ed Carter, who had managed the Bridge-port plant of LeBaron, had been placed in charge of production at Detroit. The task of getting the car ready in time fell on him, and since I had worked closely with him in the East, some of it fell on me.

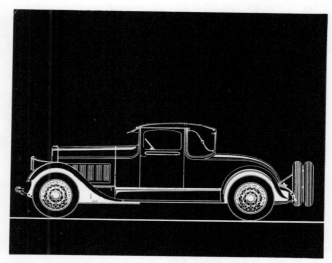

1928 Pierce-Arrow Series 36 Coupe by Judkins, ex-hibited at 1927 Salon. From Pierce-Arrow advertise-ment in Salon Catalog.

We had only been in Detroit a few weeks, and we occupied adjoining rooms in a small hotel not far from the plant while looking for more permanent quarters. New Year's Eve fell on a Tuesday, and the Show was to open in New York on Sunday. I can remember spending all of New Year's Eve in the final assembly shop with that Pierce-Arrow. Just before midnight, Carter and I drove down to our hotel, had a drink together, and yelled "Happy New Year" out the window to anybody who might be listening. Then back to the plant, and back to work.

We finally got the car finished around noon, when it was loaded into a Railway Express Car, transferred to the Michigan Central Station, and hooked onto that evening's Detroiter bound for New York. Fortunately, at the New York end the car could be unloaded almost directly into elevators leading to the Biltmore Hotel Lobby, where it was displayed during the Show.

At this time, arrangements were made with Pierce-Arrow similar to the ones we had set up with Packard a few months before. We built some small series of bodies for which they would supply chassis. There were five body styles—a Sport Coupe, Club Sedan, Convertible Victoria, Convertible Sedan and an Enclosed-drive Limousine. Twenty or twenty-five of each style were started, and I prepared a special supplement to the Pierce-Arrow dealer's catalog, to help

1931 Pierce-Arrow Club Sedan by LeBaron. Note sloping front edge of front door, following angle of windshield, explained in Chapter 44. Photograph courtesy the owner, Harrah's Automobile Collection.

sell the cars before any were actually completed.

Hardly had these catalogs reached the dealers, when I received a phone call from St. Louis. There had been some highly publicized threats to kidnap the young heir to the Busch fortune, and his father insisted—for the safety of the family—that the very first of the Limousines be made over with extensive changes and rushed to completion for him.

I arranged for a conference in my office with the sales manager of the Western Automobile Company the next morning. When he explained the changes to be made, I was amazed. The elder Mr. Busch was a large man, and first of all he wanted the roof several inches higher for adequate headroom. The next requirement was even more surprising. The car was to be fitted out to carry a regular arsenal. A shotgun was to fit into a pocket in the right hand cowl, in easy reach of the guard who would always ride next to the chauffeur. Several pistol holsters were to be put in inconspicuous yet easily accessible locations.

I pointed out that with all these items to consider, it would be much better to start from scratch with a new design, but this was ruled out. Appearance was not important, but time was of the essence and Mr. Busch knew that we had already started work on these bodies.

Finally I agreed to make the changes on the first limousine body, after convincing Mr. Busch by phone that bullet-proof glass would be a doubtful asset unless the whole car were armor-plated. While the latter change could also have been made, it would have delayed the car several months.

Normally, the first body in a series would be the one on which we worked out any problems. In this case, No. 1 became practically an individual body, and No. 2 became the prototype. Actually, the changes were not quite so difficult as they had first sounded. The extra height was added entirely above the belt-line, some in the windows and some by increasing the crown of the roof. It did mean some redesigning, and new patterns for the castings and frames of the V-type windshield.

The gun emplacements were not too much of a problem. I was given the dimensions of the shotgun, and this would ride in what was essentially a heavy leather pocket in the cowl panel. One day I received a package with a nice pistol holster as a pattern. The pocket for one was set in the left cowl panel, where the chauffeur could reach it easily, and several more pockets were recessed into the upholstery of the rear compartment, covered with inconspicuous flaps so as not to alarm any guests who might ride in the car.

Not all of the 100-odd bodies in these series were completed during the 1931 model year, and some were mounted on the 12-cylinder chassis introduced by Pierce for 1932. It is possible that some additional convertible sedans were started later, as this style seemed to sell best, but at least a few of some of the other models were never completed. Ralph Roberts told me recently that when Pierce-Arrow went into bankruptcy in 1938, they still owed LeBaron close to a million dollars.

A fair proportion of these LeBaron–Pierce-Arrows have survived. Photographs of a few are reproduced herein, which were taken by me at the various meets where they were shown. Probably the most unusual is the town car owned by racing driver Phil Hill. This was adapted from the convertible sedan, and built specially for Mr. Hill's aunt. It has been in the family since it was delivered to her in August 1931.

The photograph of this car was taken at the Concours d'Elegance at Pebble Beach, California, during the Summer of 1967. The red ribbon showing is the award it won for second place among classic cars at this Concours. To the right one can see part of the 1933 LeBaron Chrysler phaeton owned by Harold Orchard, and behind Mr. Hill's Pierce-Arrow is the green Marmon 16 Convertible Coupe, restoration of which had just been completed by its owner, Bill Harrah.

1931 Pierce-Arrow Convertible Victoria by LeBaron. Photograph by the author at Hershey, 1965, of car then owned by Mr. Alan Bittner of Camp Hill, Pennsylvania.

21
Stutz

ANOTHER car which has not survived, but on which some smart custom bodies were built, is the Stutz.

The firm was started by Harry C. Stutz in 1909, and its first car was completed in time to compete in the Indianapolis 500 of 1911. The Stutz entry finished second to Ray Harroun's Marmon "Wasp" and from then on their nameplate carried the slogan "The Car That Made Good in a Day."

Stutz had already made some money with the combined transmission and rear axle he had developed, and which remained a feature of all Stutz cars during his control of the company. They became famous for the Bearcat, the outstanding American sports car before and for a short time after World War I. Similar in some respects to the Mercer Raceabout and the Marmon Speedster, it was somewhat less expensive. College students then as now had to consider their families' budgets when buying a car, and the Stutz Bearcat invariably brings back memories of raccoon coats and football weekends.

The company suffered financial reverses during the 1921 deflation, like many of its contemporaries, and control passed to a group of bankers headed by Charles M. Schwab, Jr., president of Bethlehem Steel. They built some less dramatic vehicles under the Stutz name, while Harry Stutz founded a new company to build the H.C.S. (his initials), a much better vehicle at the time but unfortunately not well financed. He later turned to making taxicabs and fire engines.

In March 1925, Stutz elected Fred Moskovics as president. He was an eminent automobile engineer as well as a good salesman. He had previously been associated with Marmon for ten years, but left them in 1924 to become vice-president of Franklin. With-

in six months he left that company in a policy dispute. He had been privately developing a new concept of the automobile, which Stutz adopted and put into production soon after he joined them.

This car had an eight-cylinder engine with overhead camshaft, and a very low chassis for the time. This was based on a worm-drive axle developed for it by Timken, with the worm below the pinion instead of above it as was customary on the heavy-duty truck axles where this type of gearing was often used. A similar axle is found on the present-day Peugeot.

The new Stutz was introduced at the 1926 Auto Show and drew much favorable comment for its engineering advances. Some of the ideas may have come from Ettore Bugatti, who was a close personal friend of Moskovics and in fact became a consultant to Stutz in September, 1926. There was also a mutual agreement between the two firms for the exchange of patent rights.

It was advertised as the "Safety Stutz" because of some of its new features, such as a very low center of gravity and adequate performance to make evasive maneuvers. It also was the first American production car with safety glass as standard equipment—in this case made by embedding wires at about 1½-inch intervals in the glass to avoid shattering on impact.

There was only one oversight. The styling was rather stodgy, although this was somewhat offset by the fact that the car was several inches lower than its competitors. Stutz did advertise that its body designs were "supervised by Brewster & Company," but Henry Crecelius told me later that Brewster's work was confined to body engineering, not styling. The New York branch of Stutz, managed by Ed Headington, sought to remedy this problem by having a few custom bodies built, and their vastly improved appearance soon brought orders for more.

Within a year after the new Stutz reached the market, a demand was sensed for something along the lines of the old Bearcat, and Headington asked LeBaron to develop such a vehicle. We came up with

1927 Stutz Blackhawk by LeBaron. This is the original version, of which about a dozen were built, on short-wheelbase chassis with large eight-cylinder engine. Later Stutz used the Blackhawk name for a smaller car.

a stripped-down two-seater, fairly light in weight, which was mounted on a special high-performance chassis. One of the problems was to keep the price of the complete car below $5,000. To economize, the little roadster was one of the few built at this period without a top as standard equipment. A concoction of iron pipe and fabric was available at extra cost—not a conventional folding top, but something for emergencies which could be dismounted and stowed in the trunk.

The cars were called Blackhawks, and the first five were sold out in short order. About a dozen more were built before the end of the model year. Luis Firpo, the ex-boxer, had become Stutz distributor for the Argentine and ordered one for his personal use. He specified that the chassis be driven from Indianapolis to our plant in Bridgeport, so it would be broken in and ready to run at speed when it reached Buenos Aires.

The success of this model led Stutz to arrange with LeBaron to act as consultants for their entire custom body program, and later to do all of their styling. They even set up a special Stutz Salon in the Ritz Tower Hotel at Park Avenue and 57th Street in New York. All the cars shown here had custom bodies from Fleetwood, LeBaron, Derham, Rollston and similar firms.

This Salon was directed by Casimir deRham, and owned jointly with his brother William. The deRhams operated the best dancing school for Society's children, which is still in the family, and of course had a wide acquaintance among potential customers for expensive automobiles. Casimir deRham, unfortunately, died in March of 1968.

One of the first styling jobs we did for Stutz was

to adapt the original Blackhawks for production. We came up with two versions—a two-passenger and a four-passenger open body, both boat-tailed. These were built by the Robbins Body Corporation in Indianapolis, who had been building most of the Stutz standard bodies.

A team of them ran at LeMans in 1928 and performed creditably, one finishing just behind the winning Bentley. Oddly enough, these were the four-passenger models, with a tonneau cover over the rear compartment. In tests at Daytona Beach, it had been found that these were faster than the two-seaters, possibly because of their smoother lines.

The Weymann body, developed in France, was pioneered in this country by Stutz, as I have already explained. While they built a few experimental bodies on other chassis, most of their work here was confined to Stutz, who supplied part of the financing for the subsidiary company Weymann set up in Indianapolis. The Weymann bodies were several hundred pounds lighter than conventional construction, which helped the performance image which Stutz was building up.

While I was in Detroit in 1931, Preston Tucker was working for Pierce-Arrow as a sort of special ambassador and trouble-shooter for their sales department. He had spent a year or two in a similar capacity with Stutz, but was now living with his family in a Detroit suburb.

One day I was asked to accompany him to Bay City in northern Michigan, where a wealthy shipbuilder was considering buying one of the Sport Coupes we were then building for Pierce-Arrow. He liked the Pierce, but like many another car buyer he had a very definite idea of the allowance that should be given for the Judkins Lincoln coupe he had been driving for two or three years, but which his chauffeur had kept in immaculate condition.

They haggled all afternoon and well into the

1931 Stutz Monte Carlo Sedan by Weymann on DV-32
Chassis. From Stutz Catalog, Floyd Marshall Collection.

1930 Stutz Sedan-Limousine by LeBaron. Later bodies
had sloping windshields as described in text. From
Stutz Catalog, Floyd Marshall Collection.

1932 Stutz Convertible Victoria by Rollston, on DV-32
Chassis. Photograph from Floyd Marshall Collection.

evening, while I listened and helped to consume several bottles of good Hudson's Bay Scotch. Tucker finally gave up, and we started back to Detroit. Just outside of Bay City he became ill, and suggested that we stop for the night at the nearest hotel. I took over the wheel and got us to Saginaw safely.

Early the next morning, a Sunday, Tucker shook me awake and informed me he had just remembered that he was scheduled to drive the pace car for a race in Chicago at noon. He felt the only way he could make it was to have his wife meet him in Ypsilanti in the Weymann Stutz which he still had. I could either go on to Chicago with them, or return to Detroit by train from Ypsilanti, which I decided to do.

We had breakfast sent up to the room, and he made the arrangements by phone while we ate. I don't think the accelerator of the Pierce-Arrow was off the floor throughout the trip. It had a top speed of 85 m.p.h., which has been my personal speed limit ever since. Those northern Michigan highways were two-lane roads then, and the northbound lane was an almost solid line of cars on Sunday excursions. Fortunately we were going South. I don't know how much faster the Stutz went after he switched to it, but he did make the race almost on time.

When the LeBaron-Detroit plant was set up, it had more capacity than was needed for our custom body business. By 1930 we were not only styling the Stutz line, but building most of their bodies. The production models were built "in the white," less paint and upholstery. That part of the work was completed in Indianapolis after the bodies were shipped there.

At the same time, we continued to build some small series of custom bodies for Stutz, which we finished completely. These had actually been designed in 1929 with vertical windshields, but as business fell off on custom-bodied Stutzes after the stock market crash, quite a few were still in various stages of completion by mid-1931. Stutz was in shaky financial position and there was no point in pushing them to take delivery, so I was asked to see what could be done to give them a new look for

1932. The simplest thing was to substitute a sloping windshield for the vertical one. I worked out the change, and this constitutes the difference between the 1930–31 LeBaron Stutzes and the later ones.

About the same time, Stutz designed a new cylinder head with dual valves and two overhead camshafts, which gave improved performance. The first prototypes of this modified engine were used in some of the cars for Stutz's second attempt at LeMans in 1929. The new cylinder head was first offered as an option for $1,500 extra, but this was soon reduced to $700. The model designations were changed to SV-16 (single valves, 16 per engine) and DV-32 (dual valves, 32 per engine). Oddly enough, this seemed to help sales of the single-valve engine. Cadillac and Marmon had just introduced their new sixteens, and V-16 had become a magic word.

Fred Moskovics resigned as president of Stutz in 1929, but continued as a director. He was succeeded as president by Col. E. S. Gorrell, who had been an aviator in World War I and had been brought into the company by Moskovics soon after he took over.

Briggs had a practice of sending a box of good cigars each Christmas to key executives of firms he did business with. We knew that Col. Gorrell did not smoke, but liked a drink. I was asked to take care of this problem, and obtained a bottle of Johnnie Walker Scotch through private sources (Prohibition was still in effect). I put it into the space behind the folding center armrest in the rear of a Stutz limousine about to be shipped to Indianapolis, locked the rear doors, and mailed the key to Col. Gorrell. He got the Scotch.

Stutz continued on for a few years into the thirties, but finally went into bankruptcy. I have been told that not all of the Stutz bodies in process at the LeBaron-Detroit plant when I left there at the end of 1931 were ever completed. At the same time, a few new ideas were started elsewhere, such as the DV-32 Super-Bearcat, the bodies for which were built by the Murray Corporation. Although a fantastic performer, it did not sell well enough to resuscitate Stutz.

22
Duesenberg

MUCH has already been written about the fabulous Duesenberg, and the brothers who conceived it. I shall try to add a few comments that may not be generally known.

Fred and August Duesenberg were in the old tradition of "tinkerers." They loved developing new ideas, but often lost interest in an idea when they had worked it out. Fred was the more brilliant and versatile engineer of the two, and before World War I had developed a powerful four-cylinder T-head engine. It incorporated the best ideas of the time, and bore some vague resemblance not only to Stutz and Mercer, but also to the current Hispano-Suiza.

Having perfected the engine, the Duesenberg brothers sold the rights to it to the Rochester Engine Works, who continued to produce it for some years as the Rochester-Duesenberg. It powered what I have always called the Three Rs of the automobile industry—Revere, Richelieu and Roamer—as well as some lesser known makes such as Kenworthy, Meteor and Phianna. All were most popular as sporty phaetons although other body styles were available. The phaetons were generally in the $4,500 price range around 1920.

The Roamer was distinguished by its Rolls-Royce shape radiator, and was by far the most successful of the group. Built by the A.C. Barley Company of Kalamazoo, it continued well into the late twenties. By 1923, most Roamers were equipped with smoother and less expensive Continental six-cylinder engines, but the Rochester-Duesenberg four continued as a more expensive option. The fours sold for about $1,000 more than the sixes.

The Revere, built in northern Indiana, and the Richelieu from New Brunswick, New Jersey, were quite similar in design, both mechanically and in styling. I believe Richelieu used the former Crane-

Simplex plant, or part of it. Neither firm lasted too long, starting just after World War I and going out of business soon after the 1921 deflation. I have run across comment in a trade magazine of the time that the Richelieu firm merged with the United Body Company of Rahway, New Jersey, in 1922. United had been building their bodies, and probably the only production after the merger was the completion of a few cars in process.

Kenworthy was based in Mishawaka, Indiana, according to Harrah's Automobile Collection, which boasts possibly the only survivor of this make. The Meteor was built in Philadelphia, and the Phianna in Long Island City. The latter was probably the most expensive of this assortment of cars based on the Rochester-Duesenberg engine.

From the big Four, the Duesenbergs proceeded to the development of a three-liter overhead camshaft straight eight for racing at Indianapolis. It met with considerable success there, as has been duly recorded, and formed the basis for the engine of the Model A, their first complete passenger car.

During World War I, the Duesenberg brothers set out to build an improved airplane engine. It was a V-16, but although they got a few engines completed, the war ended before it reached the full production stage. At the time, they were working in the Elizabeth, New Jersey, plant built for war production by John N. Willys, who gave them financial backing. As soon as the war ended, they set about developing the passenger car, based on a detuned version of their racing engine. The first Duesenberg Model A was built in Willys's Elizabeth plant in October 1921.

It was fitted with a Town Brougham body by Fleetwood and shown at the 1921 Salon. The body was being built while the first chassis was being assembled. This was not unusual, as custom body builders often worked from chassis blueprints before the first chassis itself had been completed.

At this point, Willys himself was having problems with his overextended automotive empire, so the Duesenbergs set up their own company in Indian-

1921 Roamer Sport Phaeton, using Rochester-Duesenberg engine. Photograph courtesy Automobile Manufacturers Association.

1921 Richelieu Phaeton, another car with Rochester-Duesenberg engine. Photograph courtesy Automobile Manufacturers Association.

1925 Duesenberg Model A Sedan by Millspaugh & Irish, from Duesenberg advertisement in Salon Catalog.

apolis. Unfortunately, they were beset almost immediately by the same financial crisis that closed many small manufacturers at this time. In spite of the Duesenberg's reputation on the race track, there was not much demand for a car selling for over $5,000 that was distinctly smaller than its competitors, even though more advanced in engineering. It has been estimated that not much more than 100 of the Model As were built, but I think this estimate is too low.

Actually, the Duesenberg Motor Company went into receivership in February 1924, but the brothers were allowed to continue in operation and turned out a few more cars in the next year or two. Most of their bodies came from the nearby plant of Millspaugh & Irish, but several cars had Fleetwood bodies. One of these was a limousine displayed at the 1922 Salon, and another of the same type was shown at the 1925 Salon. These Fleetwood-bodied Duesenbergs sold for about $8,000.

In January 1926, E. L. Cord and the financial interests backing him and the Auburn Automobile Company took control of Duesenberg and invested new capital. Fred and August Duesenberg were kept on in charge of engineering and development. They set out immediately to develop a car for the expanding luxury market. They jumped from their 183 cubic inches to 420, larger than all but a handful of American cars and certainly the most powerful of all even if the claimed 265 horsepower was somewhat optimistic.

The new car was to be marketed in the manner of the most famous European makes. Duesenberg would build the chassis only, which would then be fitted with custom bodies from the foremost coachbuilders, usually to the order of the individual purchaser. Even the price was set according to this plan, with the chassis of the Model J set at $8,500, the same as the

Isotta-Fraschini. It has been reputed that the actual cost of manufacture was even more. When the supercharged Model SJ was added, it sold for $1,000 more.

In line with this policy, the new Duesenberg was launched at the New York Salon in December 1928. Four were shown, a phaeton by LeBaron, a sedan and a town car by Holbrook, and a roadster by Murphy. Each of the cars was striking, and they caused an immediate sensation.

While a large proportion of the custom bodies mounted on other chassis were town cars, this was not true of the Duesenberg. Nearly all we built at LeBaron were phaetons or convertible sedans. One now in a collection in Florida was originally built for Mr. W. F. Ryan of Washington, D.C. I have been told by Ray Wolff, the Duesenberg historian, that it was raced in Europe by the owner's cousin, Thomas Fortune Ryan. I do remember that W. F. Ryan took me to lunch one day at the Stork Club, and arranged for me to obtain one of Sherman Billingsley's elegantly gold encrusted cards of admission. A color rendering of this car was used in LeBaron's catalog for the 1929 Salon and is reproduced herein.

I also recall a convertible sedan which we built for an attorney who had participated in the negotiations leading to Cord's taking over Duesenberg. He had stipulated that part of his fee was to be a new Duesenberg, but when he went to the factory to pick it up, it turned out to be a rather massive limousine more suited to an elderly dowager. Mr. Gill immediately came to LeBaron to have the body replaced with something more to his liking.

Other body builders similarly built probably more open cars and convertibles for Duesenberg than any other types. This may be one reason such a high proportion of them are still in existence, commanding in recent years a price well above their original cost of $14,000 to $18,000.

1929 Duesenberg Model J Phaeton by LeBaron, exhibited at 1928 New York Salon. This is illustration from LeBaron catalog for that Salon.

1929 Duesenberg Model J Convertible Sedan by Le-Baron for Mr. Robert J. Gill. Photograph by Mr. Thomas Landreth of Gault, Ontario, Canada, when he owned the car in 1961.

By 1931, Duesenbergs began to appear that were exact copies of earlier ones by leading custom body builders. We referred to them as "factory bodies" and I do not recall that the earlier ones carried any body-builder's nameplate. At the 1931 Salon, however, one was exhibited by a firm calling itself Le-Grande. This had been built in a subsidiary plant of the Auburn-Cord-Duesenberg combine, as mentioned earlier.

Actually, Duesenbergs were not a towering success among the wealthy East Coast families, who felt them to be rather ostentatious. They did become popular in Hollywood, often with bodies from Murphy's nearby plant. This was perhaps fortunate since during the early thirties that was about the only place where people could and did still spend money by the bucket.

One of Duesenberg's best customers in New York was the dapper and popular Mayor, Jimmy Walker.

He had several of them. There was some speculation about this, since even one cost more than his annual salary.

A word about the other two products of the same company—Cord and Auburn—seems appropriate here. Not many custom bodies were built on the Cord. The original L-29 had a Lycoming straight-eight engine, and since this sat behind the front-wheel drive, it left very little body space. LeBaron built one town car on it, and Murphy built another as well as other types. There were also some experimental bodies by Weymann and by Hayes, the latter a coupe designed by Alex de Sakhnoffsky for his own use, and now owned by Brooks Stevens.

The Auburn dated back to the early days of the industry, beginning in 1902, and in the early twenties their "Beauty Six" was one of the better known medium-priced cars. They never were in the category of vehicles fitted with custom bodies, in fact in 1930 their lowest-priced model was selling for less than $1,000.

Some of my friends owned Auburns at this time, and I recall one especially that was fitted with a spotlight between the front frame horns, attached to the steering tie-rod in such a way that it swiveled as the wheels turned. Auburn promoted this light, although it was an accessory made by another firm. It appears that a similar idea is being touted again.

Although the Auburn, Cord and Duesenberg companies have long since been dissolved, another part of the combine, the Lycoming Motor Company, is still actively in business as a unit of the Avco Corporation.

23
Marmon

HAVING just written about Stutz and Duesenberg leads me naturally to that other pride of Indianapolis, Marmon. Nordyke & Marmon had been machinery manufacturers; they built their first automobile in 1902. They acquired an early reputation for performance, Ray Harroun having won the 1911 Indianapolis 500 in the Marmon Wasp. Incidentally, he carried the first rear view mirror in this race, to check on his competition, which was usually behind him.

Col. Howard Marmon was an excellent engineer, and he had some able assistance from people like Fred Moskovics. When he retired from Stutz, Moskovics donated funds for a medal to be presented in his name for outstanding achievement in the field of automotive engineering. The first presentation of this medal by the Society of Automobile Engineers, in 1931, was to Col. Marmon for his development of the Marmon Sixteen.

Around 1915, Marmon introduced the Model 34, which had a number of innovations. It used aluminum extensively, and was considerably lighter than other vehicles of comparable size. It also had a unique massive steel running board, extending up at either end to the top of the frame, to which it was riveted. It was intended to serve as a side bumper, an idea which has recently been suggested as an innovation.

In 1918, my brother was working as a chauffeur for a family who had just purchased a Marmon 34, and I got an occasional ride in it. I admired it greatly.

This fine car was continued with minor changes, including elimination of the side-bumper running boards, which did not fit newer styling trends, into the mid-twenties. Later versions had the same six-cylinder overhead valve engine of 340 cubic inch displacement, but were designated as Model 74 and then Model 75.

The Marmon was considered a medium-priced car, but some custom bodies were fitted. For a time, Brewster sold Marmons with Brewster bodies which ran close to $10,000. There were also others, including the Hume sedans, which as mentioned in an earlier chapter led to Marmon's hiring Mr. Pierce, Hume's designer, as a consultant. Later they took over the Hume firm.

Although the Model 75 remained the top of Marmon's line until 1928, they had in the meantime added two smaller eight-cylinder cars. One had an engine very similar to that of the first Locomobile Junior Eight. Barney Roos, who had developed the latter, spent a few months with Marmon after leaving Locomobile and before becoming chief engineer of Studebaker.

Finally, in 1929, Marmon replaced their tried and true six with the Big Eight. This sold reasonably well, but they were having trouble with the sales of their smaller cars, which by now included the Roosevelt in the $1,000 price range. It is my impression that Marmon's troubles at this time stemmed from the fact that they continued a six-cylinder engine, even though a good one, long after their competitors had switched to eights. By contrast, they used eight-cylinder engines in their smaller cars, which were competing against lower-priced sixes. Even the graceful styling of Alex de Sakhnoffsky, who was responsible for their Hayes bodies, was not much help.

Col. Marmon in the meantime was hard at work on a completely new concept which incorporated some brilliant engineering—the Marmon Sixteen. It was a jewel of an engine, neat in appearance and very smooth in operation. Unfortunately, it made its bow at the New York Salon in 1930, just a year after the stock market crash. Like other American chassis manufacturers, Marmon could not exhibit at the Salon themselves, and the first Sixteen was shown on LeBaron's stand, as mentioned in my chapter on the Salon.

In discussing the Sixteen with some of its enthusiasts, I have found much uncertainty about the source of its bodies. As I have assured them, practically all were built at the LeBaron-Detroit plant. However, we looked on them as just another production job, like the standard Stutz bodies we were building at the

1923 Marmon 74s at the New York Auto Show. A Hume Sedan in foreground, with a Brewster Sedan-Limousine partly visible at right rear. Note side-bumper running boards curved up at each end. Photograph by Nathan Lazarnick, courtesy Automobile Manufacturers Association.

same time.

The styling of the Sixteen was credited to Walter Dorwin Teague, although it has been claimed that his son did the actual work. When the sketches were sent to us for conversion into working drawings, we suggested some modifications. We felt the lines were too square and slab-sided. Marmon refused to permit any changes, and Teague's sketches were followed exactly. We were never altogether happy with the result, although they have been much admired by others.

Actually, the Marmon Sixteen work was already well under way when I moved to Detroit and I had little personal contact with it. It is my recollection that most of the bodies were shipped to Indianapolis "in the white" but that some were finished completely at the LeBaron plant. In fact, a few of them were mounted on their chassis there.

The American Legion Convention was held in Detroit in 1931, and Marmon for promotional purposes arranged to have a Sixteen placed at the disposal of each of the top national officers. These were all completed at the LeBaron plant, and were of various body types. All were finished in rather bright colors.

That was a fairly wild convention, and each of the cars was returned to the LeBaron plant by the end of the week for sundry repairs. I remember one convertible sedan that had suffered a direct hit by a pillowcase full of water dropped from one of the upper stories of the Book-Cadillac Hotel. Fortunately no one was in the car at the time, but an en-

The New York Marmon Showroom sometime in 1931, with a display of six different body styles on the Marmon Sixteen, all built in the LeBaron-Detroit plant. This showroom was on the East side of Broadway at 64th Street. The structure barely visible in the background is the Ninth Avenue "L" which then ran up Columbus Avenue, and the rather shabby stores behind occupy the site of what is now Lincoln Center. Photograph courtesy of Mr. William R. Gibson.

tirely new top had to be installed.

A very few custom bodies were mounted on the Sixteen, two of them being open phaetons on special long-wheelbase chassis for Colonel and Mrs. Prentiss, the daughter and son-in-law of John D. Rockefeller. The bodies were built by Waterhouse. One of these is in the collection of Governor Winthrop Rockefeller, and the other in the careful custody of Mr. Ed Robinson of Morrisville, Pennsylvania.

Another was the last body I designed for LeBaron. It was a 4/5-passenger Sedan-limousine. Mr. Michael L. Benedum, an oil tycoon living in Pittsburgh, wanted it especially adapted to long-distance touring, for use on inspection trips of his holdings in Oklahoma and Texas. I stopped off in Pittsburgh en route to the New York Salon in 1931 to discuss this with him in company of the local Marmon distributor.

When I returned to Detroit, I worked out the design and specifications. The latter are reproduced in Chapter 43 of this book.

The order was not actually placed until after I left LeBaron a month later, but I was told subsequently that it had been built on the special short-wheelbase chassis which had been specified by Mr. Benedum to get somewhat better performance.

While at Mr. Benedum's home, I was treated to a rare visit to the North Wing of his garage. His chauffeur swore me to secrecy—as far as Mr. Benedum was concerned. His son had joined the Lafayette Escadrille during World War I, and had been killed in action. The North Wing of the garage was reserved for the son's last cars, each one of which was immaculately kept in running condition. They were an outstanding group of the finest sports cars of their day, including a Mercer Raceabout and an Isotta-Fraschini Roadster. I have often wondered what ever became of them after Mr. Benedum's death.

I don't know what became of his Marmon either. My friend Bill Gibson has been spending some of his spare time trying to track it down, but so far without success.

1931 Marmon Sixteen Phaeton by Waterhouse on
special long-wheelbase chassis, built for Col. E. R.
Prentiss. Photograph courtesy its present owner, Mr.
E. L. Robinson of Morrisville, Pennsylvania.

24

Franklin - Locomobile - Studebaker

THE heading of this chapter may seem an odd combination, but there are links which lead from one to the others of these firms, as will be seen.

Franklin had been in existence since early in the century, and as is well known was America's leading exponent of air-cooled engines. Mr. Franklin himself was a fine gentleman of rather conservative tastes except in his engineering, which was often quite advanced and unique.

Although the H. H. Franklin Company retired from automobile production soon after the depression started, they were reorganized and continued to build small airplane engines for a time. While in Syracuse a couple of years ago, I was pleased to note a building with a sign reading "Franklin Engineering Company." Unfortunately, it was a Sunday and I could not make any inquiries about it.

Quite a few custom bodies were mounted on the Franklin, which was an ideal car for use about town because of its easy ride, due partly to the full-elliptic springs they used for many years, but also because of its laminated wood chassis frame which absorbed a good deal of road shock. Being also light and maneuverable for a car of its size, it handled well in traffic.

Frank deCausse had set up a consulting business in 1922 to design bodies for various firms, much as LeBaron had done a year or two before. His largest customer soon was Franklin, and within a few years he had not only restyled their entire line, but set up a small custom-body shop at their factory.

At this time, much attention was being given to better visibility, and several custom builders, including Brewster and LeBaron, were using cast bronze windshield posts on many of their closed cars to achieve this. DeCausse also experimented with such posts, and his associate Henry Emond applied for a patent on the idea of using windshield pillars thinner than the average distance between a person's eyes, which he defined as 2⅜ inches. With cast pillars, this was quite feasible.

At the suggestion of Richard Vail, editor of *Autobody* magazine, I wrote a letter, which he published, pointing out that the practice was quite general, and that Mr. Emond was endeavoring to obtain a patent on a definition of clear vision, rather than on a structural method of accomplishing it. The principal thought seemed to be that by keeping the pillar narrower than the inter-pupillary distance, the driver could see around both sides of the post. William Brewster wrote a similar letter, in addition, calling attention to his own patent for a clear-vision windshield. Although the Emond patent was granted, no effort was made to enforce it.

During the next few years, Franklin ordered several small series of bodies from Derham, Dietrich, Locke and others. Several of the Dietrich designs were adapted to production and became standard Franklin models, built at the Walker Body plant. One of these was the Pirate, described and pictured in my chapter on Dietrich.

Before setting up as a consultant, deCausse had been chief stylist for Locomobile. This company had been set up in the 1890s to take over the Stanley Brothers' patents and had started with steam cars. One has been for some years in the loving hands of my late friend and neighbor Bob Bohaty, and several others exist. One of them is pictured in an earlier chapter.

Having experienced some difficulty in manufacturing, and faced with competition from the Stanleys, who had returned to making steam cars of a much improved design, the Locomobile Company engaged A. L. Riker, who had already had some success with an electric truck of his own design. He soon developed a gasoline-powered car to replace the steamer. By 1910 or so this had developed into a massive automobile rated at 48 taxable horsepower, the size of the mid-range Pierce-Arrow, and of the finest quality.

The Locomobile plant in Bridgeport built chassis only, with the bodies coming from various custom

1928 Franklin Town Car by Dietrich, exhibited at 1927 New York Salon. Note wide sill molding used by Dietrich to make car look lower. From Franklin advertisement in Salon Catalog.

1930 Franklin Town Car by Dietrich. From Franklin Custom Body Catalog, Floyd Marshall Collection.

1921 Locomobile Town Brougham, designed by Frank deCausse. Body builder not identified, and similar bodies were built by various firms. Photograph courtesy Automobile Manufacturers Association.

builders to designs by deCausse. While many were built in the nearby plants of the Bridgeport Body Company, the Blue Ribbon Body Company and the New Haven Carriage Company, Locomobiles sold in other parts of the country often had the bodies, of almost identical design and finish, fitted by local concerns.

Like many others, Locomobile had difficulty adjusting to the 1921 recession and went into receivership. Frank deCausse left to set up his consulting business, but Delmar G. "Barney" Roos stayed on as chief engineer.

At the same time, W. C. Durant had just been ousted from General Motors and was endeavoring to set up his new automotive empire. In October 1922, the courts approved the sale of the Locomobile Company to Durant. He expressed the intention of continuing to build cars of the same fine quality, and immediately engaged LeBaron to restyle the entire line.

At the 1923 Salon, three of these new Locomobiles were shown—a Town Brougham by Locke, a Collapsible Cabriolet by Demarest (pictured in an earlier chapter), and the most striking, the new Sportif, also built by Demarest. Each had been designed by LeBaron.

Some of the subsequent bodies were built by the Bridgeport Body Company, and as related earlier, this led to the merger of this firm with LeBaron. For some time thereafter, a fair number of Locomobile bodies were built there, but without the LeBaron nameplate even though they had originally been designed by us.

However, we also built a few individual bodies on Locomobiles that did carry our name. One was a town car for Roy W. Howard of the Scripps-Howard newspapers. He was always nattily dressed, and I recall that when he came to our office to discuss some detail, he always stood near a window that overlooked 58th Street and Eighth Avenue. It was not until some time later that I realized that this window also overlooked the Hearst offices across the street.

For a time, Locomobile made only the one chassis, but in the mid-twenties they added some smaller cars. The first was Model 90, a six-cylinder car of more modern design but still about the size of the Lincoln. It could hardly be called low-priced, since it was in the $7,000 price range, but this was less than the Model 48, which sold for $12,000 and up at the same time.

1927 Locomobile Model 90 Town Car, from Locomobile advertisement in 1927 Salon Catalog.

However, Locomobile set out to develop a less expensive car, and the first Junior Eight chassis I saw at their Bridgeport plant had an overhead-valve engine designed by Barney Roos in collaboration with Harry Miller. This turned out to be rather expensive to produce, and since Locomobile was not selling its larger cars too well, stock engines from Lycoming and Continental were soon substituted. Another factor in this change may have been the departure of Barney Roos to greener pastures in the West.

Since the Locomobile with the larger Lycoming eight listed at about $1,000 more than the Auburn using the same engine—and in fact a bit more than the Packard Six—it did not become an immediate success. It was not too long before Locomobile folded again, along with the rest of Durant's second empire.

"Barney" Roos went from Locomobile to Marmon, where he designed a small eight similar to Locomobile's, as I have described. He stayed there only a few months before he moved to Studebaker as Chief Engineer. Later, of course, he went on to Willys-Overland, where he acquired fame as the "Father of the Jeep." On a business trip to Toledo in 1945 I telephoned "Barney." He had just returned from a trip to Washington that morning, and could not take time for a visit because, as he put it, he had to run up to Detroit that afternoon and "teach the boys at Ford how to build automobiles."

Now I know that Studebaker is not a name generally associated with custom bodies, although they had the reputation of building a solid, durable car in the 1920s. Actually, they had gotten into the automobile business by building bodies for the Detroit Electric in the 1890s while still in the wagon business, and by association with E.M.F. and Mr. Flanders finally wound up making complete cars.

In the middle twenties their sales manager, Harold Vance, decided they needed more prestige. A custom-body division was set up under a very effective salesman, Foster Rozar. He ordered an assortment of bodies from LeBaron and a few others, and arranged a five-year lease on the Rose Room of the Plaza Hotel in New York.

The first custom-bodied Studebakers were shown there in December 1925, following which Rozar arranged for special showings in Palm Beach and Miami. Some people will recall that this was a time when a hurricane wiped out some buildings in that area, and also the Florida land boom. I think it must also have wiped out the Studebakers on exhibition there, because I never heard of them again.

They had not been too well received, because people who could afford to spend $5,000 or $6,000 for a custom-bodied Studebaker could just as easily add another thousand or two and get a more prestigious Lincoln, Packard or Cadillac. In fact, they could get a standard-bodied car of any of these makes for less.

I never did learn just what became of that five-year lease with the Plaza Hotel, but I suspect it may have been an option rather than a firm lease. It did enable Studebaker to get some nice publicity, and to use a beautiful background in some of their advertisements of the period.

25
Other American Chassis

A few other American cars were fitted with custom bodies during the twenties, although not to any great extent. I have referred several times to the 1921 deflation, and its toll on the American automobile industry. It led to a greater concentration of production among relatively few large manufacturers, a process that has continued to this day.

Quite a few firms concentrated on war production during 1917 and 1918, and either did not make the conversion back to automobiles, or took several years to accomplish this, so that their new cars did not reach the market until 1921. Often they had purchased large quantities of parts and materials just before prices collapsed in the middle of that year, and were left with a high cost inventory which could not be manufactured into cars except for sale at a loss. Some other companies sprang up just after World War I and were faced with the same problem.

Another factor was the change in emphasis in society's attitude toward the automobile at this time. It was no longer the plaything of the rich, but something accessible to the average man, whose earnings had increased sharply during and just after the war. The companies making low- and medium-priced automobiles for this market prospered, some very well indeed; those catering to the high-priced trade did not do so well except for the few who survived into the late twenties. Part of the reason, of course, was the fact that the cheaper cars had improved radically in design from prewar days, and mass production had reached the point where a standardized car of reasonably good quality was available at a low price.

The net result was that between 1919 and 1923 the number of makes of American automobiles was cut by more than one-half. A few other well-regarded makes struggled on until 1925 or so, but never again reached the stature they had enjoyed earlier. Had this "shake-out" not occurred when it did, the number of automobile manufacturers going out of business soon after the 1929 crash would have been much higher. As it was, there weren't that many left by then.

Among the smaller companies, Wills Ste. Claire comes to mind immediately, since I personally admired this smaller copy of the Hispano-Suiza. C. H. Wills was an excellent engineer and a great metallurgist, and I can remember the emphasis in his advertising on the use of molybdenum steel.

If his business acumen had been as great as his creative skill, if he had concentrated on building cars at a profit instead of to the best of his ability, and if he had spent less time on the social progress of his model town on the shores of Lake Ste. Claire, perhaps the car would have been the success it should have been. As it is, he continued to make many contributions to the progress of automotive design, and especially materials, during his subsequent career on the staff of the Ford Motor Company.

The Wills Ste. Claire originally had a V-8 engine with overhead camshafts, and was relatively light because of the extensive use of alloy steels. Most of the custom bodies built for the Wills were mounted on this chassis, as the lower priced and less imaginative six which replaced it was not in the same category.

LeBaron designed some bodies in 1922 and 1923 which were built by other firms on the Wills Ste. Clair, and Willoughby showed an attractive town car at the 1925 Salon and built a few more of the same type. The Wills ad in the Salon catalog for that year had some brief but cogent copy—"Ask the concierge at the Ritz, the Bellevue-Stratford, the Copley-Plaza or the Los Angeles Biltmore—they know who owns them."

Stearns-Knight from Cleveland also had quite a bit of prestige, and was probably the finest car built in this country with sleeve-valve engines. As indi-

1922 Wills Ste. Claire Town Car designed by LeBaron, Carrossiers.

cated by the name, these were of the Knight type. Charles Knight's patent was not granted in this country until late in 1910 although he had obtained earlier patents abroad and several European manufacturers had already been licensed under these. I presume there is some difference in the laws here, since every American car using his patents had the word "Knight" in the brand name. This was not true in Europe, where Daimler, Panhard & Levassor, Minerva and others used sleeve-valve engines under his license. Mercedes did, however, call theirs the Mercedes-Knight.

Stearns made an eight-cylinder car as early as 1918, but these were V-type. By the 1920s they were building a straight-eight with a somewhat larger engine, and quite a few custom bodies were mounted on this chassis. There was usually at least one Stearns-Knight in the Salons of this period, several I recall being shown by Brunn.

John N. Willys bought a controlling interest in the company late in 1925, but kept it entirely separate from his other companies. The Stearns-Knight and the Willys-Knight were quite different in concept, the latter being concentrated in the lower-middle-price field.

Actually, Willys-Knight had earlier taken a fling at a higher-priced car in 1918, when they also introduced a V-8, but it sold for just over $2,000,

1927 Stearns-Knight Town Cabriolet by Brunn, exhibited at 1927 New York Salon. From advertisement of F. B. Stearns Co. in Salon Catalog.

1918 Willys-Knight Town Car. Photograph courtesy Automobile Manufacturers Association.

which was about $1,000 cheaper than the comparable Stearns-Knight. My father bought one, used, in 1921 for $1,250. It wasn't the best looking car in the world, but it was smooth and quiet. Like most V-8s of the time, it had dual exhausts.

A few custom bodies were mounted on this Willys-Knight chassis, including some town cars, but not very many. It was continued only for a year or two, and later cars from this firm were too low-priced to encourage custom building.

Mercer was outstanding as a sports car in the period before World War I and briefly afterwards. So much attention has been focused on their Raceabouts that some people are not aware that they also built a longer chassis with the same four-cylinder motor. Several town car and limousine bodies were mounted on this. Mercers were built in Trenton, New Jersey, and named after Mercer County, in which this state capital is situated.

Priced at upwards of $3,250, which was the list for the Raceabout in 1918, they were in competition with the six-cylinder cars made by Marmon, Winton and Dorris, which had a wider appeal for the average motorist. Mercer set out to develop a six of

somewhat more conventional design than the four, but lacked the capital to carry through the program. They went into receivership in 1921.

The following year, E. S. Hare, who had been a Packard salesman and had some financial backing, formed a syndicate to follow in Durant's footsteps and build an automobile empire. He had some sort of option on the majority stock of Mercer, Locomobile, Crane-Simplex and Kelly-Springfield, as well as several accessory manufacturers who were in financial straits. All of these companies were in receivership at the time, and control rested with the creditors rather than the stockholders.

His grandiose scheme failed to attract sufficient capital, and it fell through. A new group was formed to take over Mercer, and they put its new six into production as well as continuing the four, but were soon again in bankruptcy. The assets of the company, except for the land and buildings, were bought by the Curran-McDevitt Company, who had been the Mercer distributors in Philadelphia, early in 1924. They completed the last few cars which had been in process when the company was forced to close its doors.

As mentioned, Durant bought Locomobile. Another group was formed to take over the Crane-Simplex, and even engaged LeBaron to design some new bodies for them. Unfortunately they never got into production.

The Simplex Company had been established before 1910 to make a car along the lines of the current largest Mercedes, which had been designated the Simplex model. Henry Crane became their chief engineer and developed new designs which were even better. Many people consider the cars built under his supervision, with the name changed to Crane-Simplex, the finest American car built before World War I. They were the size of a Rolls-Royce, with an even larger and more powerful engine, and such unique features as ball-jointed rear spring shackles.

The company turned to making Hispano-Suiza airplane engines during the war, and seemed unable to decide what course to pursue when it was over. When they went into receivership, Henry Crane became a consultant to General Motors. He was then well along in years and I imagine had no great interest in starting anew with fresh designs.

LeBaron designed two bodies on Crane-Simplex chassis in 1923 for Mrs. Theodate Pope Riddle, daughter of the architect and herself an accomplished one. This was before we had our own factory, and the bodies were built by Demarest in New York. One

was a Coupe-Landaulet and the other a Sedan-Limousine, and both had completely new radiators, hoods and fenders to make the cars look quite current. This quite disguised the fact that the chassis themselves had been built in 1915.

Stevens-Duryea was another firm, one of the oldest automobile manufacturers in the United States, which concentrated on arms production during the war. In fact, the company was actually the Stevens Arms Company, making cars originally from the designs of Charles Duryea.

They did not resume building cars until 1921, when they introduced a new model very similar to the Locomobile, even in appearance. The price was also similar, and while some very lovely bodies were built on it—I can recall one by Healy with exquisite wood panelling in the interior—it did not reach any sizeable production and the firm gave up the automobile business within a couple of years.

The Daniels V-8 was built in Reading, Pennsylvania, and as mentioned earlier many of their bodies came from nearby Fleetwood. I recall some quite attractive town cars. As early as 1918 they had a four-seater with bucket seats in front and a narrow seat for two set into the rear deck, which they called the Sportif, a name later borrowed by LeBaron for their Locomobile sport phaeton. Daniels's engines came from Herschell-Spillman, who built similar ones for several small-volume, high-priced cars, and also made

1916 Crane-Simplex Phaeton by Holbrook with many nautical features, including cowl ventilators. Photograph courtesy of its present owner, Harrah's Automobile Collection.

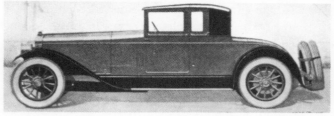

1915 Crane-Simplex with Coupe-Landaulet body by LeBaron added in 1924, with redesigned radiator and hood. One of the two cars rebuilt for Mrs. Theodate Pope Riddle.

airplane and marine engines of advanced design that powered some high-speed boats.

In 1922, Paul duPont bought a substantial interest in Daniels, and planned to merge the company with his own and move the machinery to Wilmington. At the time, duPont cars were being assembled in the Indian Motorcycle plant in Springfield, Massachusetts. They were of more conventional engineering, with a chassis made up largely of stock components such as Continental engines. DuPont was credited with designing the bodies for many of his cars, and at one point claimed they were built in his own

shop. However, I believe most came from Merrimack, and as mentioned earlier, the announcement of the establishment of Waterhouse specifically mentioned that they would build bodies for duPont. Their factory was only fifty or sixty miles from Springfield.

White had built steam cars early in the century which were highly regarded, then switched to gasoline power. Their cars were fairly large and expensive, so naturally quite a few were fitted with custom bodies. However, the company had given up the manufacture of passenger cars even before World War I to concentrate on trucks and busses. They had evolved from the White Sewing Machine Company in Cleveland, and just recently there have been reports of an impending merger between the surviving company, White Industries, and the Hupp Corporation, another old automotive name. I don't recall any custom-bodied Hupmobiles although they did build some attractive medium-priced automobiles.

Winton and Peerless were other Cleveland firms of some prestige. Alexander Winton started building,

1915 Stevens-Duryea with Convertible Sedan body of probably later vintage. Post-war Stevens-Duryeas were very similar. Note Westinghouse Air Springs.

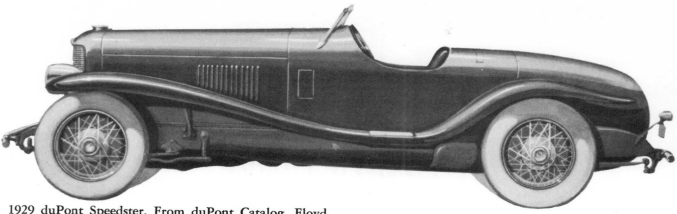

1929 duPont Speedster. From duPont Catalog, Floyd
Marshall Collection.

and racing, automobiles before the turn of the century. He was an early advocate of the six-cylinder engine, and by 1918 these were being made in two sizes, the 33 with a 348 cubic inch engine, and the 48 with a 525 cubic inch engine the size of the Locomobile. Prices were moderate considering the size and quality of the cars, with open models beginning at $3,000 and $3,500 respectively.

A number of Wintons were fitted with custom bodies, and the factory also offered a standard limousine for about $1,000 more than the open cars. I imagine that Winton did not find passenger car production profitable at these prices, for by 1925 they discontinued it in favor of the development of Diesel engines for marine and stationary use. This business was eventually sold to General Motors.

Peerless, who had started in 1900, was somewhat lower priced than Winton. However, by 1918 they looked quite a bit like the Cadillacs of the same era, and also had V-8 engines, but at a price some $500 less. Some were fitted with special bodies, and they usually were shown at the Salons of the early twenties. By 1926 or so, however, they had concentrated on less expensive cars with Continental engines. While the bigger eights were still in production in 1928, the company was fast losing ground and gave up when the depression hit.

Premier also came from Cleveland, and during its later years had an electric push-button shift. Not an automatic transmission in the present sense, but an early attempt in that direction with electromagnets moving the gears in a sliding transmission. Its appeal was more to the owner-driver, and for this reason not many custom bodies were built on it.

More advanced was the Owen-Magnetic, which was something of a sensation in the days just before and after we entered World War I. It had an electromagnetic transmission which could more truly be considered a forerunner of today's automatics, although it worked on an entirely different principle.

The car was built by Baker, Rauch & Lang, who had extensive experience with electric cars as well as substantial manufacturing facilities for both mechanical components and bodies. Each of the cars produced was virtually custom built, with a goodly proportion of town cars among them. Unfortunately, the mechanism was both heavy and expensive, so that its manufacture proved unprofitable and the venture was dropped by 1919.

Lastly, Cleveland also was the home of Leon Rubay's attempt at complete automobile production. As mentioned in the section describing his body-building activities, he tried to market a car embodying the latest European ideas in 1922. Unfortunately, he misjudged the American public, which wanted bigger and cheaper cars at this time. Several others made the same mistake, and all succumbed.

1923 Rubay Victoria Coupe. From *Motor Magazine*,
December, 1922.

26

Some Smaller American Manufacturers

CUNNINGHAM

FINALLY, I come to a group of American cars that never reached substantial volume and have long since disappeared from the market, although some examples of a few still exist.

The American Underslung had a good reputation and some racing success during the early part of the century, but never reached the same position again after World War I. As its name implies, the frame was hung below the axles, a distinct advantage in the early days of high wheels, but which lost much of its attraction as wheels grew progressively smaller.

The Biddle was built in Philadelphia, long the home of the family that gave it its name. The early ones may have had Rochester-Duesenberg engines, but by 1918 a Buda engine had been substituted. Buda built mainly truck engines, and they were massive and durable. The Biddle had a pointed radiator somewhat like the Mercedes, and while some open cars and sedans were built, I recall them mainly as town cars. Bodies were supposedly built in their own factory, but bore quite a resemblance to the Fleetwood bodies of the same period. Although somewhat smaller, the car sold in the Cadillac price range.

The Cole V-8 was another medium-priced car with a good reputation. They had started with fours in 1910, but by 1920 were building only the eights which had a 346 cubic inch Northway engine and quite good performance. A sedan sold for $4,350 that year. Willoughby built several small series of custom bodies for Cole around 1921, but I do not recall any but regular production models thereafter.

James Cunningham Sons & Company were carriage builders in Rochester and early in the century built some custom bodies for automobiles. By 1910 they were making their own car, and in 1916 introduced a V-8 engine, which they continued into the 1930s. They built all their own bodies and these included some very attractive phaetons. In the early twenties these had rather rounded sides, splash pans covering the chassis, and usually individual steps in place of running boards.

They also built some attractive town cars which sold in the $8,000 bracket, or slightly more than a comparable Packard or Lincoln. There was not much business in this price range after the stock market crash of 1929, and like Brewster, Cunningham built a few town car bodies on Ford V-8 chassis around 1934. Recently I have heard that the company is still in business, making garden tractors and power mowers.

Dorris was St. Louis's contribution to the fine car field. They started with a four-cylinder car in 1906, but introduced a six in 1915, which was continued until 1923. It had a 377 cubic inch engine, somewhat smaller than the Pierces and Packards of the time, and sold for about $6,000 in sedan form. Some cus-

1925 Cunningham Town Car, from their advertisement in New York Salon Catalog. Later models had less rounded radiator.

tom bodies were fitted, mostly by Midwestern build-ers, as their sales were highest in that area. Dorris did not find motor cars profitable after 1921, and decided to liquidate in 1923.

Fergus is a name still known along New York's automobile row. In 1920 they introduced a car of their own, but not many were ever built. Like the imports with which the company has long been asso-ciated, it was available only in chassis form, on which the purchaser would have a body built by one of the local custom builders. The chassis were built in New-ark, New Jersey.

There was an American Fiat, a duplicate of the cars they were building in Italy just before World War I. Just after hostilities started in Europe, the company put up a factory in Poughkeepsie, N.Y., so that the name could be carried on even though pro-duction in Italy was converted to war materiel, in-cluding airplanes and engines.

Fiat found it difficult to compete here after 1921, and the factory was shut down. There was some talk that Lancia would take over the buildings in 1928 and assemble cars in this country, but this failed to materialize.

Charles B. King started building multi-cylindered cars quite early in the history of the automobile in-dustry, and by 1918 had a medium-priced V-8, but its appeal was to the younger element rather than the older and wealthier people who bought custom bod-ies.

Kissel of course built some very attractive cars, nearly all with their own bodies. Their two-passenger open Speedsters were as much admired then as now. Not many people may be aware that in 1918 they introduced a V-12. It had a Weidely engine, which was also used by the H.A.L. and the Austin (no con-nection with the English company), and in modified form in the Heine-Velox which was briefly produced in San Francisco a year or two later.

C. W. Nash set up the Lafayette Motor Company in 1919 to make a high-priced eight-cylinder car. Its quality and prices were close to those of Henry Le-land's new Lincoln, and quite a few custom bodies of various types were built on it. Nash did not find this new venture profitable, and unlike Ford, who continued the Lincoln as a losing proposition, he de-cided to discontinue it. An effort was made to sell the company to Pierce-Arrow in 1922, but it fell through and production ceased soon afterwards. Nash did, however, retain the right to the Lafayette name and used it for an inexpensive car some years later.

1921 Lafayette Limousine. Photograph courtesy Auto-mobile Manufacturers Association.

I have already mentioned McFarlan as body build-ers and later manufacturers of complete automobiles. The history of the car has been compiled by my friend Alvin Arnheim in his book, *What Was the McFar-lan?*

Although they built other models of more modest size, their claim to fame is based almost entirely on the huge twin-valve six which was produced from 1920 until the company closed in 1929. It had the largest engine of any production car of the period. One magnificent town car shown at the Chicago Auto Show of 1923 had gold-plated exterior and interior hardware and a price tag of $25,000, considerably higher than most McFarlans. Arnheim's book men-tions that it was not sold until July of that year, some five months after it was first shown, and that "According to one delicately phrased news report, 'It was purchased by a lady from Oklahoma City whose family acquired wealth from oil.' " My own recollection is that those news reports identified the lady as a recently widowed Indian.

National was one of the better cars of the early part of the century, and by World War I was build-ing a good and not too expensive Six. In 1918 they also introduced a V-12. There was a rash of these at the time. A few custom bodies were mounted on this Twelve, and also on the Six. E. J. Thompson dis-played one at the 1921 Body Builders' Show, held concurrently with the New York Auto Show.

Noma is a name which people associated with Christmas tree lights for many years, but in 1920 the same firm introduced a car, one of the few being

1922 McFarlan Town Car. Photograph courtesy Automobile Manufacturers Association.

built in New York City at the time. It had an assembled chassis with Continental engine and other stock parts, but came with rather attractive bodies paneled in aluminum and often left unpainted. Their open cars were quite good looking.

The Standard was built by the Standard Car Company of Pittsburgh, manufacturers of railroad cars, which later merged into the Pullman Company. It used the same V-8 engine as the Daniels, made by

Herschell-Spillman, but was somewhat less expensive. A few special bodies were built for it, several by Thompson in Pittsburgh, but the company gave up automobiles in the early twenties to concentrate on their major business.

Stanley Steamers were quite the rage early in the

1919 Body Builders' Show in New York. Rolls-Royce Coupe by Blue Ribbon in foreground. Part of a Noma can be seen behind it. Photograph courtesy Automobile Manufacturers Association.

century. Although the brothers sold their patents to Locomobile before 1900, they were soon back in the automobile business with a more modern design. By 1906, one of their cars with a special streamlined body had been driven at 127 miles per hour by Fred Marriott at Daytona. A little later he wrecked the car while trying for a still higher record. His speed when he hit a depression in the sand and sailed off through the air has been estimated at 190 m.p.h. by observers.

Currier & Cameron in Amesbury built the bodies for the early Stanleys, and later some limousines of rather conventional appearance. With the improvement of internal combustion engines, steam lost much of its appeal after World War I, and the company gradually declined until it went into bankruptcy in 1923. Syracuse interests bought the company from the receivers, and continued production for a couple of years, but that was the end.

Doble was a small manufacturer of steam cars in San Francisco between 1914 and 1924, and a few of their chassis had custom bodies from Walter Murphy.

Finally, sight should not be lost of the custom bodies mounted on such unlikely chassis as the Chalmers and the Model T Ford shortly after World War I. These included some town cars. During a talk to the Classic Car Club, Enos Derham showed a picture of a Model T town car they had built. He explained that the family chauffeur, formerly their coachman, had never learned to drive any car but the Model T. Rather than find a new chauffeur, the family arranged with the Derhams to build an appropriate body, which cost around $5,000. The chassis on which it was mounted was under $500.

Actually, a number of small production runs of special bodies were available for the Ford, usually in body styles not included in the regular line, which was quite limited in those days. Many of these were fairly sporty looking roadsters and coupes. There was even an occasional Ford by Brewster around 1915 or so, one or two of which are still in existence.

PART IV

PART IV

27
European Luxury Cars

ANOTHER of my articles for *Motor Trend* was entitled "Ten Great European Classics." Much of the material in the next few chapters is an expansion of this.

Between 1920 and 1932, a considerable number of European cars were imported, mostly in the luxury class. There may have been fewer in number than in the past dozen years, but their value, in current dollars, may have been greater.

There is no question that connoisseurs of the time considered the Hispano-Suiza and the English Rolls-Royce the world's finest automobiles. A chassis of either marque cost $14,500 landed in New York, without body or fenders. This brought the price of the complete car well over $20,000. To duplicate either of these fine cars today would easily cost three or more times as much.

The others I selected as members of the "Top Ten" were only slightly behind these two—Isotta-Fraschini, Minerva, Mercedes, Renault, Panhard & Levassor, Voisin, Lancia and Farman. Most of them sold for upwards of $10,000, partly because the European firms built chassis only in this Luxe category. Either they were purchased with a custom body built in Europe, or the chassis only was imported and fitted with an appropriate superstructure by one of the top American coachbuilders.

In compiling my article, I confined myself to those cars actively imported during the 1920s. There were others brought in on a smaller scale—Excelsior, Hotchkiss, Lanchester, Maybach and Steiger all had distributors here at various times.

In my introduction to the *Motor Trend* article, I said that readers would look in vain for such famous names as Alfa-Romeo, Bentley, Bugatti, Horch and Wanderer, since none of these were imported at the time. A few were purchased in Europe by wealthy Americans and shipped here after touring the Continent. Many more have come over recently, being eagerly sought by collectors. I shall make some comments on these in the following chapters.

There were other names famous in Europe that had a place in the American market before World War I, but were not sold here to any appreciable extent later on. Austro-Daimler, Fiat, Napier, Sunbeam, the English Daimler, Delage, Delahaye, Delaunay-Belleville, Steyr and Graef & Stift all fit into this category. Some of these firms are still in business, or at least were until quite recently, and the often-revolutionary vehicles they built in the 1930's have been especially sought after.

Many European companies built a considerable range of models simultaneously, some with the same high quality throughout, and others with a rather extensive variation to suit different markets. Most of them built relatively small cars after World War I for the European market. Gasoline costs and taxes were extremely high there, and placed the operation of a large car beyond the means of all but the very wealthy.

The huge luxury models shipped here were often aimed primarily at the American market, and just as our manufacturers at this time produced "export" models, which were identical to the domestic ones except for substantially smaller engines, so these European firms produced some cars for sale here with larger engines than were generally available in their home countries.

As has been the case with Jaguar in recent years, more than half of whose production has been exported, some of these manufacturers shipped more than half of their largest models overseas. This does not mean that they all came to the United States, as there were some extremely wealthy nabobs in India and the oil-rich Middle-East. And of course, South America was not without a few who could afford them, too.

There was also one small sports car imported during the 1920s—a forerunner of the MG and its various competitors. This was the Amilcar from France, handled here by Fritz von Meister, who was the American representative for Maybach.

131

The Amilcar was introduced at the 1925 Salon, and was an immediate success. At $1,850 delivered in New York, and promising 75 miles per hour and 40 miles per gallon, it was a good value. It had a 1300 c.c. engine, a two-seater body with rather good streamlining, and definite style, looking somewhat like a miniature G.P. car. Quite a few were sold, and I remember seeing them in various parts of the country. Several survive, which is somewhat surprising considering their rather fragile appearance.

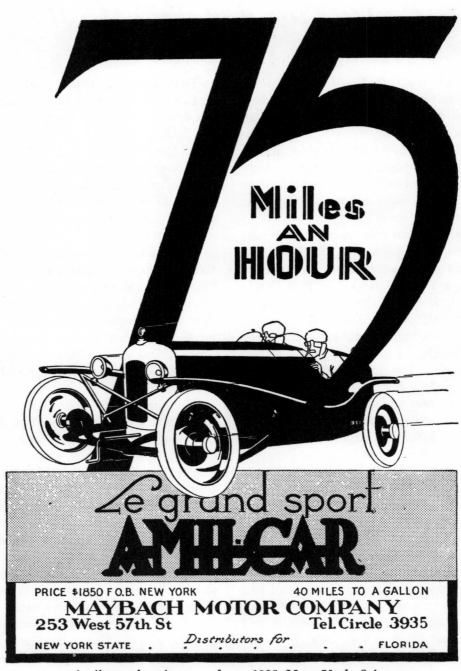

Amilcar advertisement from 1925 New York Salon Catalog.

28
Hispano-Suiza

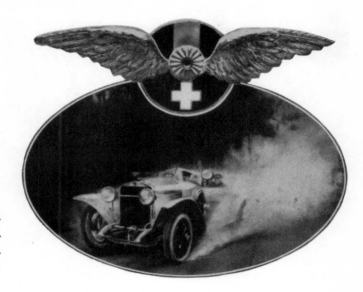

MANY experts consider the Hispano-Suiza, especially the H-6 models, the finest automobile of all time. Designed by a Swiss engineer, Marc Birgkit, who had moved to Spain, the name was a combination of those of these two countries.

Production started in Barcelona, in 1904, and some of their early prestige was gained in racing. King Alphonso XIII of Spain was a great enthusiast and encouraged the racing program. He drove a Hispano-Suiza as his own personal car, and allowed the company to call duplicates the Alphonso XIII Model. This was a light, fast car which even in those days sported a short boat-tail. It was a far cry from the monstrous, heavy cars that dominated early auto racing.

In 1911, a branch factory was opened outside Paris, which soon far outstripped the original one in Spain—at least in automobile production—and became the principal source of cars shipped to America. With the outbreak of World War I, Marc Birgkit turned his attention to airplane engines, and designed a V-8 that was one of the best engines the Allies had. Before the war ended, it was being produced under license in many countries, including the United States. Later a V-12 was designed, but the war ended before volume production started.

In 1919, Hispano-Suiza resumed production of automobiles, with an extremely advanced engine which was essentially half of that V-12 aero engine.

It had an aluminum crankcase, aluminum-alloy block with screwed in steel cylinder liners, and an overhead camshaft. The bore and stroke of 100 x 140 m.m. gave it a displacement of 6½ liters, or just about 400 cubic inches.

In the mid-twenties, an enlarged version was introduced with the bore increased to 110 m.m., boosting the displacement to 463 cubic inches or 10 percent more than the Duesenberg Model J. A modified engine of this type in a short chassis won the Coupe des Voitures race at Boulogne, and subsequent duplicates were known as the Boulogne model. Even this short wheelbase was still 134 inches. A few of these chassis were imported, and were guaranteed to top 100 miles per hour with open bodywork, the first non-racing car I can recall with such performance.

Most of the cars that reached these shores were, however, the normal 145-inch wheelbase, which served as a foundation for impressive town cars as well as more sporting vehicles. Besides being well engineered, they were manufactured under the highest standards. The engine had tremendous torque and performed beautifully in high gear from 6 m.p.h. to a maximum up in the 90s. As an example, the crank-

1927 Hispano-Suiza Town Car, probably by Million-Guiet. This is a movie still taken about 1933, after its first restoration. The car is again being restored by Mr. Ray Radford of Vancouver, Washington. Photograph courtesy Mr. Malcolm Willits of Hollywood.

shaft was machined from a solid billet of alloy steel weighing more than 750 pounds. The finished shaft weighed only 99 pounds.

One of the distinctive features of the Hispano was the "Flying Stork" radiator emblem. This was inspired by the badge of Captain Guynemer's squadron of Spads during World War I, which had been powered by Hispano-Suiza engines.

Throughout this period, Hispanos were also being built at Barcelona. Most of these were smaller four-cylinder cars but some sixes were also produced. These were available throughout Europe, but few, if any, came to the United States.

During the 1930s, a V-12 was built in France, with a square engine of 100 x 100 m.m., or nearly four inches in both bore and stroke, giving a displacement of 575 cubic inches. Some people consider this the most magnificent Hispano of all, but others prefer the earlier H6B and H6C. Road tests of the twelve by the English magazine *Autocar* showed it could go from 0 to 60 in 12 seconds—not bad for a

5,000 pound car in 1930. Not many of the Twelves came here new during the depression, but there are several in this country now in various collections, including Briggs Cunningham's.

Hispano-Suiza were never adequately represented in this country, although the car was well known to many wealthy clients. It was shown at the 1921 Salon and once more later. Through the mid-twenties, we built several bodies on Hispano chassis, which arrived here through the mysterious ministrations of the Best brothers, Leo and Jack. They had a small showroom on Central Park South in New York. One of my first assignments with LeBaron was to walk down the block with R. L. Stickney and take all the vital measurements of a Hispano chassis they had just imported for G. Maurice Heckscher.

Later Clarke D. Pease was appointed the American agent, and maintained for a while a showroom on 57th Street near Sixth Avenue. He was a close friend of Rene LaCoste, the tennis star, whose family at this time controlled Hispano. For some reason, he never established close relations with any American body builder, and most of the cars he brought here were fitted with bodies by Hibbard & Darrin or some other French firm. Throughout the existence of his company, chassis were still coming in through clan-

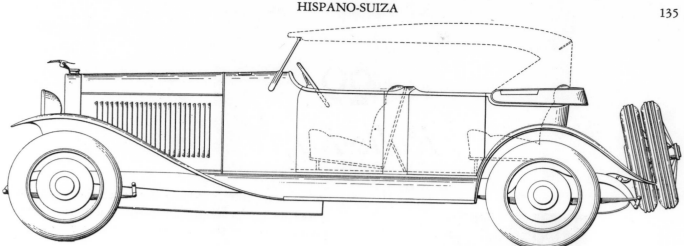

1926 Hispano-Suiza Phaeton by LeBaron, built for
Mr. Lewis Hirshon. Reproduction of original design
sketch submitted to customer.

destine sources.

Pease was given control of the Hispano-Suiza trademark, which had been registered in this country. He took advantage of this by filing suit against every individual who owned a Hispano that had not passed through his hands. Since this brought him into conflict with people like the Mellons, who owned several, most of the suits dragged on and I believe were still not settled when he went out of business in the early thirties.

Early Salon catalogs carry an advertisement that reads simply—

John B. Mezey
Motor Car Maintenance
Hispano-Suiza Specialist

Brief and to the point. I think Jack Mezey did the servicing of just about every Hispano we built a body for, if not almost every one imported. They required some special attention, since the cylinder sleeves were deliberately ground slightly oval, and not too many mechanics were aware of this.

In the middle forties, his son Jim formed Mezey Motors, which took over the Lincoln dealership that for many years had occupied the corner showroom at 247 Park Avenue. Later he moved to Huntington, Long Island, to become our local dealer. He has recently retired, but we often visited and spent some time discussing various individual "Hissos" we both remembered.

Hispano built only chassis, and these were fitted with bodies from the finest coachbuilders the world over. Rarely was more than one of a design built, since the clientele constituted the elite of the world, who wanted individuality above all else.

We built several sporty phaetons on Hispanos, as well as superb town cars, but one I recall especially was a two-passenger coupe for Col. H. H. Rogers. It didn't even have a rumble seat, and was planned especially so his chauffeur could get the Colonel to Southampton in rapid time for his long weekends there. I also recall that his chauffeur referred to the then new Phantom Rolls as an "overgrown Buick" and would have no part of it.

29
Rolls-Royce

SINCE much has already been written about Rolls-Royce, still considered among the world's best even though some of its admirers feel that current models have slipped somewhat from their peak, I shall try to add some comments that may be new to many people.

While Rolls-Royce of America maintained a factory in Springfield, Massachusetts from 1921 to 1933, many people felt the cars built there were not quite the equal of those from the Derby works in England. Also, the Phantom was introduced in England a year or so before production of this model started in Springfield. As a result, quite a few Rolls chassis were imported from England in the twenties even though the cost was several thousand dollars more than for an American one.

For some reason, the American company was reluctant to import any of the English chassis, even though these were built by an affiliate. Possibly this was an effort to refute the opinion that the English product was better. Some people bought theirs in England and shipped home either a complete car, or the chassis, to which an American custom body would be fitted. Quite a few came through the Best brothers, whom I have already mentioned in connection with Hispano-Suiza.

The Rolls-Royce Silver Ghost had been continued almost unchanged since the first one was built in 1906, with an almost square L-head engine of 4½ x 4¾ inches. Like Hispano, Rolls-Royce concentrated on airplane engines during World War I, and this undoubtedly influenced the design of the Phantom. It was one of the few instances where a more modern engine increased the stroke-bore ratio, to 4¼ x 5½ inches.

With its 470 cubic inch displacement, this was one of the largest engines of its time when production started in 1925. However, Rolls-Royce then as always was more concerned with silence and smoothness than with performance, and the engine was less advanced in design than the Hispano's. The big engine contributed to Rolls's goals by operating under very low stress under almost any conditions.

The first Phantom engines were installed in a chassis essentially that of the Silver Ghost, with 143½ inch wheelbase, and cantilever springs at the rear. With this arrangement, one end of a semi-elliptic spring was attached to the rear axle, and the other to the chassis frame a little aft of the middle. The center of the spring was mounted on a pivoting trunnion attached to the frame. It allowed considerable movement of the axle and a soft ride.

For 1928, a new chassis was introduced with 150-inch wheelbase and normal semi-elliptic springs, but continuing the torque-tube drive, which had been essential with the cantilever springs. This was designated the Phantom II, and the earlier cars, which had been known simply as Phantoms, now became known as the Phantom I.

Subsequently, during the 1930s, a 12-cylinder model was introduced as the Phantom III. Any Rolls-Royce aficionado is of course aware that all Rolls model names have had Ghost, Phantom, Wraith, Shadow or something similar to convey the impression that the car moves silently.

In 1924, it was announced that Brewster had resumed selling Rolls-Royce chassis with Brewster bodies, something they had done earlier when the chassis all came from England. After the American Rolls-Royce factory was established, Brewster had for a time imported Lanchester chassis, as well as selling Marmons and Packards with Brewster bodies.

1921 Rolls-Royce Silver Ghost Landaulet by Brewster.

A year or two later, the Brewster family sold their business to Rolls-Royce, as explained in my chapter on their company. The Brewster building in Long Island City became the service depot for Rolls-Royce. For a time it was expected that all body building activities would be transferred to the Rolls plant in Springfield, but this proved not to be feasible and instead, in 1928, all body building was moved back to the Brewster plant.

In 1925, Rolls-Royce asked LeBaron to illustrate a forthcoming catalog. Some of these renderings by R. L. Stickney are reproduced herein. Several of the designs obviously originated with Brewster and were continued almost unchanged for several years.

Just as we all borrowed good ideas from Brewster, they would also adopt one when it was advisable. We did not like the deeply crowned fenders Rolls-Royce was using, and which are shown in the catalog illustrations. We had developed our own style with a lightly crowned, slightly flared shape which we thought blended better with the square-cornered radiator and hood.

A month or so after we delivered one car with such fenders to Mr. Philip M. Plant, he asked me to check on some detail while the car was being serviced at the Rolls-Brewster building. When I got there, there was much confusion about the location of the car. After some delay, I was taken to an upper floor of the building. Not only was the car there, but Carl Beck and several Brewster workmen were busily removing drawings, templates, etc. A couple of months later, all new Rolls-Royces sprouted more modern fenders, exactly like those LeBaron had been using. Incidentally, the body of Mr. Plant's car was a close copy of a Hibbard & Darrin design, at his request.

Even though the Phantom radiator was higher and narrower than that of the Silver Ghost, it was still not high enough to blend smoothly into the high beltline favored by LeBaron and some other body builders. Quite a few Rolls-Royces had their radiators rebuilt and new higher shells made. This in itself was quite an expensive process, costing more than a new Ford car at the time.

One of the last Rolls-Royces we built at LeBaron, a town car for Nicholas M. Schenck of Loew's, was the most expensive body we ever built. The price included fenders, running boards, and some work on the chassis, and cost over $8,000, bringing the complete car to about $23,000.

One of the changes we made was to cover the beautiful nickel-silver radiator shell with a dummy of brass, which was then nickel-plated and finally chrome-plated, to match the new-fangled chrome plating on the body hardware. The interior had very modern wood panelling lacquered to match the exterior colors.

Modifications on Rolls-Royce chassis were done

1926 Rolls-Royce Silver Ghost Pall Mall Phaeton. From Rolls-Royce Catalog illustrated by LeBaron.

1931 Rolls-Royce Phantom II Convertible Roadster by Brewster, exhibited at 1930 New York Salon. The rounded boat-tail deck had a one-passenger rumble seat.

for us by the Van Cura Machine Works, still in existence a few blocks from the old Brewster plant in Long Island City. Emil Van Cura had been chief mechanic for Rolls but left the firm to set up his own shop. He was one of the people who felt the English chassis were better than the American ones, and he specialized in servicing them.

Emil, now in his seventies, is still working. When I stopped by one morning recently, he was "supervising" the grinding of a connecting rod bearing seat, and seemed to be doing most of the work himself. Like other old-timers, he complained of the difficulty of getting competent help, and that his older employees were dying off, getting infirm, or otherwise leaving him in the lurch.

I gathered that Mr. Van Cura is also not too happy to work on more recent Rolls-Royces, but that his eyes light up when one of the early Phantoms comes along.

30
Isotta-Fraschini

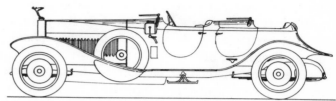

1924 Isotta-Fraschini Sport Phaeton. Original design by the author for LeBaron.

OF the cars imported in greatest volume during the classic period, Isotta-Fraschini was one of the most versatile. There were almost as many roadsters, phaetons and convertibles built on it as there were massive town cars and limousines, all on the same basic chassis.

Like Hispano-Suiza and Rolls-Royce, Isotta had started building automobiles in the early 1900s, and before the first World War they had already achieved some fame on the race course. During the war, they gained much engineering knowledge and experience building airplane engines, and like the other two, they continued this activity for some years—in fact through World War II. Some hope was held that they would resume automobile production in the late forties, and in fact a prototype rear-engined V-8 was exhibited at Milan and Geneva, but not enough capital was available.

Isotta was one of the first cars to carry four-wheel brakes, as early as 1908 as optional equipment. One of their cars placed second in the Vanderbilt Cup race that year, behind George Robertson's Locomobile. Their later advertising mentioned that four-wheel brakes had been standard since 1910. One of our neighbors, when I was still quite young, had a 1914 Isotta with brakes on the front wheels. They were the first I had ever seen.

Their Chief Engineer, Giustino Cattaneo, who had designed their airplane engines, developed the Tipo 8, which was introduced in 1921 and continued with minor changes into the 1930s. This was an overhead valve straight-eight with dual carburetors. The early versions had a bore and stroke of 85 x 130 m.m. for a displacement of 360 cubic inches, and were quoted as delivering 85 horsepower at 2,400 r.p.m.

Later, the Tipo 8-A had the bore increased to 95 m.m., enlarging the displacement to 450 cubic inches. At the same time, about 1925, a sport engine was added, with higher compression and better breathing giving somewhat more power for an extra $500. There was little advertising of horsepower at this point, the assumption being that customers would know that a car of this calibre had adequate power.

Like Hispano, Isotta built a sport chassis of shorter wheelbase, but not many were imported to this country. Quite a few cars did arrive, however, with the sport engine in the standard 146-inch wheelbase. These sold in chassis form for $9,000 and from $15,000 up with a limousine or town car body.

The Isotta-Fraschini showroom on Fifth Avenue near Sixtieth Street in New York, where the Sherry-Netherland Hotel now stands, was actually factory-owned. It was presided over by Captain Ugo d'Annunzio, son of the famous Italian poet and patriot. Most of the actual selling and promotion, however, was handled by his manager, Elmo di Paoli.

Many of their cars came with European coachwork, especially by Castagna and Sala, both of whom were located in their home city of Milan. There were also frequent displays with bodies ordered by Isotta from Fleetwood, LeBaron and others. Naturally, a great many were built to order to meet the requirements of individual customers.

The wood frame bodies of those days did not seem to survive ocean voyages too well. Often LeBaron—and other builders—were approached by customers who had just taken delivery of, say, an Isotta with a Castagna body. We would be asked to replace the body because the owner just couldn't stand the squeaks and rattles. This would add several thousand dollars more to the cost of the car.

In my chapter on Fleetwood, I have described the town car built by them for the 1925 Salon, which was purchased by Rudolph Valentino. Actually, di-Paoli had been trying for several years to get Valentino to buy an Isotta, and had made it a practice to place a car at his disposal whenever he came to New York. This may have led to various rumors of one or another Isotta having also belonged to Rudy, since he had been seen in it and probably even photographed with the car.

There was another Isotta built for him, but unfortunately not completed until after his death. It was a roadster which had been designed for him by LeBaron in late 1923. At that time, we were not yet building bodies, and diPaoli sent the drawings to Fleetwood to get a quotation on the body. Valentino did not buy it then, having just placed an order for the Voisin which was delivered to him a few months later.

Finally, after he bought the town car, he ordered the roadster, which was duly built by Fleetwood. It had rather unusual fenders and a pair of very thick running boards which were really full-length tool boxes. Valentino was quite a good mechanic and diPaoli knew he would be impressed by the idea of having a complete set of tools along if any roadside repairs should be necessary.

The car was completed soon after Valentino's death in 1926, and had been fitted with his cobra mascot. To get its maximum publicity value, Isotta displayed it at the 1926 Salon complete with a sign stating that it had been specially built for Rudolph Valentino. Recent reports indicate that it is still in existence.

There was another Isotta customer who had five or six with LeBaron bodies, each one specially designed for him. Three of the bodies were at different times on the same chassis. This was one of the first available with the new sport engine, and it was fitted with a very close-coupled town car body. A few months after it was delivered, it was turned over in a ditch. There was considerable damage to the body, but fortunately very little to the chassis or to the chauffeur, who was alone in the car.

Mr. Piperno did not want to give up using the car for four or five months while a new body was being built, so we concocted a sort of open surrey for him, which was put together in short order. By fall, the new convertible coupe was ready, and for several years the car was brought back to our shop regularly in Spring and Fall to have the bodies interchanged. There was a rumor that the owner once played polo in it, while the surrey body was in place. He claimed the car was as agile as his ponies, but couldn't turn quite as short. I saw it a year or two ago with the convertible coupe body, boat-tailed. I wonder if its present owner is aware that this is the third body built for that chassis.

The Tipo 8B, a further refinement, was introduced in 1931, but by that time the market for such cars in this country was sharply reduced. In the late thirties, the company went back to producing airplane engines.

As mentioned, after the war an experimental rear-engined car was shown in Europe, but never got into production and another fine old name faded from the scene.

1925 Isotta-Fraschini Phaeton by LeBaron, the first of several Isottas for Mr. George Piperno. Although appearing close-coupled, this body had jump seats in the rear to hold seven passengers.

1929 Isotta-Fraschini Sport Sedan by LeBaron, exhibited at 1928 New York Salon, described in Chapter 15.

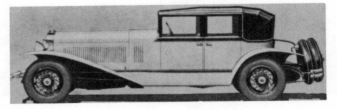

1926 Isotta-Fraschini Roadster by Fleetwood for Rudolph Valentino. The original design by LeBaron was slightly modified. Photograph taken just before the car was exhibited at 1926 New York Salon. Note Valentino's Cobra mascot on radiator cap.

31
Minerva

THE other car imported extensively during the 1920s was the Minerva, built in Belgium. In Europe they built quite a range of models, including some fairly small cars, but the only one shipped to this country to any extent was the largest 30 h.p. six.

European model numbers at this time were often based on taxable horsepower. Formulas varied from country to country, and this is one reason there has been a certain amount of confusion. The authors of many articles have referred to reports in European motor magazines of the period without realizing that what was a 24 h.p. car in Germany might be called a 35 h.p. model in England. Germany used a formula based on displacement, one horsepower for each quarter-liter, and France and Belgium a similar one but with one-fifth liter per horsepower. England used a formula based on the bore and number of cylinders, and the same formula was used in this country and many others for some years. These formulae had nothing to do with actual power, but were merely a basis for assessing license fees, which were substantially higher in Europe than here.

In the very early twenties, several European manufacturers, including Minerva, tried exporting some of their smaller cars to this market. They did not meet with any enthusiasm, and were soon dropped here. Since most of the cars sent over thereafter were the largest ones made by each firm, even model designations were generally eliminated in their advertising and publicity material in this country.

All Minervas had sleeve valves, as did quite a few good cars of this era both here and abroad. The Knight engines were quieter and smoother than poppet-valve engines, and operated quite satisfactorily at the lower engine speeds which were normal then. Such things as hydraulic valve lifters were just beginning to be experimented with then.

The 30 h.p. model had a six-cylinder engine of 95 x 140 m.m., for a displacement of 363 cubic inches. With its 149-inch wheelbase and a weight close to 6,000 pounds, this did not give flashing performance. However, the car was very comfortable and rode well with its cantilever rear springs. In 1930, an optional straight-eight engine was introduced of somewhat greater power, but by that time the luxury market here had practically disappeared, and very few were imported.

The unique compound curved radiator shell blended well with dignified body designs. It was copied in the late twenties by Diana, built by the same firm in St. Louis that built the Moon with a copy of the Rolls-Royce radiator. The Diana was quite a different car from the Minerva, however.

During the twenties, the building at 247 Park Avenue—only recently torn down to make way for a taller one—housed some of the finest automobile showrooms in the world. They were elegantly appointed, to go with the cars displayed. On the 46th Street corner was Park Central Motors' Lincoln showroom, Minerva just beyond, and Mercedes at the other corner. For a while, duPont and Duesenberg snuggled between them.

Paul Ostruk, who headed the Consolidated Motor Car Company, distributors of the Minerva, had a close working relationship with LeBaron. We built many of his bodies without our nameplate, and as previously mentioned, I can recall signing "Paul Ostruk" to many a design sketch. In addition to their Park Avenue showroom, a service station in the West Sixties occupied what had been the Brooks-Ostruk body shop. Some repair work was still being done

1930 Minerva Sedan, from Minerva Catalog, Floyd
Marshall Collection.

1925 Minerva Town Cabriolet by LeBaron, sold as
with "Body by Ostruk." A dozen or more were built,
one for Flo Ziegfeld. The Friml car described in the
text was a later variation with "All-Weather" front
including windows in front doors. Photograph from
George Moffitt Collection.

there, but I do not believe any complete bodies were built after about 1923. Ostruk also had branches in Boston and Chicago.

Late in the twenties, he also purchased Hibbard & Darrin's Paris Minerva agency, largely because they had been consistently underselling him. Many prominent Americans found it cheaper to buy their Minervas in Paris while on a trip abroad.

Ostruk and his staff had a wide acquaintance in theatrical circles, and Florenz Ziegfeld was one of their best customers. We built several cars for Ziegfeld, including one Rolls-Royce town car which he purchased through Ostruk. I have no idea how that little maneuver was arranged.

Once Ziegfeld ordered a Minerva town car for Rudolf Friml, then his favorite composer, with a regular piano keyboard—but no strings—built into the partition behind the chauffeur. I can remember expressing surprise at this request, but Ziegfeld, whose office was then in his new theater a block from our office, explained that Friml's imagination was enough. The keyboard was just to help him visualize a score and jot it down if he happened to think of a tune while en route to the theater or on some other errand.

Most of the Minervas I can remember were town cars or limousines. We did build one group of sim-ilar, but not identical, sport sedans. The first of these was shown at the Salon, and had the built-in bar previously described. It even had a brass rail around the top of the cabinet, to keep the drinks from sliding off.

While LeBaron built the bodies for the majority of Minervas sold in this country, some of our other custom builders also worked on this chassis. Quite a few came in with European coachwork, especially from Hibbard & Darrin. The rolled-belt treatment, which was almost Hibbard's trademark, blended especially well with the rounded hood and radiator. There were also some elegant limousines by d'Iete-ren Freres, considered possibly the finest body builder in Belgium, and an assortment of bodies from Van den Plas as well.

Some of the earliest experiments with a pennant-shaped raised panel on the hood, which LeBaron adapted to other chassis as well, were done on either Minervas or Isottas. One version, which I developed for a Minerva for the 1926 Salon, swept down behind the side-mounted spare wheels.

Like some other old firms, Minerva was finally absorbed into a merger of several Belgian firms during the depression, and another fine name vanished.

1930 Minerva Drop-head Coupe by Van den Plas. From Minerva Catalog, Floyd Marshall Collection. While the catalog identifies this as a "6-litre Speed Six," length of hood indicates it may be one of the new eight-cylinder models.

32
Mercedes-Benz

FORTY years ago, Daimler-Benz, newly amalgamated out of the two oldest manufacturers of automobiles, was able to advertise: "Mercedes engineers have spent forty years in constant research work and automotive improvement to produce the cars which are on exhibit today. The keynote of the Mercedes is perfect dependability born of quality as expressed in materials, workmanship and design." That statement may be just as true today, after eighty years.

Daimler-Benz is descended directly from the two firms established by Gottlieb Daimler and Karl Benz in the 1880s. Each of them tested a motor-driven vehicle in 1885 or 1886, and started building more of them. Although the two experimenters were both in South Germany, not too far apart, it has been insisted that neither knew of the other's experiments.

In his early work, Daimler was assisted by an excellent engineer, Wilhelm Maybach. They had an agent in Nice, Emile Jellinek, Consul-General for the Austro-Hungarian Empire and a wealthy financier, who raced frequently under the pseudonym of Mr. Mercedes, taken from the name of his daughter. He made some suggestions which Maybach developed into a revolutionary automobile in 1900, with much of the basic arrangement that has been considered normal ever since. Jellinek ordered a number of them, with the stipulation that this be called the "Mercedes" model.

Daimler had already licensed his French agents, Panhard & Levassor, to produce engines and vehicles according to his patents, and they in turn arranged to let Peugeot build automobiles as a sub-licensee. So several of the oldest names in motordom grew from this beginning.

The Mercedes soon acquired quite a reputation by

winning races, and also as a much-admired vehicle for the wealthy. A branch was set up in Austria by Paul Daimler, son of the founder, which grew into the Austro-Daimler Company. They soon acquired the services of a brilliant engineer named Frederick Porsche. In 1923, he moved to the main Daimler plant in Stuttgart. Later he went on to even more impressive contributions to the design of the automobile.

Daimler had a licensee in England, although the Daimler Motor Car Company, Ltd., was never actually affiliated with the German Company. At one time, there was also an American Mercedes. William Steinway, the piano manufacturer, had early become interested in Daimler's engines and was his American agent. As mentioned in an earlier chapter, he set up a factory not far from the still extant piano factory in Long Island City. The cars built there were basically assembled from parts shipped over from Germany, but fitted with some American accessories and with coachwork from local plants.

As mentioned in the preceding chapter, Mercedes had a showroom at Park Avenue and 47th Street in the twenties, under the direction of Richard Schilling. The first cars imported after World War I were principally the 28/95 model, as it was designated in Germany. It had a 6-liter six-cylinder engine with overhead camshaft, designed before the war by Paul Daimler. Like many others, Daimler was too busy reconverting to peacetime production to start immediately on new designs.

Soon afterwards, Dr. Porsche moved up from Austria, and with a series of improvements developed the engine to the point where, with a supercharger, it produced 250 horsepower. This is the form in which it was used in the celebrated SSK.

There seems to be some confusion over the Mercedes model designations during the late twenties, with the letters K and S recurring. Since K is the initial of the German word for supercharger, *Kompressor,* many people erroneously believe there is a

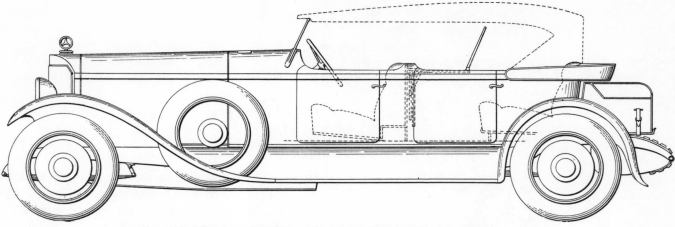

1926 Mercedes-Benz Model K Phaeton by LeBaron,
first of two Mercedes built for Mr. W.A.M. Burden, Jr.

connection. Some earlier Mercedes models had been fitted with superchargers, and they were generally known abroad by a combination of horsepower figures, the first being the taxable horsepower, the second the unblown, and the third the blown power. As Germany and England used different formulae for computing taxable horsepower, the first figure varies between countries and this has led to further confusion.

Porsche's first new engine was designated the Model K, and the following one of the same series of large engines, Model S. The intervening letters had been used for concurrently produced smaller models. When a sport version of the Model S was produced, it was called the SS, for S Sport. Then a short chassis for high speed touring and racing was added, and called the SSK. The K here stands for *Kurtz,* the German word for short. Finally, a modification of this with the chassis drilled for lightness came along, used for racing only, and called the SSKL. The L was added for *Licht,* German for light, and referred to the reduced weight.

During 1922 and 1923, some Benz cars were imported, and LeBaron designed bodies for several. When the two firms, Daimler and Benz, started cooperating about this time, Benz disappeared from the American market. In 1926, the two firms were merged into the present Daimler-Benz A.G.

Most Mercedes full-sized passenger cars came over in chassis form, and were fitted with bodies by the leading American custom-body firms. German coachwork at this time tended to be massive and not especially suited to American taste.

One particularly interesting one LeBaron built

for Mrs. H. E. Manville was a convertible sedan with disappearing chauffeur's partition. It had auxiliary seats in the rear so seven people could be carried, but was carefully designed to give the appearance of a 4/5 passenger car.

Some convertibles were imported with bodies by Saoutchik, which were rather more sporting in appearance than most German designs, and a few from Castagna. Saoutchik also supplied the bodies for many of the SSKs imported. This model was extremely low, with the top of the hood barely clearing the engine. Functional and very necessary louvres were provided in the top of the hood.

At LeBaron, we built only one body on an SSK, a roadster for William A. M. Burden, Jr. He felt the German designs were not well proportioned with their very low hood, and we had a new radiator built several inches higher than the original.

While the body was being built, Mr. Burden took a trip to Europe. He brought back a fabulous col-

1925 Mercedes 28/95 Convertible Sedan by LeBaron,
built for Mrs. H. E. Manville.

lection of instruments—speedometers, tachometers, an airplane compass, and various other goodies. Burden and I spent an entire afternoon at the LeBaron plant in Bridgeport, shuffling these about on a walnut plank that would become the instrument board. It was necessary not only to decide where each one would be placed, but which ones would be used. I think he had at least three different speedometers in the collection.

Surprisingly, not too many of the Mercedes imported during the twenties, and to which bodies were fitted here, seem to have survived. Most of those I have seen at various meets seem to have come over from the Continent fairly recently and carry European bodies.

1928 Mercedes-Benz SSK Convertible Coupe by Castagna, with its original owner, Al Jolson. Photograph from George Moffitt Collection.

1928 Mercedes-Benz SSK Roadster with an English body reportedly designed by Van den Plas. Photograph by the author at Morristown Grand Classic of car then owned by Mr. Charles J. Mulhearn.

33
Renault

PEOPLE familiar only with Renault's small cars, which they have been importing recently, may be surprised to learn that the largest car coming out of Europe in the twenties was a Renault —one model had a wheelbase of 157 inches!

Even then they were building small cars as well, and a few of their little touring cars were shipped here. Anyone who has read Ernest Hemingway's *A Moveable Feast* may have noticed the picture of Zelda and Scott FitzGerald in the little Renault which was the subject of one chapter.

Louis Renault took part in many automobile races of the early part of the century, on cars of his own design. Most of the early Renaults, in fact those right up to the thirties, had the radiator mounted behind the engine, or rather surrounding the rear portion of it. The earlier models had a curved hood, but by 1923 a more streamlined design had been adopted which was continued for quite a few years. When Renault finally moved the radiator out in front of the engine, they still kept the sloping front.

Quite a few Renaults were imported before World War I, many with bodies from Kellner or Rothschild. A large part of these were town cars. Renault built one chassis especially for this purpose, a smaller four-cylinder model with a double-drop frame. The side-rails swept down amidships to permit a low entrance to the tonneau.

One such belonged to Mrs. William May Wright, Jr., who arranged with LeBaron to replace the body sometime in the mid-twenties. The new body was deliberately made almost a duplicate of the old one, a town brougham finished with cane panelling. The vanity case had been made by Cartier in Paris and was transferred to the new body. I remember taking it to Cartier's New York shop to have the perfume bottle caps replated, in gold.

The Renault showroom in New York was then on Fifth Avenue, only a block or two from Cartier's, giving this area quite a feeling of Paris in New York. Many of the cars displayed had French bodies, and this was especially true of the smaller chassis. There was usually a town car or two on one of the four-cylinder models, or the smaller six. Because of their relatively compact size and easy maneuverability, quite a few of these could be seen on the streets of New York. Renault was about the only European manufacturer who had any success here with their smaller cars.

At one time, Renault came up with an idea that might have had a beneficial effect on New York's traffic. Since their early days they had built many taxicabs, which found a ready market in most parts of the world. Around 1926 they built a small one with a body similar to the horse-drawn hansom cabs which were to be found near the Plaza Hotel, the area where carriages are still available for a ride around Central Park. Unfortunately, Renault could not persuade the powers-that-be to license these vehicles for taxicab use.

Probably half of the cars imported during the twenties were the large six-cylinder model, called the 45 h.p. by French ratings, which signifies a 9-liter engine. Even in those days, the French could not agree with the English or the Germans on such a non-controversial item as horsepower ratings for tax purposes.

It was one of the largest production engines of its time, quite in keeping with the massive size of the car. Although a shorter wheelbase was available, most custom bodies built here were on the long chassis, first with 153-inch wheelbase, and later 157-inches. Some were streamlined phaetons with French bodies, featuring pointed tails and often wood panelling on the outside of the body. A few similar ones

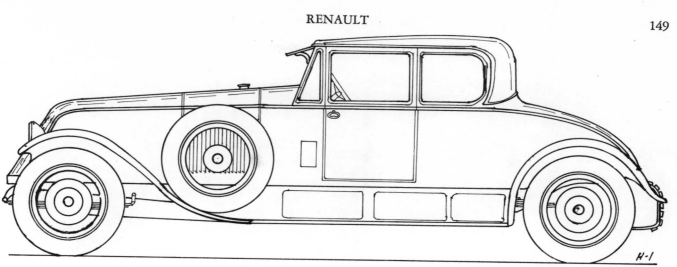

1924 Renault Six-cylinder Victoria Coupe. This is the author's first original design while working for LeBaron.

1923 Renault Town Brougham on small drop-frame chassis, probably by Kellner. Exhibited at 1923 show of Foreign Automotive Association.

1928 Renault 45 Sedan by Weymann, exhibited at New York Salon. From Renault advertisement in Salon Catalog.

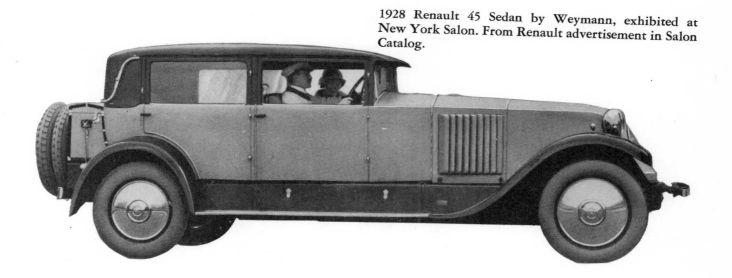

1928 Renault 45 Torpedo Phaeton. From Renault Catalog, Floyd Marshall Collection.

were built in the country, but I believe the idea originated with Henri Labourdette in France, who had built wooden airplane fuselages during the war.

In 1924, LeBaron designed a smart convertible coupe for Renault, which was placed in production in France by Kellner. It is one of the few cases I can recall where a European manufacturer came to this country for a design. The idea was that a body designed by an American firm would sell better here, but actually most of the bodies were sold in Europe.

Louis Renault was quite inventive, and introduced many ideas later adopted by others. One was a servo-mechanism for powering brakes, etc. It was so good that Rolls-Royce took out a license under his patents when they decided to put four-wheel brakes on the Phantom.

1924 Renault Convertible Coupe, designed by LeBaron and built by Kellner. Photograph of rendering by R. L. Stickney for LeBaron.

34
Panhard and Voisin

SOME people may wonder at the grouping of these two names, but there is a good reason. Both made excellent cars with Knight-type sleeve-valve engines for quite a few years, and both turned in some fine racing records although at different periods.

Panhard & Levassor is one of the oldest names in the automobile industry. They were Daimler's agents in France before he built his first automobile, and they controlled the rights to his patents there. They had started as machinery manufacturers in 1864, and one of their old catalogs claims that the first automobile was built in their shops. However, they licensed the firm of Peugeot to build automobiles under Daimler's patents, and only when these proved successful did they start manufacturing their own.

In the 1890s, they were already winning races, with two-cylinder, Daimler-type engines fired by glow-plugs. By the early years of this century, their cars kept growing bigger and more powerful. People familiar only with the small two-cylinder Panhards of recent years may be astonished by their advertisement in the 1920s, which must also have been read by Pontiac:

> The Panhard model displayed is especially adapted to long distance touring. The unusually long wheelbase, 148⅝ inches, and its *Wide Track* of nearly five feet, allow the building of a roomy, comfortable body. (The italics are mine—author.)

In France, Panhard produced several small- to medium-sized cars, largely with four-cylinder engines, but the only ones I remember reaching the United States were the large straight-eights whose size is outlined above. All of their cars at this time had sleeve-valve engines. The engine blocks were exceptionally neat, aided by the fact that no access plates had to be provided to get at the valve gear.

The 309 cubic inch engine of this eight was somewhat smaller than those of other cars of similar size at the time, but it was considered efficient enough to give smooth, flexible performance within the accepted limits of the day. It was reputed to be able to cruise for long periods at sustained high speeds with a minimum of attention.

Another unique feature was that the frame side-rails were downswept some two inches just behind the engine compartment, making it possible to build relatively lower bodies. Actually only a few American custom bodies were fitted, since Panhard had access to most of the leading French firms. The bodies I recall, although built in France, had lines close to some of the better American designs of the time.

Voisin came on the scene considerably later, just after World War I. The name of the firm, Avions Voisin, indicates its origin. They had built airplanes during the war, notably some good heavy bombers.

Throughout their career, Voisins were powered with sleeve-valve engines. This was not unusual, for even Mercedes were building some at the same time that also performed creditably in races. Voisin won at least one 24-hour race at LeMans, and set all kinds of records. At the 1923 show of the Foreign Automotive Association, which competed with the Salon that year, Voisin showed a sport phaeton, which their advertisement describes:

1923 Panhard & Levassor 8-cylinder Conduite Interieur or Sedan-Limousine, exhibited at 1923 Show of Foreign Automotive Association.

1923 Panhard & Levassor Touring Car, from their advertisement in catalog of Foreign Automotive Association show.

This body is the result of the startling discoveries made by M. Voisin in the recent Grand Prix of France at LeMans. The body is built with a view to eliminate air resistance in accordance with the latest aviation practice.

I can remember the car quite well because it made a deep impression on me at the time. It had a boat-tail, a disappearing top, and unusual flared fenders, which combined nicely with the sharply pointed radiator that was a Voisin feature. It also made a distinct impression on Rudolph Valentino, who ordered

a duplicate with some slight modifications. This was reputed to be his favorite car and it was still in his possession when he died a few years later.

Although it had a relatively small four-cylinder engine, about 240 cubic inches, the car was quite fast, as it must have been to win at LeMans. It came with a choice of wheelbases, the shorter one being used for the phaetons mentioned above, while a longer one was available for more luxurious coachwork.

Later, this four was replaced by a somewhat larger six. As early as 1920, Voisin had built a few twelve-cylinder cars, V-type, and also with sleeve valves. Around 1930, they produced a new twelve, but this had the cylinders all in line, one of the few of this type ever built. The last two cylinders actually projected into the driver's compartment. This engine was of smaller displacement than the more widely sold six, under six liters. It must have been quite a

1924 Voisin Phaeton with its owner, Rudolph Valentino. Photograph courtesy Mr. Al Michaelian of Petersen Publications, who worked with Mr. Valentino in the movies.

job to assemble those 24 sleeves and the array of eccentrics which moved them up and down to expose the valve openings.

The Voisin agency here, in the twenties, was the Robertson-Stelling Corporation, with a showroom on West 57th Street. Yes, that was George Robertson of Vanderbilt Cup fame, who later left the firm to join Lincoln.

Probably the greater proportion of the Voisins imported here were the long chassis fitted with four- or six-cylinder engines. A few had bodies fitted in this country, but the majority came with coachwork from France's leading carrossiers. Some were town cars from Kellner or Rothschild, but the most attractive were phaetons, convertibles and sport sedans.

Some of these, including the Valentino Phaeton, came from Voisin's own body shop, which was con-

sidered in France to be one of the leading carrossiers, although they did not work on other chassis than their own. They often won prizes in Concours d'Elegance in Europe against the competition of the leading custom builders.

This brings to mind the fact that 57th Street, where their showroom was located, was then as now an area of smart shops. Since our office was just around the corner, I frequently walked along that street on my way to one of the imported car showrooms located there, or to one of the domestic ones further West on Broadway. The street would be lined with fashionable cars whose chauffeurs were waiting for their owners to come out of Henri Bendel, Revillon, Milgrim or one of the other stores. I often counted over a million dollars worth of automobiles in just that short stretch.

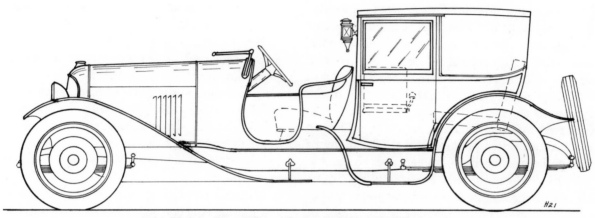

1925 Voisin Panel Brougham. Original design by the author for LeBaron.

35
Lancia and Fiat

WHILE my *Motor Trend* article included Lancia but not Fiat, this was only because Fiat was not a factor in the American market during the 1920s. The earlier history of these two marques had a distinct connection, since Lancia was one of Fiat's great race drivers in the early part of the century as well as one of their best engineers.

Fiat started building cars before 1900, and soon began to take an active part in racing. Like many of their competitors, they built bigger and bigger engines to achieve higher speeds. Eventually they came up with one of the largest four-cylinder engines ever fitted into an automobile, displacing 28 liters or about 1,700 cubic inches. That was in 1913.

In the meantime, they continued to build a large variety of passenger cars, including some luxury vehicles which found a ready market in this country prior to World War I. They were distinguished by a graceful radiator, coming almost to a point at the top, which was copied by several American manufacturers such as Daniels.

As was mentioned previously, with the start of hostilities in Europe, Fiat's owners, the Agnelli family, built a moderate sized factory in Poughkeepsie, New York, and continued to assemble cars here to some extent. These were more or less identical to the 1914 models built in Italy, which had been most successful here, with a 240 cubic inch four-cylinder engine in a fairly large chassis. Quite a few were to be seen in New York, mostly town cars.

After the war, Italy's economy was in rather poor shape, and Fiat concentrated on trucks and inexpensive small cars, which were more in demand there.

They did develop a medium-sized six and made an effort to sell these on the American market, but without much success. The improved American cars of the same size, but with much larger engines, were more to our taste, and cheaper.

Fiat abandoned their efforts here until after World War II, when their smaller cars achieved a prominent place in the new market for tiny European cars.

In the meantime, Lancia had set up his own firm and began, soon after 1918, to introduce some quite revolutionary ideas. One was the narrow V engine with a 14 degree angle between adjacent cylinders, first in four-cylinder form and later as an eight. This continues to be a feature of Lancia engines. They are not V-type in the sense of having separate blocks, but have a squarish block with the cylinder bores running at this slight angle. It is interesting to note that this gives an out-of-phase damping effect similar to what Leland achieved with a 60 degree angle between blocks.

In 1922 Dr. Lancia introduced a completely new automobile concept with his Lambda model. It had a combined body and chassis, with all four wheels independently sprung. Although it had a relatively small engine, a four of only 156 cubic inches, it was capable of very high speeds for the time. The novel suspension gave it excellent road holding.

Lancia opened a branch here in 1924, with a showroom at 140 West 57th Street in New York, near Carnegie Hall. The Lambda met with considerable success here, and quite a few were imported in the next few years. In 1928, Lancia announced plans to assemble cars in the former Fiat plant in Poughkeepsie, which the Agnelli family still owned. Although their ad in the 1928 Salon catalog listed "Works in Poughkeepsie, N.Y., and Torino, Italy," nothing ever came of this, and soon afterwards the New York showroom was closed following the stock market crash.

Most of the Lambdas sold here were open touring cars, for the entire structure was designed for this type. The basic framework made up an open car body

1915 American Fiat Roadster. Photograph courtesy of its owner, Harrah's Automobile Collection.

1922 Fiat Limousine-Landaulet by Hooper. From *Motor Magazine,* December, 1922.

1931 Lancia diLambda Convertible Coupe by Castagna. Photograph courtesy of its owner, Harrah's Automobile Collection.

1929 Alfa-Romeo Model 6-C Sport Spider, from Alfa-Romeo Catalog, Floyd Marshall Collection.

with the front and rear door openings already formed. It was not only a light but a very sturdy structure, proved by the fact that quite a few are still in existence.

Unfortunately, this arrangement made for certain difficulties in trying to design other body types around it. A few closed cars were imported from Italy, with a superstructure built up on the basic framework. Since the door openings had to conform to the original design, these sedans had two rather narrow doors with a window between, and some had a fourth window in the rear quarter. If any of these survive, their owners at some stage probably removed the superstructure, as the closed bodies were not very attractive.

At LeBaron, we attempted only one design on this chassis. It was a town car with open chauffeur's compartment. It was not an aesthetic success.

In the late twenties, Lancia added another model, the di-Lambda, with an eight-cylinder engine and a more conventional separate chassis. This was more suitable for custom bodies, and quite a few were built in Italy and France. By the time it was available, the car was no longer imported here. I believe that nearly all the di-Lambdas now in this country arrived at some later date, along with other classic European cars "liberated" during or since the last war.

Alfa-Romeo was already celebrated for its racing cars in the early twenties, but had no representation here. The few cars that reached here at the time were bought in Europe and shipped here by their owners. Most of these were the GT type, only slightly modified from Alfa's racing cars. I can recall seeing an occasional one, usually with open four-passenger bodies. More Alfas, too, have been liberated more recently.

36
Farman and other French Cars

FOR my *Motor Trend* article, I included Farman as the Tenth European Classic for two reasons. I liked the car, and I had several good pictures, which are reproduced herewith. Due to a change of editors, my pictures had not been used with the article. Actually, there were only a few Farmans imported, and these by their individual owners.

Henri Farman was an early automobile enthusiast. He won the 1902 Paris-Vienna race on a Panhard. In World War I, he and his brother built airplanes, including one of France's best biplane bombers.

After the War, they turned to building automobiles, and they were among the finest, close to the Hispano-Suiza in engineering and quality. The engine, in fact, was almost a duplicate of the Hispano in size and design, with the same bore and stroke. I have never been able to find out whether the Farmans bought their engines from Hispano, as they did earlier for their bombers, or if it was simply a copy.

The company existed from just after the war until the middle thirties. Only one basic model was built, and it was strictly a luxury car. This may account for its demise when millionaires went out of fashion.

From the beginning, the car had a pointed radiator which blended well with smooth, flowing body lines. I do not believe there was any such thing as a production body, and quite a few of the custom bodies fitted were rather extreme. One such was built for Capt. Charles Nungesser, the French Ace of World War I, and Farman followed airplane lines in designing this torpedo phaeton.

In the mid-twenties, Jay Hyde Barnum, artist and illustrator, bought a used Farman in France and shipped it to this country. It had a limousine body, which he asked LeBaron to replace with a phaeton. He had seen the Nungesser car in France and admired it.

We followed some similar ideas, with a boat-tail and disappearing top, but worked out rather more

sweeping fender lines and running boards, which made the car look lower than the original French model. After we had worked out the details of the design, Barnum made a couple of water color sketches of it, photographs of which are included here. The raccoon coat graces one of his few self-portraits.

When this car reached the painting stage, we worked out with Mr. Barnum by experiment a special mixture of oil paint and sand, which proved quite durable and had an unusual texture. It also created quite a problem when it finally became necessary to repaint the car.

The Farman differed from the Hispano in having cantilever springs at the rear. This gave it a softer ride, but made it less stable at high speeds. Unlike many of their close competitors, Farman did not participate in racing.

Two of those competitors, Delage and Delahaye, date back to early motoring days, and had already developed a reputation in the road races of the time. For some reason, neither was represented in this country in the twenties, so the few cars that reached here had been purchased in Europe and brought over by their owners. At this time, both were of similar size with six-cylinder engines of about 4 liters capacity, and 135- and 137-inch wheelbase respectively.

They had rather attractive radiator and hood lines, and were favorites of the smaller and more enterprising French carrossiers. By the mid-thirties, both had done more successful racing, and their passenger cars were to all intents detuned versions of their racers. Along with this, some interesting experiments in streamlining were done, on both chassis. They were among the most advanced passenger cars of those days just before World War II.

Brasier, Darracq and deDion-Bouton are other names that played a prominent part in early automobile racing. Each had a number of successes, Brasier possibly the most. They continued to build a rather large passenger car for some years, but did not last out the twenties.

1922 Farman Torpedo with its owner, French Ace Captain Charles Nungesser. From Paris Salon issue of *L'Illustration,* October, 1922.

1923 Farman with Torpedo body by LeBaron built in 1926. Photograph of water-color sketch by Mr. Jay Hyde Barnum, for whom it was built.

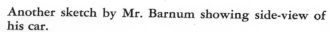

Another sketch by Mr. Barnum showing side-view of his car.

1935 Delage Convertible Coupe by Leturneur & Marchand, once owned by Mr. Herb Lozier. Photograph courtesy of Automotive History Collection, Detroit Public Library.

1937 Delahaye Roadster by Figoni & Falaschi. Photograph courtesy of Automotive History Collection, Detroit Public Library.

Darracq came up with some excellent designs, and the first cars built by Fritz Opel in Germany were exact copies, built under license. The French automobile industry was running to some extent along the same lines as French politics in the years between the wars, and the car became the Talbot-Darracq and eventually the Sunbeam-Talbot. In fact, at one time it was being marketed under one name in France and another in England.

Count deDion was building steam cars before the turn of the century, and subsequently came up with many innovations. The recently revived "deDion rear axle" is one of these, although he used it only for a short time around 1900. It consisted of a flexible, jointed axle shaft to transmit power, and a separate offset rigid tube to keep the wheels aligned and to carry the weight.

His early steam vehicles were large for their time, but later gasoline-powered ones varied from small to medium size. Just after World War I, his firm was building a high-quality V-8, about the size of the Delage.

Another fairly early French racing success was the Mors. Some of their cars prior to World War I had really huge engines, something that was generally true until another Swiss engineer, M. Henry, came up with a design for Peugeot in 1913 that proved a small, light car, highly maneuverable, could win races from the prevailing monsters. Mors reentered automobile production in 1918 with a sleeve-valve engine of moderate size, but could not seem to recapture their former glory.

Another quality French car of the early part of the century, long since vanished, was the Delaunay-Belleville. In 1918, they built a six-cylinder car with a displacement of 486 cubic inches, the largest of any French car that year. Delaunays had been imported here extensively before the first World War, and had a good reputation, but I believe the company experienced internal dissension in the 1920s and dissolved.

Delaunay-Belleville were primarily manufacturers of marine engines, but they also built a line of trucks and buses. The first motor-driven buses to operate on Fifth Avenue in New York came from their shops. I believe General Motors made an arrangement during World War I to use their designs, and from this beginning came the GMC Coach Division.

There were other French manufacturers of high-quality cars, none of which were imported to America to any extent. These included Leon Bollee, Chenard & Walcker, Cottin et Desgouttes and Lorraine-Dietrich among others.

Finally, I come to one which almost, but not quite, made the American market. It was the Picard-Pictet, which actually originated in Switzerland. Its basic design was aimed at this country, with a sleeve-valve engine of V-8 type and displacing 358 cubic inches, in a 126-inch wheelbase chassis. That was a much bigger engine than most of its European contemporaries boasted.

The firm actually set up a subsidiary in this country, and arranged with LeBaron in their early days to design a series of bodies specifically for American taste. They even did some market research, and decided that the name was a bit exotic for this country. The car was to be sold here as the Pic-Pic.

I do not know the exact reasons, but the plans failed to materialize, probably due to lack of capital, and a year or two later the car disappeared even from the French market. Not more than two or three had actually been shipped here.

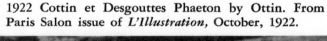

1922 Cottin et Desgouttes Phaeton by Ottin. From Paris Salon issue of *L'Illustration*, October, 1922.

37
Bugatti

EARLIER I mentioned that I had not included this famous name among my "Ten European Classics" simply because practically none of them came to this country in the twenties. One or two were brought over in the thirties, principally by Hollywood personalities. One, still in existence, probably arrived in chassis form, since it has a body by Walter Murphy of Pasadena.

Actually, Bugatti concentrated largely on racing cars in his early years, along with ventures into areas other than automobiles. He was a close friend of Fred Moskovics, President of Stutz, with whom he worked out a cross-licensing agreement.

In June 1926, Bugatti announced the production of a new chassis to sell for about $11,000, or around $18,000 for a complete car. The engine was to be based on the eight-cylinder 142-cubic-inch design of his successful racing cars. The expectation was that a majority of the 100 or so cars to be built in the next year would be sold in the United States. Nothing seems to have come of this project, at least in this country. Perhaps the fact that Bugatti became a paid consultant to Stutz later the same year had something to do with it.

In the late twenties, Bugatti developed a high-speed rail car which it was hoped would revolutionize French transportation. For it he developed a large eight-cylinder engine incorporating many of the same features as his small racing engines. The vehicles proved quite fast and reliable, but like any product of Bugatti's domain in Alsace, quite expensive. After one or two prototypes had been built, the French government, which had underwritten the project, abandoned its support.

This left Bugatti with several of the big engines on his hands, and he proceeded to design a car

around them, to be the largest and most luxurious motor car ever. It was called the Royale, and reputedly seven were built. In the Summer of 1967 I had the rare privilege of examining five of these in various collections.

The town car pictured herein may well be the first Royale chassis built, which originally sported a Packard Phaeton body transferred from the car Ettore Bugatti used for long-distance touring. Later, this was replaced with the elegant town car body by Binder for the use of his daughter. Possibly because of his great concern for the safety of his family, the body originally was fitted with armor-plate beneath the well-shaped body panels, and with bullet-proof glass.

Many legends have grown up about the Royales, the most popular being that any prospective purchaser had to visit Le Patron and be socially acceptable to him before being permitted to make the purchase. I am inclined to doubt this story somewhat.

Of the seven cars built, three were originally used by members of the Bugatti family and only four were sold. At the time, it was known that only a few of the engines existed and it was doubtful that more would be built during those troubled times. Very probably there was some competition among the handful of people who could afford them, and there may have been other factors than having the money available in deciding who would get the prizes.

Later the railcar was redesigned by a firm specializing in this field, and more of the Bugatti engines were produced to power them.

In the early thirties, Bugatti added the Type 57, of which possibly more were sold than any other model. It was not regularly imported into this country, but was available in England at a price of 875 pounds for the chassis, or roughly $4,375 in those days. With a closed body, the price of the complete car would have been around $10,000—not a low price for the 1930s.

It is my impression that the majority of the Bugattis now in this country arrived during the past twenty years. Many of them were no doubt hidden away in various parts of Europe, especially France, during the war. Considering the French reputation for thrift, their owners probably planned to drive them again when conditions permitted. As they be- gan receiving offers close to the original cost of the cars new, enough to allow them to replace them with newer vehicles and leave something over, many succumbed to the temptation.

1927 Bugatti Royale, with Binder Coupe de Ville body fitted in 1933 for Mr. Bugatti's daughter. Photo- graphed in Paris just after new body was completed. Courtesy Automotive History Collection, Detroit Pub- lic Library.

The same Bugatti Royale as recently restored. Photo- graph courtesy of its present owner, Harrah's Auto- mobile Collection.

38
Bentley and other English Cars

LIKE Bugatti, W. O. Bentley had concentrated largely on racing cars at first. It must be remembered that the European races of this period were often road races, and the cars basically high-powered touring cars rather than the type developed here for Indianapolis and the board tracks.

Bentley started off with a three-liter car because this was the racing formula at the time. Later he built larger ones, first the 4½-liter, then the Speed Six, and finally the 8-liter model, which he was still trying to perfect when the company ran into financial difficulties in the early thirties and was sold to Rolls-Royce. Since that time, the Bentley has been essentially a Rolls-Royce with a different radiator shell, the early ones using the smaller 25 h.p. chassis.

Bentley himself joined Lagonda, and most of their excellent cars of the middle and late thirties were of his design. These included a six-cylinder 4½-liter and a superb V-12. Lagonda at one point advertised their cars as Bentley-Lagondas, but this was stopped by Rolls, who had purchased the rights to the Bentley name along with his company.

It is no accident that most of the true Bentleys in this country are open two- or four-seaters. Most of the cars they built during their dozen years as an independent company were of this type. A few had closed bodies mounted, especially the 8-liter model, and many of these were custom-built under the Weymann system by one of the English firms licensed under these patents. The lightweight Weymann bodies did not affect performance too much.

Bentleys were fast, but except for the final 8-liter model they were not too comfortable or docile for driving around town. Since most of the expensive cars imported here in the 1920s were for this purpose, very few Bentleys were shipped over then. The few that did arrive were brought over by aficionados of the fast car and driven mostly in the country.

There were, however, two other distinguished British cars that were seen around New York occasionally. One was the Napier and the other the Lanchester. Both were of similar size, about that of a Rolls-Royce, and in the early twenties had similar six-cylinder engines of 4-inch bore and 5-inch stroke, with overhead camshafts. At this time, the Napier chassis was slightly more expensive than a Rolls, in England.

The Napier had been developed originally by S. F. Edge as a racing car. David Scott-Moncrief, in his book *The Three-Pointed Star,* refers to the first Napier as having been built in a dingy workshop in a Lambeth slum—a district in London roughly equivalent to New York's Lower East Side of the same period.

Napier developed a luxury car before World War I, and I can recall seeing a few of them on the streets of New York in my youth. During the War, they built airplane engines like so many of their competitors, and kept on with this activity later. Although they again made some automobiles, there was no effort to export them to this country, and after a few more years they concentrated entirely on the aircraft engines. Some of these did power automobiles, but these were the specially built record vehicles built by Railton.

Lanchester was represented here for a time by Brewster, who in the early twenties sold a few with bodies from their own shop. The arrangement was terminated a year or two before Brewster merged with the American Rolls-Royce company. In the late twenties, Lanchester was also building a smaller six and a straight-eight, but retained the unique worm drive for their overhead camshaft, which had replaced an earlier drive by eccentrics.

Another English car sold here to some extent in the twenties was the Sunbeam. They had also made a reputation in racing, and by this time were building

Four Winning Bentleys: the cars which won at Le-Mans in 1924, 1927, 1928 and 1929, with their drivers —F. C. Clement, S. C. H. Davis, Dr. J. D. Benjafield, B. Rubin, Woolf Barnato and Tim Birkin. The 3-liter at left was fitted with closed body after retiring from racing. From Bentley Catalog, Floyd Marshall Collection.

some excellent fairly large cars for town use as well. Dario Resta, who was born in England of Italian parents, was their most brilliant racing driver. He was placed in charge of a showroom they opened here at 22 West 57th Street in 1922. Price of their six-cylinder chassis was $6,500 in New York. Since this brought the complete car to over $10,000, they were not a howling success and the showroom was closed a year or so later.

One of the most distinguished British cars, the Daimler, was seen here only rarely. The company started under a license from Gottlieb Daimler in the 1890s, and the then Prince of Wales, later King Edward VII, showed an interest in their first automobiles. His influence helped the campaign to repeal the old "locomotive laws" in Great Britain, which had required a man on foot to precede any self-propelled vehicle. For many years thereafter, Daimler supplied nearly all the motor cars for the King and Queen.

In the mid-twenties, they acquired the services of the distinguished engineer Laurence Pomeroy. He began work on developing the "Fluid Flywheel," which Daimler introduced in 1930 and which was the forerunner of modern torque converters. Since he was also a consultant to Chrysler, he worked with the latter firm in adapting the idea to mass production.

Another good English car which comes to mind is the Alvis. Medium-sized, they were well built and well engineered, although not revolutionary except for one front-wheel-drive model produced for a year or two around 1929. Earlier models had four-cylinder engines, but about 1928 they concentrated on progressively larger sixes. The Alvis seems to have been especially popular in Switzerland, where a number of attractive custom bodies were fitted by Graber.

The last British car I shall mention is the A.C., which had some success here in the 1950s. The six-cylinder engine used in their first postwar models was very similar to the one they were marketing in England in 1920. Later this was replaced with a more modern six of the same two-liter capacity built by Bristol but based on designs by B.M.W. While quite successful as a sports car in England in the twenties, only an isolated A.C. appeared here at that time, privately imported.

1929 Bentley 4½-liter Supercharged Open Four-seater by Van den Plas. From Bentley Catalog, Floyd Marshall Collection.

1931 Bentley Speed Six with Weymann-type body by Van den Plas. Photograph courtesy of its owner, Harrah's Automobile Collection.

1922 Napier Enclosed-drive Limousine by Brewster.

1930 Lanchester 8-cylinder 30 H.P. Saloon. From Lanchester Catalog, Floyd Marshall Collection.

THE   FIVE   YEARS   GUARANTEE

*I*N Consideration of..

....

agreeing to purchase from..

Chassis No... Engine No..which is sold subject only to and with the benefit of the following express warranty which shall exclude all conditions warranties and liabilities whatsoever whether statutory or otherwise which might exist but for this provision Messrs.

*B*ENTLEY MOTORS LIMITED agree with him to supply new or repair free of charge any part of such Chassis other than proprietary articles such as electrical fittings, lamps, shock absorbers, detachable wheels, or other such accessories or

fittings, that may fail on or before the..day of...19............, owing to defective materials or faulty workmanship provided the defective part is returned to their works at Cricklewood, carriage paid with the claim for repair or replacement, or the chassis is delivered at such works free of expense.

*I*T must, however, be understood that this guarantee in no way affects such repairs or renewals as may be occasioned by fair wear or tear.

All rights or liability shall immediately be forfeited or cancelled if :—

(a) The Chassis is used for racing or other competition work without the written consent of the Company, or

(b) Any repair is done to the Chassis by any firm or company, other than Bentley Motors Limited, or an Authorised Service Agent, without the written consent of the former, or

(c) The weight of the completed car with equipment exceeds 36 cwts, or

(d) The dimensions of the body exceed the limits specified on the Company's "Coachbuilder's drawing" in respect of the 4½ Litre Chassis, or

(e) If the Chassis is used for hire purposes of any description.

*T*HE benefit of this agreement is not transferable except with the consent of the Company. Anyone desiring such transfer may obtain it by sending the car at his expense to the Company or an Authorised Service Agent for inspection and by subsequently placing an order for any repairs and adjustments that the Company may consider necessary. After these repairs have been completed the Company will transfer the Guarantee, on payment of a fee of £5 which does not include the charge for any repairs or adjustments.

For and behalf of BENTLEY MOTORS LIMITED

....

Director.

Oxgate Lane, Cricklewood, London, N.W.2...19..............

T E R M S   O F   B U S I N E S S

PRICE AND SPECIFICATIONS   All prices and specifications are subject to alteration without notice. The price to be paid for each chassis or complete car is that current at the date of notification that the chassis or complete car is ready for delivery.

TERMS OF PAYMENT   A deposit equal to 20 per cent. of the list price of the chassis or complete car is to be paid with each order, and the balance on notification that the chassis or complete car is ready for delivery.

DELIVERY   All prices quoted are for delivery at the Company's works at Oxgate Lane, Cricklewood, London, N.W.2. The cost of delivery elsewhere is chargeable.

GUARANTEE   All chassis are sold with and subject to the Company's FIVE YEAR GUARANTEE.

EXHIBITING   (a) The purchaser shall not exhibit any Bentley chassis or body and accessories supplied therewith at any Exhibition held in the United Kingdom of Great Britain or Ireland, without the previous consent in writing of the Company and further guarantees that no one who may acquire title under or through him shall so exhibit the same. (b) In the event of any Bentley chassis, body or other accessory being exhibited contrary to the provisions of clause (a) of this condition, the purchaser shall pay to the Company the sum of £250, such sum being the agreed damages which the Company will sustain. Any sum in respect of such damages may be assigned by the Company.

**The Bentley Five Year Guarantee as of 1929. From
Bentley Catalog, Floyd Marshall Collection.**

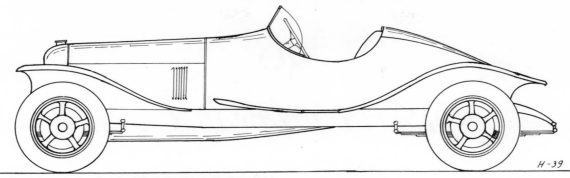

1924 Sunbeam Six Speedster. Experimental design by the author for LeBaron.

1922 Daimler Limousine by Hooper, for a member of Britain's Royal Family. From *Motor Magazine,* December, 1922.

1928 Alvis 12/50 Two-seater with Polished Aluminum body and fenders. From Alvis Catalog, Floyd Marshall Collection.

39
Other European Cars

FINALLY, I come to a small group of cars, some of which were imported here briefly, but which made their reputations primarily in Europe.

From Belgium came the Excelsior, which was reputed to be more highly regarded in its native country than the Minerva, which was better known here. The car had a moderate-sized six-cylinder engine in a well-built chassis of 150-inch wheelbase. It was represented here for a year or two by the Isotta-Fraschini branch. Their advertisements at the time stressed the fact that the Excelsior was used by the Belgian Royal Family. They also played up the smooth ride achieved by the use of an Adex Stabilizer. This was a torsion-bar added to the rear suspension, and I believe represents its first use in an automobile.

Several interesting cars were built in Austria during this period. There were a few Austro-Daimlers to be seen, but I believe the majority were imported by Detroit manufacturers who wanted to study the latest engineering advances of Dr. Porsche and his successors. At least, I am reasonably sure this was true of the Alpine model produced in the late twenties, with a tubular backbone chassis. It was rumored at the time that three of this model were imported, one each by Chrysler, Ford and General Motors.

Before the first World War, one might see an occasional Graef & Stift, a truly magnificent vehicle. They were still building excellent automobiles up into the thirties, but I do not remember any coming to this country after 1914. Steyr was a high-quality Austrian car, but this too was imported mainly for study. On the other hand, a few of a similar name, the Steiger, were brought over in the twenties by James Martin, who sought to add to his already well-established tire business. The Steiger was unique in having a stroke 2½ times its bore, and was built in South Germany.

Locke & Company for a while represented the Hotchkiss here, as mentioned in the section on that

1924 Excelsior Town Car by d'Ieteren Freres. H. M. Queen Elizabeth of the Belgians with her personal car. From Excelsior advertisement in 1924 New York Salon Catalog.

body firm. The French company ran into problems, and was merged with Talbot-Darracq, which in turn became affiliated with Sunbeam. At times, this combine was marketing and in fact assembling automobiles in different countries under different names.

Other than Mercedes and Benz, and later the product of the combined company, the only German car to reach this country to any extent in the twenties was the Maybach. The company by this time was owned by the Zeppelin firm.

William Maybach had started building engines for Count Zeppelin after leaving Daimler, and his son went on to develop the car that bore their name. Unfortunately, there were some rude comments here that the cars with their massive German bodies looked as big as a Zeppelin. Fritz von Meister, their agent in New York, was aware of this and arranged for a few bodies to be built here, mostly by Fleetwood. They made no effort, however, to disguise the rather massive hood and radiator.

We had drawn a few designs for him, but none

1930 Austro-Daimler Model ADR Chassis, showing its tubular backbone. From Austro-Daimler catalog, Floyd Marshall Collection.

1923 Steiger Touring Car, exhibited at 1923 show of the Foreign Automotive Association.

1930 Maybach Zeppelin 12 Convertible Victoria. From Maybach Catalog, Floyd Marshall Collection.

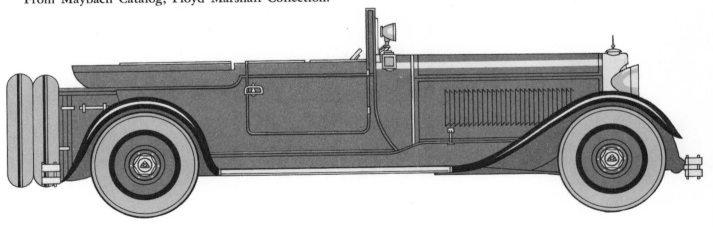

resulted in orders. Sometime in 1930, I suggested that a different radiator design would make the car more acceptable to this country, and I drew up a suggestion von Meister liked. It had some resemblance to our favorite Hispano-Suiza, but differed in some details. I made a water-color rendering which he planned to take to Germany with him, but before this could be done the depression had caught up with the market for expensive cars.

Actually, von Meister spent more time promoting Maybach's aircraft and marine engines than he did on their automobiles. I believe he was more successful in this field.

There were two other cars being built in Germany at this time which were quite highly thought of—the Horch and the Wanderer. In the early thirties, they merged with Audi and D.K.W., both of whom built small, inexpensive cars, to form Auto-Union. By 1934, they decided to challenge Mercedes's racing supremacy. Dr. Porsche was already working independently on the design of a new racing car at the time, and they took over his entire project, which became one of the most successful if hard-to-manage racing cars of all time.

In the late twenties, the Horch was more like our American cars than most European vehicles. They had quite good performance, and they seemed to grow larger every year. Not many, if any, came here at that time, but since 1950 a number have been shipped over, many with carefully documented histories attesting to the fact that they were the personal cars of various Nazi bigwigs just before or during the war.

Finally, there was the Rumpler, the rear-engined car developed by Germany's most celebrated airplane designer in the early twenties. Too far ahead of its time, it was not a commercial success. It was carefully studied, however, by many American engineers in the thirties, when there was a flurry of interest in rear-engined cars. Except for experimental prototypes like Buckminster Fuller's Dymaxion, nothing came of these ideas at the time.

PART V

PART V

40
Production Designs by Custom Body Builders

NO history of the custom body era can be complete without some comment on the influence of the custom designers on the production cars of the time.

In general, few of the automobile manufacturers had a true styling department in the early twenties. The exceptions were often medium-priced cars whose makers prided themselves on being style leaders. Most bodies were designed by the body manufacturers, who were usually independent firms and built bodies for more than one make of car. Even the highly publicized Art and Color Section, which Harley Earl founded in the mid-twenties, was a function of the Fisher Body Company rather than General Motors.

A few makes of the time were essentially the product of body builders who assembled chassis from stock components on which to mount their creations. Auburn, Elcar, Gardner and Jordan fell into this category, as well as Kissel, who did build a bit more of the basic chassis themselves.

Murray Corporation in Detroit was one of the first body builders to set up a design studio, under the direction of Amos Northup. Soon afterwards, they lured Ray Dietrich to Detroit to serve as a consultant. Northup had previously worked for Wills Ste. Claire, and brought with him a young assistant, Julio Andrade, who later became known for his design of the 1934 LaSalle as a member of the General Motors staff.

When Briggs purchased LeBaron, it was primarily to obtain our services as stylists. About the same time, they took over some smaller production body firms, Phillips and Robbins among others, to get the services of their skilled executives rather than their manufacturing facilities.

I have already mentioned how Lincoln bodies were designed by various custom body builders as early as 1925. This was probably the first instance of any

manufacturer getting outside help of this sort in their styling. Others hired consultants, Marmon with W. E. Pierce of Hume, Franklin with deCausse, and at one time Cadillac with Hibbard.

Frequently, too, various manufacturers simply adopted design ideas that had been worked out on custom bodies. For obvious reasons, these came especially from bodies that had been built on their chassis, and which were available for study when taken to one of their dealers for service. However, their stylists and sales chiefs always visited the Salons to see what new ideas were being shown. Often these turned up a year or two later on a production model.

Some of the ideas which LeBaron developed for Briggs have rather unusual stories. Before starting his own company, Walter Briggs had been manager of the Ford body plant, and rumor has it that he set up his own business after telling Henry Ford that he could build bodies cheaper on his own. Ford immediately turned over part of the Highland Park plant to Briggs and told him to go ahead.

As a result, a large share of the Briggs business came from Ford. Naturally they were closely identified with the development of the Model A, although I do not believe most of the styling came from the LeBaron Studios, which had only just been started in Detroit.

However, Ralph Roberts was asked to develop a special show car for display at the Model A introduction at Madison Square Garden in New York. A scaled-down version of a Lincoln sedan we had built for Herbert Bayard Swope the year before was chosen, and at the Garden it occupied a place of honor atop a pyramid. I was not present, but was told that when Henry Ford arrived with Mr. Briggs just before the show opened, he took one look at the showpiece and announced, "Walter, there's our new Fordor sedan." I do know that it was six months before this model

1930 Ford Model A Sport Coupe, with design based on earlier LeBaron bodies. From Ford catalog, Floyd Marshall Collection.

appeared in dealers' showrooms, and even that was remarkably quick work.

Since quite a few of them remain, it is obvious that the lines of this Fordor sedan were completely different from other 1928–29 models, and formed the basis of the body designs for the 1930 and later Model As.

Another early LeBaron design for Briggs was the Graham-Paige. When Dillon-Read bought out Dodge in 1926, a substantial part of the multi-million-dollar purchase price went to Joseph W. Graham, who with his brother had been building trucks out of Dodge components and a few years earlier had merged their company into Dodge. Graham immediately invested the proceeds in the then-slipping Paige-Detroit Motor Company and approached Briggs to style him an entirely new car to be called the Graham-Paige.

Since the Detroit studio had not yet been fully staffed, Roberts assigned the preliminary design to Stickney and myself in New York. We created the original design including the curved-front radiator shell. The Detroit studio then expanded our basic design to cover the various chassis sizes and body styles.

At that time, space in the New York Automobile Show was assigned by the National Automobile Chamber of Commerce (now the Automobile Manu-

facturers Association), on the basis of the dollar volume of each member firm's sales during the preceding year. By pure chance, Graham-Paige and Hupmobile were assigned space on opposite sides of the same aisle.

When I visited the show, I could not help smiling at the comments of people who stood between the Hupp and Graham exhibits and made remarks about how everybody in Detroit was copying everybody else. I was one of the few people there who knew that the Hupmobile, with a Murray body, had been styled by Amos Northup and his staff in Detroit, while Stickney and I worked out the Graham-Paige in New York. Neither of us had any idea what the others were doing.

Of course, a considerable amount of copying did go on, but many similar designs came from different people simply because design is essentially a process of evolution. One idea suggests another, and it is not unnatural for more than one designer to get the same inspiration at the same time.

On the other hand, there were cases where a manufacturer simply took over a design that had been created for his chassis by some custom builder. Usually this was done without any thanks or even an apology. The first we would know of it was usually when we saw a production model that was an exact copy of a custom body we had built earlier. Design patents were not feasible protection, since a minor change might lead to enough litigation to offset any possible benefits.

1931 Jordan Speedway Sedan. Photograph from Floyd
Marshall Collection. It had been sent to him in lieu of
a catalog as they could no longer afford to prepare one.

41
How Custom Body Orders Developed

THE beginnings of a custom body were various. Each coachbuilder had a following of loyal customers who would approach them to design their latest purchase for them, occasionally (but rarely) even leaving it to them to suggest the chassis most appropriate for the particular use they had in mind.

More often the inquiries came through the dealers for various luxury cars. Their salesmen were generally above average, and the dealership usually had at least one who was quite familiar with the leading body builders and their capabilities. For some years, the sales manager of the leading Lincoln dealership in New York was Alan Buchanan, who had previously been a salesman for Brewster.

In either case, a very influential go-between was the family chauffeur. They still had some of the aura that had surrounded them when any proper family with a car hired an engineer to operate and care for it. It was well known that many of them exerted a vital influence on just which chassis or body-builder would be decided on. Frequently the chauffeur received a fee from both the chassis dealer and the body builder. Actually this was not just a bribe—there were always numerous minor adjustments necessary on any new car, especially a custom-built one, and a friendly chauffeur would take care of these without his employer even being aware of them.

Some manufacturers maintained a custom body department to take care of such business, place orders with body builders, and keep an eye on the results. I have mentioned Grover Parvis at Packard's New York branch, as well as the department maintained for a while at the company's headquarters by Horace Potter. Lincoln's custom body purchases were handled by George Walker, although Edsel Ford took a great personal interest in this phase of the business. In general, these people concerned themselves with purchasing series of bodies, five or more of a style.

Very few dealers could afford to buy bodies in series, but where the parent company did so, they sometimes would order one for stock, to be displayed in their showroom until it was sold. In this way they also stimulated the sale of additional cars of the same design. Most of the better dealers, in New York at any rate, kept files of sketches that had been submitted for various of their customers, photographs of completed cars, and similar material. These might furnish the basis for discussion of an individual design.

The next step would be a meeting with one or more of the custom builders who might be considered. Sometimes this was arranged at the body builder's office or plant (several custom body plants were right in New York City), or the body builder's representative might meet the customer at the dealer's showroom, or in the customer's office or home. Here the details would be discussed and enough information obtained to permit the designer to prepare a sketch for submission at a later interview.

I spent quite a bit of time circulating among the various dealers, factory branches and importers in New York, along with an occasional trip to Boston or Philadelphia. Jim Derham did the same for his company, as I have mentioned.

Once a year the Salon was held, and this naturally always brought a flood of new inquiries. One person would want, say, a Lincoln town car but with some changes from the one we exhibited. Another might like the body we showed on a Stutz, but fitted to a Packard chassis. The local dealers always had some of their most dignified salesmen on duty at the Salon, and these inquiries were usually handled through them. Often a discussion would take place right at the Salon, involving some marching back and forth between different exhibits.

Some business did originate in other parts of the country, as I have indicated. I recall particularly the Crocker family of San Francisco, for whom we built several bodies. Every once in a while we would get a letter from the Lowe Motor Company, the Lincoln dealers there, that one or another of the Crockers was

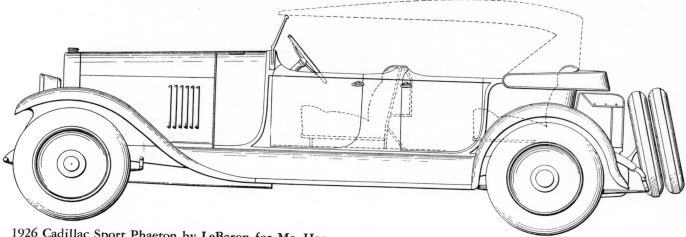

1926 Cadillac Sport Phaeton by LeBaron for Mr. Harold Russell Rider. This was a modification of car shown at 1925 New York Salon and pictured in Chapter 18. This is how proposed designs were submitted to customers.

coming to New York, where they maintained apartments. One of our extra duties was to arrange with J. P. Carey to have a limousine ready when they arrived. Carey used only Packards in those days, and had several with LeBaron bodies.

I also remember the little old lady down in New Orleans. At least, I always pictured her as a little old lady, although I never met her. Every year we would receive a letter from the local Pierce-Arrow dealer, asking if we could build her a town car to match the attached fabric clippings, which ranged from pale lavender to purple. I always wrote back that we could paint it to match her samples, and would do our best on the interior although it might be necessary to have the fabrics dyed specially. There the matter would rest until the next year, when we would get an almost identical letter with samples cut from the same pieces of cloth. We never did get an order for her.

Actually, a very large part of the custom bodies built during the twenties were town cars or limousines. Partly this was because such bodies were not usually available in regular production models. Also, there were a great many more chauffeur-driven cars in those days.

The first step toward any order was a scale drawing of the proposed design, either a completely new concept or a revision of an earlier one. At LeBaron, we did these on a scale of one inch to the foot, and it was my impression that most other firms used the same scale.

Each such design sketch was assigned a number. When I joined LeBaron in December 1923, these numbers were just above 1,000, indicating that some 500 sketches had been drawn since the firm started three years earlier. It was not considered fashionable to start a series with 1, and LeBaron's design numbers started with 501. By the end of 1930, when we closed the New York office, the series had reached 2,300, or nearly 200 designs a year. Actually not all of these were completely different. If we adapted a design to a different chassis, it got a new number, but if we merely modified the design slightly, we added an "R" to the old number. Not all of these designs were built, by any means.

At LeBaron, we were careful to make these preliminary sketches complete, to scale, and entirely practical. We often worked out structural details with scale models before incorporating them into our design. This would not be a full scale model, but one of a portion of the body. Sometimes we cut from cardboard replicas of the top mechanism so we could see just how it would fold.

The first step was, of course, to lay out the chassis. In most cases we had blueprints with dimensions, which we would transpose to our standard scale. For American cars, this would include the shape of the standard fenders, as well as the radiator, hood, etc. On European cars, the fenders were not included with the chassis and we always made these up to suit our body design. Occasionally we designed special fenders and other items for American cars as well. In a very few cases, such as the Hispano-Suiza mentioned earlier, we had to get our information by actually measuring a chassis.

Once we had put a chassis into proper scale on

a sheet of tracing paper, the essential details for the design in question were traced on a fresh sheet, and the original layout filed in a special drawer for reuse as necessary. We were most careful to include in our chassis layout the exact shape of the frame, including the kickup over the rear axle, which would affect seat positioning, and for the same reason the precise location of the steering wheel.

Some chassis, notably the Rolls-Royce, could be obtained with the steering column in different positions. In such cases, we at LeBaron normally used the lowest, most sharply raked one (called the "D" post by Rolls) as this would permit the longest cowl line. This was in contrast to many chauffeur-driven English bodies, which used the highest or "A" position.

Once the chassis tracing was down on paper, the next step was to lay out the seating, depending on the type of body being planned. Here, too, we tried to be as accurate as possible, taking into consideration requirements of legroom and headroom, thickness of cushions, etc.

Normally we allowed a clearance of 7 to 8 inches below the bottom of the steering wheel to the cushion, and 14 to 15 inches to the seat-back. We had determined these dimensions as best suited to the average person, but often they were modified to fit the prospective purchaser or his chauffeur. Adjustable seats were not generally used in custom bodies. It was more feasible to design the seat to fit the individual. On a coupe or roadster, the seat might be set a bit lower since this was the determining feature for the overall height of the car.

Whenever possible, on a 4/5 passenger car, we placed the rear seat ahead of the rear axle. In this way, it could be lower, and we also found that this position gave a more comfortable ride. The distance from the front to the rear seat could vary somewhat, but we considered 20 inches at this point desirable. Sometimes this had to be reduced a bit to fit the chassis being used.

Since a large proportion of custom bodies were town cars with auxiliary seats in the rear compartment, these ran somewhat longer. Space also had to be provided for the glass partition behind the chauffeur, which took up several inches. Rarely, on a smaller car, we used a sliding window with the auxiliary seats folding under it.

We preferred what was called "Opera Seating," which was reasonably comfortable for four people in the rear. A wide rear seat held three of them, and a folding seat faced sideways for the fourth. This had a lightly padded backrest and an armrest, both of which also folded. A second folding seat was also provided, but was really only for emergencies. The person using this rode backwards and had to find room for his feet as best he could. With this arrangement, a distance of 27 or 28 inches from the partition to the rear seat was considered ideal.

Finally, in a full seven-passenger car with forward-facing auxiliary seats the distance from partition to rear seat had to be at least 36 inches to allow enough kneeroom. At first this arrangement provided two folding seats with a space between them, but during the late twenties we began to use two wide seats close together. They could even seat three in a pinch and were much like those still being used on Fleetwood Cadillacs.

The other immovable object was headroom. We thought 36 inches the minimum and only rarely brought this down to 35 inches for a sport model. For a town car 37 or 38 inches was preferred. These dimensions could be varied to suit the purchaser, and for very tall people the headroom might be increased an inch or two. Sometimes we were asked to make it even higher because of some physical problem the buyer might have, or because he wanted to wear his top hat to the opera.

Once these limiting dimensions were marked out, which meant that the seats were actually sketched in, the design could proceed. The outline of the body would be drawn, like an enclosure for the passengers who were to occupy it. The doors and windows were located, and any decorative treatment such as moldings, raised panels, or whatever else would make each design distinctive, was worked out. At LeBaron, we preferred to have the front doors considerably wider than the rear ones, which we felt gave better proportions.

When we had some spare time, we might jot down an idea for a new design with only a rough idea of its actual size and shape, but most of our designs were drawn to specific requirements. The new ideas used often grew out of the needs of the moment, although they might be modifications of something we had thought of earlier.

Our only concession was for the optical illusion created by the rounding off of the body. We would draw the roof one or one-and-a-half scale inches lower than its true center line, and the rear of the body two or at most three inches shorter. We called these the "cheat lines." With the more deeply crowned roofs and well rounded backs of those days, they came close to what one actually saw in the finished car.

Often a design would be revised several times before the prospective purchaser was satisfied with it. In some cases, plan views or perspective sketches (especially of interiors) were made if some especially unusual feature was to be incorporated.

I have given here the standards that Stickney and I followed in our drawings at the New York office of LeBaron. Not everyone was equally careful, and I have seen presentation or catalog drawings from other sources which were not as close to the truth. Many were quite a bit off scale, usually much longer and lower than the cars would actually be built.

42
Renderings

ONCE the design was perfected, the next step, when desirable, was a color rendering by R. L. Stickney. Not every design rated one of these. Each rendering was three or four days' work, although it did not occupy him continuously for this period. Often he would put it aside to permit one section to dry before going on, and turn to something else in the meantime.

Besides the renderings of our own designs, he illustrated a number of catalogs for others. One was done for Rolls-Royce in 1925, a few copies of which still exist besides my own personal one, some of which is reproduced herein. Anyone who has a copy will be aware that the title page carries the legend "Color renderings by LeBaron Studios, New York."

Another for whom we performed a similar service was Lincoln. Each year, the issue of the *Lincoln Magazine* closest to the time of the Salon was devoted to a description of the cars to be exhibited there by the various custom builders. A few months ahead, Lincoln would send us sketches of each, together with paint and upholstery specifications. Stickney would prepare a rendering of each, and also interior views of some of them. These were reproduced in the Lincoln magazine and the illustrations were often used by Lincoln dealers and the body builders in their advertisements in the Salon catalogue. Once or twice we could not handle this extra chore and the work was done by others, with not nearly as good results.

Another customer was the Fairchild Airplane & Engine Company. Sherman Fairchild personally had several cars with LeBaron bodies. When he was building private planes, he consulted us on color schemes, etc., and had Stickney make several renderings of planes showing the various colors that would be available.

The usual fee for such a rendering was $150 in the mid-twenties. I believe it went up somewhat as Stickney's salary increased.

It was not usual to make a rendering of an individual design, except those specially developed for the Salon. Sometimes we did so at a dealer's insistence and often at his expense, when he wanted the picture for display in his showroom. More usually, they were made up when a small series of bodies was being ordered by, say, Packard or Lincoln.

Stickney's renderings were also to scale, and the first step was to prepare a drawing of the car which was then transferred to the Bristol Board on which he painted. The scale was an arbitrary one to fit the 9 x 12 inch sheets, and worked out to roughly ⅝ inch to the foot. We made up our own rulers in this scale.

Sometimes I got to do these scale drawings, which formed the basis for the paintings, and on rare occasions I might help with the actual rendering. I was never able to come even close to Stickney's technique. Everything was done in water color, and he generally used a wash background. In some cases, especially for the *Lincoln Magazine,* he filled in a light, not too distracting scene with a few trees. Mostly he used a pale blue sky and a tan foreground to set off the car.

The work was quite painstaking, since he showed chassis details quite accurately down to the highlights on rivets and wheel-spokes. Wire wheels were quite a chore, since he strove to get the proper variations in tone for the different way the light would hit each spoke.

As each rendering was finished, we had it photographed. Stickney was quite an excellent amateur photographer himself, but since this was his hobby he never did any professional work in this field. However, he did consult with our photographers on the lighting used, and worked out with them an arrangement that successfully concealed the brush marks, which might be visible in the original rendering.

As a result, I have had great difficulty in convincing people that reproductions of his renderings, whether in color or in black and white, are not photographs of the actual cars. There have even been cases where someone has insisted that he saw a cer-

1924 Mercedes Sedan-Limousine. Photograph of an R. L. Stickney rendering.

tain car that I knew had never actually been built, although an illustration appeared in one of our Salon catalogues and was later widely reproduced.

Bear in mind that almost invariably these renderings were made before the body was built. While we might have had some help from photographs of similar models in determining where and how the highlights should appear on the hood and fenders, those on the body had to be interpolated from Stickney's imagination. In some unusual cases we had fairly long discussions of these before he painted them.

I tried a few times to duplicate his technique and while I feel rather proud of some of my best efforts, they did not come even close to his. I never did a complete rendering for LeBaron that was submitted to a customer, with the exception of the Maybach radiator suggestion.

One thing I have often been asked is whether Stickney used an airbrush in his work. At least at LeBaron I know that he definitely did not. Sometimes he did use a ruling pen for parts of the work, but most of it was done with camel hair brushes of which he maintained a nice assortment down to the very finest.

After we closed the New York office of LeBaron in

1930, Stickney declined an offer to move to the LeBaron Studios in Detroit. Instead he joined Judkins up in Merrimac. I have a letter from John Dobben, who was then Chief Engineer for Judkins, stating that Stickney's work was the finest he ever saw, and I heartily concur.

While he did some color renderings for Judkins, the only work of his that I have from this period is in a catalog of sales trailers which Judkins started to build during the depression. These were black and white sketches and some of them appear earlier in this book.

Stickney was equally at home with such pen and ink sketches, and while we occasionally used these ourselves, the ones I particularly recall were done for J. P. Carey's Packard Limousine service. They had several LeBaron Packards, and hired us to sketch these for their newspaper and magazine advertisements.

Later on, Stickney joined Henry Dreyfus and Associates as an industrial designer, a career which he continued until his retirement a couple of years ago. He was able to devote part of his time to independent work, which included some renderings for Rollston and for John Inskip during the late 1930s. Another of his private clients was the architectural firm of Harrison & Abramovitz, for whom he did a number of renderings including those for nearly all of the buildings in Rockefeller Center.

Speaking of Stickney reminds me of our mutual friend George Hildebrand, who has for some years been a designer for Republic Aircraft. He was in charge of their recent project to develop a safety car. George first came to LeBaron as a boy of twelve or so, to show us some sketches he had drawn. We felt they showed promise and encouraged him to continue in the field of design.

CUSTOMER'S SPECIFICATIONS

DATE December 8, 1931.

NAME Mr. M. L. Benedum

ADDRESS Pittsburgh, Pa.

LeBaron
DETROIT
COMPANY

3100 MELDRUM AVE.

BODY 6-Pass.Sedan-Limousine

CHASSIS Marmon

DESIGN NO. D740   MODEL NO.   BODY NO.

---

(1) Chassis Specifications

WE SHALL SUPPLY ONLY ITEMS MARKED (*).
ALL OTHERS TO BE SUPPLED WITH CHASSIS BY CUSTOMER.

MAKE	Marmon		RUNNING BOARDS	Std. Marmon shortened to fit		
MODEL	16		SIDE SPLASHERS	" " " " "		
WHEELBASE	136 inches		REAR APRON	" " altered for special		
TIRE SIZE	Std. Marmon		BONNET	" " (gas-tank filler		
SPARE TIRES	Two, on wheels, with metal covers		COWL BAND	None		
TIRE CARRIER	Std. Marmon side-mountings		COWL LAMPS	"		
WHEELS	Six wire		INSTRUMENT BOARD	Std. Marmon but with door added		
FENDERS	Std. Marmon		TOE BOARDS	" " (to center glovebox		
CHASSIS FINISH	Surfacer coat, to be painted by LeBaron		FLOOR BOARDS	" " (by LeBaron & all		
STEERING COLUMN	Special position, bottom of wheel 20" above		TRUNK RACK	" " (instrument bezels		
	(chassis frame			(satin nickel finish		

TAIL LIGHTS- Special, similar design to std. Marmon, but with
colored lenses in outer sides as well as rear

(2) Body Construction

UNLESS OTHERWISE SPECIFIED, ALL LE BARON BODIES WILL
BE BUILT OF BEST QUALITY HARDWOOD FRAME, SECURELY
IRONED, AND PANELLED WITH STEEL OR ALUMINUM, AS SPECI-
FIED HEREIN.

COWL PANELS	14-gauge aluminum, per design		FRONT SEAT	Non-adjustable. Dimensions per design	
FRONT DOORS	" " " " "		REAR SEAT	Medium soft. " " "	
REAR DOORS	" " " " "		BODY WIDTH	Same as Marmon Model 159	
LOWER BACK PANEL	" " " " "		EXTRA SEATS	Rostand type, concealed, rear facing	
UPPER BACK PANEL	" " " " "		ARM RESTS	Ea. side of rear seat & folding center	
ROOF SIDE PANELS	" " " " "		REAR WINDOW	8½x25", round corners(with special	
ROOF DECK	Regaleather, colored to match body		RUMBLE SEAT	None (flap	
WINDSHIELD	Fisher VV ventilating type		GOLF DOOR	"	
WINDSHIELD STANCHIONS	Per design, painted		DECK GRIDS	"	
DIVISION	Glass to drop flush. No header, minimum side posts		SCUFF PLATES	Std. Marmon style	
VENTILATORS	Two in top and two in sides of cowl		DOOR HINGES, FRONT	Heavy exposed type	
WINDOW REGULATORS	Best type		DOOR HINGES, REAR	" " "	
GLASS	Non-shatterable throughout		DOOR LOCKS, FRONT	Lever locks	
GLASS FRAMES	None		DOOR LOCKS, REAR	" " remote control	
TOOL SPACE	Under front seat		DOOR LOCKING DEVICE	Ea. l.h. door. Yale lock ea.	
CANOPY SPACE	None		DOOR HANDLES	Std. Marmon (r.h.	
TOPBOOT SPACE	None		CABINETS	None	

(3) Standard Equipment, Exterior

OUTSIDE VISOR	Skeleton type, per design, colored glass		STEP LIGHTS	None. Rear dome light operated by
CHAUFFEUR'S CANOPY	None		LANDAU JOINTS	None (automatic door switch
TOP	"		SIDE CURTAINS	"
TOP BOOT	"		LUGGAGE	Cowhide trunk to fit std. Marmon rack.

LUGGAGE — Exterior colored to match body, and
to be easily detachable. Fitted
with two black cowhide suitcases
& hatbox. To be attached by means
of metal clamps & thumbscrews.

(4) Standard Equipment, Interoir

WINDOW MOLDINGS	Similar to Stutz Salon car but walnut finish			
WAINSCOT PANELS	" " " " " " " "			
TOILET CASES	Built into side armrests, similar to std. Marmon			
INTERIOR HARDWARE	New LeBaron pattern, satin nickel finish		CIGAR LIGHTER	Wireless type, in smoking case
DOOR PULL-TO HANDLES	Loop-type		CLOCK	Sterling, in partition wainscot
LIGHTS	Two dome and two corner		FOOTREST	Triangular hassocks (panel
LIGHT SWITCHES	Rear dome on r.h. rear body pillar, also door		ROBERAIL	Folding metal rail, cloth covered
	automatic switch. Corner l.h. rear pillar		TOGGLE GRIPS	Arm loops (to be bolted on
COMMUNICATION DEVICE	Telephone		CARPET	Front & rear, also rubber mat rear
WINDSHIELD WIPER	Waycross type		POCKETS	In each cowl quarter
REAR VIEW MIRROR	Double, non-glare type		INSIDE VISOR	Folding, cloth-covered, extra lg.(8")

HEATERS - Hot water type, front & rear. Reat outlet to be
mounted in rear seat heelboard. Separate
controls.

FIRE EXTINGUISHER - Pyrene, mounted in most
convenient location in front comp.

(5) Paint and Trimming

DETAILED SPECIFICATIONS TO BE COMPILED LATER.

PAINT:- Entire car Dupont Buckingham Gray #244-5526, including radiator, lamps except rims. Dupont Cornice
Gray #244-6159 for window reveals, wheels and hubcaps except center octagon. Silver stripe on body,
also on tire covers ¼" away from edge of top section. Hood hinge including extensions on cowl and
radiator in std. chrome-plated finish. All interior chassis parts including control levers satin n
nickel finish.

TRIM: - Wiese #1802 striped broadcloth. Plain panels, well-tailored, semi-loose cushion effect. Cushions &
backs straight and medium soft. Extra pillow for driver's seat only, 2-3 inches thick. Doors
trimmed in leather to match cloth. with single narrow riser formins 2½" crowned border. Carpet kick-
pads on all doors. Curtains on all windows including front doors. Laprobe to be made of trim cloth
with plush backing to match extra interlining. Monogram MLB in block letters with border. Self-
colored letters with black piping.

MONOGRAM - On doors, to be removed from Cunningham and installed on new car by Marmon.
LeBaron to supply chrome-plated plate for radiator with initial B engraved in black.

ANY ADDITIONS TO OR ALTERATIONS IN THESE SPECIFICATIONS WILL BE CHARGED AS EXTRA TIME AND MATERIAL AT ADDITIONAL COST.

ACCEPTANCE OF SPECIFICATIONS: DATE:
(CUSTOMER PLEASE SIGN)

Specifications for Mr. M. L. Benedum's 1932 Marmon
Sixteen Sedan-Limousine by LeBaron.

43
From Design to Reality

WHEN the design had been completed, we drew up a set of specifications for the body. LeBaron had a special printed form for these, with spaces for the important items to be covered. The layout of the form was revised in details from time to time, but in general it was the same from the origin of the firm, and it was also used by the LeBaron-Detroit Company later on.

Reproduced herewith is a copy of the specifications for the last individual body I designed for LeBaron. I had visited the customer, Mr. Michael L. Benedum, a Pittsburgh oil operator, en route to the New York Salon in late November 1931, and typed out these specifications when I returned to Detroit. At the same time, I worked out the design on the special short wheelbase chassis he had specified for better performance.

This particular specification sheet includes details of paint and trim, although normally these would be covered on a separate sheet. One reason was that several copies would be needed for the paint, trim and purchasing departments. Modern duplicating machines were not yet available, so we typed these on tracing paper and had blueprints made as needed.

Reference to the specification sheet will show how it is broken up into sections. The first one deals with the chassis, and any modifications such as special fenders and running boards would have been noted here.

On an individual body designed for its purchaser, a contract was drawn up. We had a form for that, too, and it would be signed by either the individual customer or the dealer who might be placing the order. The price would range anywhere from $3,500 up, depending on the body style and the extent of extra work such as chassis modifications.

Our standard contract called for a deposit of one-third of the price to be paid in advance. This was not so much to insure against the customer cancelling his order, something I do not recall ever happening, as to provide working capital. Body builders were not wealthy even though their customers might be.

When a series of bodies was sold to a chassis manufacturer, it was customary for them to issue a regular purchase order, and of course payment was made when the body was delivered. During and after 1930, as I have mentioned, we did some business on a different basis of necessity.

Lincoln had a set of standard specifications covering many structural details, which had to be incorporated into any body built for them or one of their dealers. In working with Lincoln we still used our own specification sheets, but for many items merely filled in "standard Lincoln practice."

It was not unusual for a customer to change his mind about various details during the construction of his body. Many of them came to the plant several times to check the progress and appearance of what was being built for them. The cost of such changes was added to the price, and sometimes ran to several hundred dollars.

The same procedure was applied to changes in one of a series of bodies. Often these were worked out directly with the ultimate purchaser. We were kept posted on the standard markups of various companies, so we could quote a retail price directly to the customer.

Once the order had been placed, the next step was to prepare the full-size body draft and working drawings. Nearly all body draftsmen had taken the same course, which included the rather unique method of developing curved surfaces. The idea was originally worked out mathematically by Andrew F. Johnson, who gave his course at the West Side Y.M.C.A. in New York. Around 1920 he retired to Gray, Maine, but continued to offer the course by correspondence. The fact that almost the same methods were used by all body engineers made things easier when they changed jobs, something they did often.

There was some variation in the amount of detail shown on drafts by various body builders. At LeBaron, we showed a bit more than most custom shops, especially during the period when we were doing the engineering but not the actual building. As I have mentioned, when I first joined LeBaron there were two drafting tables, and I occasionally worked at them. Later, when this work was being done at Bridgeport, I frequently went there to discuss details with the draftsman, and when I moved to Detroit I also found myself spending quite a bit of time in the Engineering Department.

The first step was to lay out the contour of the chassis frame and such fixed items as the dash, which in our parlance was what is now usually referred to as the firewall at the front of the body. In those days, the hood ended at the dash, and everything from there back was part of the body. Cowls were often intricately shaped to blend from a hood line, which could range from the Rolls's square corners to a very rounded one, to the belt line, which we usually tried to keep high. There were often double compound curves in this portion, which we called "Ogees."

The design of the body was then reproduced full size, and the details gradually worked out. Side views and cross sections were superimposed on each other, sometimes by using different colored inks to avoid confusion. Sections in various places were laid out much as in ship lofting.

Often details were transferred to separate tracings for easy reference in the shop. In my first year or two at LeBaron I did quite a few such tracings. It was important for a designer to know just how a body was constructed. We didn't come up with ideas that could not be built, nor did we have specialists who worked on only one phase of a design.

The body draft showed the actual framing of the body—each individual piece of wood was shown so templates could be made directly from the draft where intricate shaping was involved, or the wood cut to fit the drawing itself. The exact location and shape of windshield castings was worked out, so that patterns could be made.

Every bit of the body—locks, window regulators, seating—was indicated in exact size and location. Most hardware and mechanisms were bought ready-made, and we had a file of blueprints of these in every size and shape manufactured. Even so, we sometimes had to design new ones and have them made specially to fit a particular application.

Most custom builders used large sheets of manila board about six by sixteen feet. Tracings might be made for special details, but all important informa-

tion was on the original draft. Draftsmen spent much of their time lying on the big tables where the manila board was tacked down. The drafts could be rolled up and stored for future reference.

In Detroit, it became the practice to use large sheets of aluminum sprayed with off-white lacquer. These were more stable than the manila board, which tended to stretch or shrink with variations in humidity. The variation might be minor on a percentage basis, but could be appreciable on a ten- or twelve-foot dimension.

Such aluminum sheets were used at the LeBaron-Detroit Company, where John Votypka was Chief Engineer. Those used for individual bodies were often destroyed after the body was completed. We simply sprayed a fresh coat of lacquer over the draft to provide a clean surface for a new one.

Many present owners of custom-bodied cars of the classic era have asked me whether the original body drafts were still available. Unfortunately, the manila ones which were rolled up and stored generally disappeared as the various body builders went out of business during the depression. The aluminum sheets used later were all sold as scrap when the war started. I have personally checked with various people formerly connected with body firms, but have not been able to find a single draft, or even detail drawing, which survives.

When I moved there, I found that the engineering department at the LeBaron-Detroit Company was vastly larger than the one we had in the East. One reason for this was the Detroit practice of requiring a part number for each individual piece of a body. Each part number had to have a corresponding drawing on file.

I pointed out that this was very cumbersome for individual bodies, which were under my personal supervision in Detroit. In the East, we had often bought parts as needed and then incorporated them into the body drafts. It took a few months, but I finally got a new system. We still had to have part numbers, but a special clerk was assigned to me and a special series of numbers prefixed with an "X."

These part numbers would be followed by a brief description, such as "Rawlings Regulator, Style A," or perhaps "Rear-view mirror purchased by H. Pfau." Often I went out and bought such items, but had to have a part number assigned before I could be reimbursed.

44
Construction of the Body

ONCE the draft was ready, work started on the actual building of the body. The first step was to construct the wood framework on which everything else was mounted. For an individual body, most of the wood was hand cut—and sometimes steam-bent into shape—to match the lines of the body draft. On a series of bodies, templates were made from the draft, and the wood then shaped to fit them.

Oak, sometimes laminated, was often used for the body sills, but in general the framework was of northern white ash. Frequently during the twenties various chassis had very intricate kickups over the rear axle. These involved building up the body sill in layers to achieve the correct shape.

A sizable area in every body shop was set aside for aging the wood. It was normal to buy kiln-dried wood, but it was allowed to age another year or so in the area in which it would be worked. This gave it a chance to adapt to the temperature and humidity conditions normal to the plant, and so avoid excessive shrinkage or swelling while the body was under construction.

Once the wood framework was put together, with glued and screwed joints, it was time to start the metal paneling. Before this, wrought-iron braces would be applied to key points to strengthen large openings such as those for the doors. These were made up in our own blacksmith shop to fit the situation. Some people, notably Brunn, used cast bronze supports at these points.

Almost invariably aluminum was used for paneling custom bodies, usually 14-gauge. The reason for this was simple—aluminum could be hand formed more easily than other metals. I imagine most metalworkers were pretty hard of hearing from the noise of their hammers beating the panels into shape.

Sometime during the late twenties, a man named Artz designed a press that permitted the use of steel in some panels such as cowls, provided the shape was not too intricate. The Artz press was really two sets of clamps, which gripped opposite ends of the panel, and a hydraulic press to push up a wooden form and stretch the panel into something approximating its eventual shape. Under this stress, the metal could be more easily hammered into the desired contour.

I recall the Artz press being used mainly for cowl panels on custom bodies. The cowl framework would be filled in with blocks of hardwood (often scraps from body sills were used) which had been shaped to the contour wanted. A sheet of steel or aluminum was bent over this framework and gripped by the clamps at the bottom of each side. It still took a fair amount of work with hammers on the metal blocks called dollies to get the sheet of metal properly shaped. Those dollies came in various shapes, and are still used by body repair men.

On a series of bodies, often a wooden form was built for the cowl on which the same procedure was followed, but one form would serve for all the bodies of the series. Often it could even be used for different body styles being built simultaneously, if the changes were all from the windshield back. This is true of the Cord cowl illustrated.

Until 1924 or so, doors were finished with T-moldings which covered the raw edges of the metal and also to close the small opening around the edge of the door. Nearly everyone thought this interfered with the clean flow of the design, and flush doors were generally used from then on. Doors were bigger on the outside, so they would close easily, and the door frame was built with two or three "steps," which helped to minimize drafts.

A 3/32-inch space between the door panel and its neighbor was considered ideal, and a good body man could hang the doors so that this space did not vary by the width of a hair, either from point to point or from door to door. The same standards should be maintained in restoring a custom body, if you can find someone capable enough.

Artz Press in use at Union City Body Company, making a Cord cowl panel in 1929.

Open or town cars, and even many closed bodies, had windshield posts of cast manganese bronze. On closed cars, these were used to improve visibility, as discussed in connection with the Emond patent. At LeBaron, we bought these castings from the Rostand Manufacturing Company of Milford, Connecticut. They would make up patterns to our drawings and cast the parts. Rostand is still in business making marine hardware, as mentioned in my comments on Rollston.

I would imagine that where such sections need replacing, any firm making custom marine hardware should be able to duplicate the parts. It might be expensive if new patterns have to be made. Actually this should be necessary only if they have been damaged in an accident, since they would practically last forever otherwise.

We often used bronze castings for the center posts of convertible sedans after we started hanging both front and rear doors from this center post. They were usually cast with a heavy base extending at least a quarter of the way across the body, and bolted, not screwed, to the underframe.

As chassis got longer during the twenties they became a bit flexible even though most of them had side members eight or nine inches deep and much cross-bracing. The point of greatest flexing was near the center of the car, and with motors positioned behind the front axle, as they then were, this was just about where the front edge of the front door was located.

We tried hinging the front doors at the rear, and found that this gave a much more stable result. This explains why many LeBaron bodies from 1928 on had all their doors hinged at the rear. It also permitted some design innovations, with the door edge continuing the sloping line of the windshield. Sloping windshields became fashionable just about then.

It also allowed more footroom getting into and out of the car, since we liked to keep the windshield as close as possible to the steering wheel to permit a long cowl line. When this arrangement was adopted for most Ford bodies in 1933, I had become a Ford salesman. I recall that our competitors were trained to point out that this resulted in a somewhat unladylike effect when getting into, and especially getting out of, the car. I was perhaps the only Ford salesman who knew the engineering reasons behind this design. It was easy to demonstrate the difference by leaning down on the different types of doors while closing them.

Although we usually used standard fenders on American cars, we often made up special ones to suit the design. We also made all fenders for imported chassis. Like the body panels, they were generally made of aluminum, but of heavier gauge. Being softer than steel, aluminum was easily dented and could even be bent out of shape by someone leaning on it heavily. On the other hand, it was relatively easy to straighten whatever damage might have been done during construction or in traffic later on. I have seen a number of these cars which are still in existence, and the aluminum fenders seem to be in very good condition.

Fenders ran about $450 per set. This cost was kept down by the fact that we had several basic styles we favored, and wooden jigs were made on which they could be easily duplicated. Several of the fender styles we originated were later copied by various car manufacturers for their production models.

Where standard fenders were used on American cars, the rear ones were usually available with varying amounts of metal in the wheelhousings. In general, a special type was made for each production body style and on some chassis they could also be ordered with a full wheelhouse panel on the inner side. It was easier to cut away unwanted metal than to add some. Anyone replacing rear fenders on an old car should bear this in mind.

Running boards for all European cars, and often for American ones, were made up in our shop of solid planks of walnut or mahogany. Our most popular design had these grooved, with nickel-silver strips mounted between the grooves to carry the weight of people stepping on them, and prevent scratching of the highly varnished wood. Holes were drilled in the grooves to provide drainage. The usual price of a pair of running boards in the twenties was around $300, but I doubt if they could be duplicated for under $1,000 per pair today.

Chassis of that time were left rather bare and functional, with much of the basic structure exposed. We often covered the gas tank with wood strips to match the running boards. These were usually two inches wide and were mounted on an iron framework made up in our blacksmith shop, which also supplied fender and light brackets and similar parts. Generally the wood strips were trimmed with nickel-silver moldings like those on the running boards.

Not too much attention was paid by chassis manufacturers to such items as batteries, tools, etc. Those who drove in those days, or own classics now, are aware that these items were often tucked under the front seat. In many cases, we built special battery and tool boxes into the running boards.

Another activity for the blacksmith shop was spare tire or wheel mounts. Dual side-mounted spares were often used on custom bodies, and the early ones had individually made brackets. Even the fender wells were made specially, although we often used a standard fender as a base.

Side-mounted spares had been used earlier without fender wells. Our 1917 Hudson Super Six had them on the right side only, riding on top of the back edge of the fender. Tires were less durable in those days and we usually carried two or even three tires side by side.

Even with rear-mounted spares, which we often used in pairs, special brackets were sometimes needed. Where a standard bracket was available with the chassis, we frequently modified it to get the angle of the spares just what we wanted to blend with the design. Sometimes we even made completely new ones. Since every custom body shop had its own blacksmith, such parts could vary considerably. Any competent blacksmith should be able to replace them —if you can find such an individual.

Headlight brackets were another job for the blacksmith, since these were usually made specially for any European chassis and often for American ones if special lights were fitted. We favored the Marchal P-100 which had exceptional power and a very clean design. Our source for these was Nil Melior, who operated a high-grade accessory store first in the West 50s and later in the new Waldorf-Astoria Hotel.

Nil Melior was also our source for Lalique radiator

ornaments. *Automobile Quarterly* recently published an article on these. Quite recently, I saw Melior's name on a gift shop at 700 Madison Avenue, and was pleasantly surprised to find him still active, although no longer associated with automobile accessories. He told me that one or two of the Lalique molds are still in existence, and that some designs are still available.

Occasionally we had a special radiator ornament made. This would usually be modeled by a sculptor and then cast in bronze and plated to match the radiator. One such was the stylized airplane on the Lincoln Aero-phaeton we showed at the 1928 Salon.

One day in 1931 I received a call from George Walker at Lincoln. It seemed that the man who finally bought the car after it had been shown around the country wanted the radiator ornament replaced. I don't recall whether it had been stolen before or after he bought the car. I said, "My God, George, it will cost a lot of money. The original clay model was destroyed after the first one was cast." It had run to several hundred dollars, and translated into retail prices it would have been a fantastic figure for a radiator ornament. Walker said he was sure the customer would drop dead when he heard the price. Since Ford was one of Briggs's largest customers, I arranged to have a new ornament made and sold it to Lincoln at substantially less than cost.

When I saw that Lincoln Phaeton in Ray Radford's garage last summer, the ornament was gone again. I would hate to have another one made up today. It might cost more than the $10,000 price tag the whole car carried originally.

45

Interiors

IN describing the process of designing a custom body, I mentioned that this was laid out around the desired seating arrangement. Most people who bought custom bodies were interested in comfort and luxury in the interiors, often more so than in the appearance of the outside of the car.

Sometimes this resulted in some rather odd looking vehicles, especially when for some reason unusually high headroom was required. Several cars built for Col. E. H. R. Green survive, and anyone who has seen them is aware that they were built at least a foot higher than normal. Col. Green had an artificial leg and insisted that his cars be built so he could get in and out of them with a minimum of difficulty.

In most cases, however, people were satisfied with upholstery that they would sink into, but not so soft that it would bottom when the car hit a bump in the road. At the same time, the angle of the seats and backs was carefully studied.

At LeBaron, we gave this a lot of thought, and also considered our own reactions when driving or riding in a car. Fairly early during my work there I remember we had a jointed dummy of masonite, made to represent the "average" human figure. This was placed on the body draft to help determine the location and position of seats, their relations to controls, and similar dimensions.

For the driver's seat, we favored a more upright position, which we ourselves felt was more comfortable for driving. Left to our own devices, we used a relatively flat seat, with the back edge about an inch and a half lower than the front, and not too deep, about 18 or 19 inches. This was to allow easy leg movement (there were no automatic transmissions then). Our normal angle between seat and back cushions for the driver was 100 degrees.

As mentioned in the preceding chapter, the position of the front seat was determined primarily by the steering wheel. However, our "dummy" allowed us to make sure that this created no problem with the operating of various pedals.

Many custom-bodied cars were chauffeur-driven, which was another factor to be considered. It was thought proper for the chauffeur to sit quite erect. Owner-drivers with any experience also preferred this position. Naturally where a body was individually designed, the physical characteristics of the most frequent driver would be taken into consideration, and the seat tailored to fit him.

In the specifications for Mr. Benedum's Marmon, included in an earlier chapter, this is evident. Mr. Benedum expected to drive the car himself a good part of the time, and he was over 6 feet tall. His chauffeur, on the other hand, was of average height. Adjustable seats were not considered suitable for a body with chauffeur's partition, and I therefore specified a separate cushion for use when the chauffeur was driving. Since the difference in their heights was largely in their legs, the cushion behind the chauffeur's back left him quite comfortable, and without it Mr. Benedum was at ease.

Rear seats were usually sloped somewhat more, with the back edge two or even three inches lower than the front, and the angle between seat and back 110 degrees or sometimes even more. For the seat back we usually used an extra-deep and soft spring.

We always used built-up coil spring seat frames, and by working closely with the spring manufacturers could get these in many degrees of softness. Most Eastern body builders obtained theirs from the F. R. Atkinson Spring Company of Hamburg, New York. Our principal source in Detroit was the L. A. Young Spring & Wire Company, and since they did a large business with Briggs, they were especially cooperative.

When I first moved to Detroit, our trim-shop foreman complained to me that he had a problem. Ralph Roberts and Henry Hund, then president of Briggs, insisted on personally trying out the seats in every prototype or individual custom body. Both gentlemen were short, and neither weighed much over 120 pounds. When a seat was soft enough for them, the foreman, who weighed over 200, would sink right down to the bottom.

I went into a huddle with L. A. Young's representative, and we came up with a solution. He made up one special spring designed to suit Messrs. Roberts and Hund. We would install this for their trial, and then substitute the spring we had planned for that particular body. I don't know whether they were ever aware of this subterfuge, but from then on we had no problems.

Since we were primarily interested in comfort, these springs averaged about six inches deep at the back, and up to eight inches at the front. This is the spring itself, without padding. In later years, as overall heights were lowered, these dimensions shrank somewhat.

Some of the springs were in two layers—a lower one of heavy wire to take the shock of rough roads, and a soft upper one of finer wire. During my last year at LeBaron, I had some experimental springs made up in which the lighter spring was set partly inside the heavier one, in an effort to reduce overall thickness without sacrificing comfort.

Much of the upholstering was done in the manner of fine furniture, with good padding and in the style suitable to the car and the wishes of its purchaser. One of our favorites at LeBaron was the loose cushion style. The springs were lightly padded, and separate down pillows placed over them, tailored to fit. Sometimes we used these only on the seat, but most frequently for the back as well.

As anyone who has a sofa upholstered in this manner is aware, down shifts about and the pillows have to be fluffed up frequently. From the standpoint of both appearance and comfort, this leaves something to be desired. We gave this a lot of thought and came up with a solution that I regret I have never seen copied in furniture. The pillows were made up with compartments shaped to fit the posterior. It was somewhat like a series of U-shaped tubes. The down could still shift somewhat, but the general shape of the pillow was retained. Of course, this added to the cost since quite a bit of extra labor was involved, but then saving money was not our primary object.

Another favorite of ours was the roll-edge style. A six- or eight-inch roll extended across the front of the seat, with a corresponding roll across the top of the back. Sometimes this was in a contrasting material, often a leather roll with the balance of the cushion

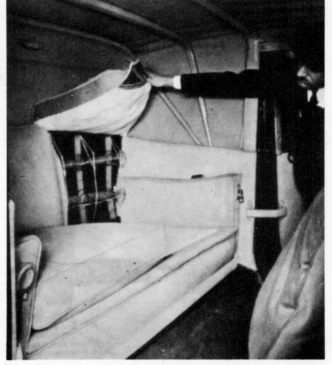

Loose-cushion upholstery in Isotta-Fraschini Cabriolet designed by LeBaron, Carrossiers, and built by Derham for 1923 Salon. Later bodies used light padding over the springs.

in Bedford Cord. The rolls were well padded, and we would vary the softness to suit the individual.

Pleated upholstery was favored by many, and we liked it especially in open or convertible bodies. While we occasionally made pleats as narrow as two inches, we generally kept them wider, sometimes even five or six inches. Often tufting was used, especially on the backs, with two or three rows of self-

Leather and cloth interior of 1925 Mercedes-Benz Convertible Sedan by LeBaron for Mrs. H. E. Manville. Note roll across front edge of seat. Bedford Cord was used for door panels and top lining.

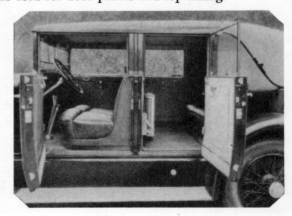

covered buttons sewed through the upholstery. These were generally spaced in a diamond pattern.

While tufted upholstery is more typical of the earlier period before and just after World War I, we used it very effectively on some Packard Convertible Sedans in 1930 and 1931. The rear seat of these was truly a pair of bucket seats with a permanent armrest between them.

Folding center armrests were used in the rear seats of many custom bodies, but often we built the seat in two sections and had a removable armrest slipped between them. This was because normally the seat would be occupied by only one or two people, and the chauffeur could easily slip out the armrest on the rare occasions when extra passengers were carried.

Literally anything under the sun was available for upholstery material, including such exotic items as specially woven fabrics and even snakeskin, but in practice we used just a few sources for nearly all of it. Wm. Wiese & Company and Laidlaw Company were the main sources for wool fabrics, and the Radel Leather Company (mentioned in Bob Turnquist's *The Packard Story*) supplied leather. We sometimes bought upholstery leather from Eagle-Ottawa or Blanchard Bros. & Lane, but they concentrated more on quantity production for Detroit.

Wiese had a very nice doeskin broadcloth, which came in a range of soft pastel shades. Beiges and greys, being neutral, were most popular. No respectable society matron wanted the upholstery in her car to clash with whatever gown she might be wearing for a particular occasion. Wiese owned the Broad Brook Mill in Connecticut. During the depression, they sold out to the Fisher Brothers, and I believe the mill is still making some of the fabrics for today's Cadillacs.

Laidlaw's cloth came largely from England, and they had a particularly fine Bedford Cord we also used extensively, often with matching broadcloth. They also had some French fabrics that earlier had been imported by the firm of A. Boyriven.

Both firms had some patterned materials, mostly fine and muted stripes. We kept in our office sample books of all their materials, and the various shades available, so our customers could select what pleased them.

On rare occasions none of the samples satisfied, and we would have some material dyed to suit the customer. Alternatively, we might work out a combination of two fabrics to get the desired effect, perhaps seats of a striped broadcloth with the balance of the interior in a solid color picking up either the background color or that of one of the stripes.

Interior of 1940 Cadillac 75 Formal Sedan by Fleetwood. Auxiliary seats in earlier bodies were very similar. From Fleetwood Cadillac catalog.

Even where bodies were built in small series, the interior was usually finished to meet the requirements of their ultimate purchasers. Often this work was not completed until a firm order at retail had been placed. Naturally, if a considerable deviation from standard specifications for the particular body style occurred, an additional charge would be made. For instance, this was done on the Lincoln Town Car with needlepoint upholstery which I mentioned as part of one of our Salon exhibits.

Leather was the most used material for upholstering open cars and convertibles. We preferred the natural color of oil-tanned top grain hide, but where desired the leather could be dyed almost any color to match or harmonize with the color scheme. Oil-tanned leather was softer and more flexible than conventionally tanned types.

Since only the best parts of a hide were used for seats and other large areas, several hides were needed for each car. The scrap was skived and used for piping, carpet binding, and the like. There was usually more than enough scrap to take care of all these items on one body, and some of the surplus was saved for those occasions when we used leather piping with cloth upholstery.

Pigskin was another leather we liked, generally in natural color although I can recall one or two instances when we had it dyed. The hides were smaller and it took quite a few to do an entire car. Although they had been carefully selected before being shipped to us, we sometimes had to discard an entire pigskin because it was not possible to cut a seat panel from it. That means a seat for one person, because no pigskin was big enough to reach across the car body.

I recall a conversation with Fred Radel about the source of his hides. Those for top-grain upholstery leather came from carefully controlled areas where the cattle were free to graze without encountering fences. Barbed wire fences used in some places left extensive scars, which marred the beauty of the leather. I believe he said the best ones, at that time, came from South America. Texas already had quite a bit of barbed wire, and the cattle would encounter more on their journey to the slaughter house.

Occasionally something more unusual was called for, as with that needlepoint Lincoln. Wiese shipped some of their fine broadcloth to France, where it was embroidered by Gobelins in the pattern they had used for a sedan chair for Marie Antoinette. While two panels sufficed for this car, a few more were made up and used in other bodies later.

By the late twenties, some experiments were being made with synthetic materials. The Stutz Blackhawk Town Car we had at the 1928 Salon had the interior done in rayon fabric in a modern, abstract design, woven by F. Schumacher. This foreshadowed the more recent trend to Nylon, Saran and similar fibres.

About the same time, some reptile leathers were introduced. Due to the small size of the skins, only the pleated style could be used. Most of the snake-skin interiors I remember were on Mercedes with bodies by Saoutchik.

Alpina Watersnake interior in a Stutz Sedan. From Alpina advertisement in 1928 New York Salon Catalog.

I have heard considerable discussion in recent years about the proper upholstery for the front compartment of chauffeur-driven cars. On an open-front Town Car, this was invariably leather and almost always black. I can recall one instance where we had some Bedford Cord dyed black and made a slip-cover for the chauffeur's seat at his insistence. In fine weather the front compartment was always open, and those leather seats could get pretty hot in the sun.

In an enclosed-drive limousine intended to be entirely chauffeur-driven, the seat and doors were again usually done in black leather, although the headlining matched that in the rear compartment. On the other hand, a sedan-limousine which would be frequently driven by the owner generally had the same upholstery front and back. Naturally the wishes of the purchaser determined this, although we were often asked to make recommendations.

Finally, I have been asked on several occasions whether the upholstery in a restored custom body was "authentic." I have replied that, especially on an individually built body, anything could be authentic. If a customer wanted pink upholstery with green stripes, we'd try to get it for him. Actually, most of our customers had very good taste and the tendency was toward the conservative. If we felt their ideas were a bit extreme, we tried to influence them in the direction of our own standards of taste—although not always successfully. I can recall a few bodies which left our plant with color schemes or interiors we felt a bit gaudy, but not very many.

46
Interior Trim

WHILE the upholstery was the dominant factor of most interiors, much attention was given by the custom builders to such details as hardware, vanity cases and paneling. Many of us obtained these from the same sources, with the result that some such items are interchangeable among various custom bodies of the period.

Our principal source of interior hardware in the East was Harry A. MacFarland. Earlier, he had set up an automobile body hardware department at Gorham, but in the very early twenties he started his own business. He never revealed his sources, so I do not know whether Gorham made the pieces for him.

In general, the hardware was made of bronze, nickel plated, in either bright or satin finish. We preferred the latter on closed bodies, but for convertibles and the front compartment of town cars we generally used the bright finish. MacFarland called the satin finish a "platinum finish."

Sometimes a customer wanted cloisonne trim on the hardware, and in such cases the pieces were made in sterling silver on which the cloisonne enamel was applied and baked. Mr. MacFarland always insisted that silver was the only suitable base for cloisonne, but I have since seen some excellent work on copper.

Occasionally gold-plated hardware was used at special request, but this was rare. Even rarer was solid gold hardware. The only car I can recall offhandedly with this added touch of luxury was the Pierce-Arrow Town Car that Brunn built for the Shah of Iran. The gold hardware was quite attractive, but also very expensive.

Our favorite pattern was MacFarland's "Puritan," very simple. The same shape was also available with an engraved design, which we also used to some extent. Sometimes for a very conservative interior, the hardware was left in natural bronze finish. In these cases we usually used the engraved design to relieve the severity of its appearance.

When the LeBaron-Detroit Company was organized, they designed and had made up hardware of an

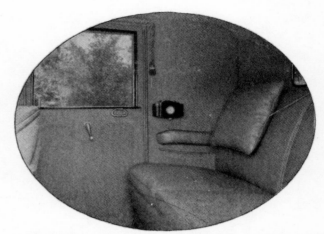

Interior of 1925 Isotta-Fraschini Sedan by Fleetwood, showing MacFarland hardware, Linden vanity cases, and a loose pillow.

even simpler and somewhat lighter shape. This is to be found in most bodies built there from 1928 until well into the thirties. Brewster also had hardware of their own design, in a rather thin straight shape. This sometimes serves to identify some of their bodies that have long since lost their nameplates.

Lincoln had a special pattern of interior hardware made for them by the Sterling Bronze Company in New York, and this was used both on their production bodies and on series built by custom firms such as Brunn, Judkins, LeBaron and Willoughby.

Harry MacFarland had a few other interests. He was an acknowledged authority on Georgian silver, and often had a few pieces in his office, on consignment from some collector for whom he would dispose of them.

At one time, he was commissioned to dispose of the bulk of the Rodman Wanamaker collection by private sale. The prices of the various items were set by a group of highly competent appraisers. For a year or so, different groups of pieces were in MacFarland's office for a few weeks while he negotiated with prospective purchasers.

I especially remember one magnificent small jade statue that I admired greatly but unfortunately could not afford. He told me some of its history. It had been part of the heritage of the Chinese Emperors, but was spirited out of their palace during the Boxer Rebellion. It vanished from sight for some years but eventually turned up in Canada, where Mr. Wanamaker bought it for his collection.

MacFarland was also our principal source of vanity cases. Those we bought from him were usually covered in suede leather, hand-tooled in gold. Several soft shades were available from stock, selected to harmonize with the most popular upholstery colors.

Some people preferred wooden vanity cases, and while MacFarland had some of these too, we more often bought them from the Linden Manufacturing Company in New York. They would make them up in almost any shape or wood we requested.

One of the cases usually contained a clock. MacFarland used mainly Waltham clocks, while Linden favored Jaeger. The Elgin Watch Company made similar clocks, but they also made complete vanity cases. Theirs were used more in the better production models than in custom bodies.

The lady's case usually contained a mirror, which might be backed with suede leather to match the case, a notebook, and a perfume bottle or two with caps to match the interior hardware. The man's case was the smoking case, fitted with cigar lighter and ashtray. The lighters were made by Casco in Bridgeport, who I believe still manufacture them. Early ones had a flexible wire on a spring reel, but later on the wireless type was developed much like those used today.

It was customary to place the lady's case on the left, since she would enter the car first, and the man's case on the right. Some very early custom bodies had the positions reversed, a carry-over from the days of horse-drawn vehicles, and this reversed position will also be found in many English bodies because of their practice of driving on the left.

In the later twenties, we began to receive requests to include an ashtray in the lady's cases as well. When the wireless lighters were introduced, which took up less room, one of these was usually put in place of one of the perfume bottles.

All of these vanity cases were attached in much the same way, with metal dovetails on their backs sliding onto matching metal strips screwed to the body frame. In most cases, it should not be difficult to transfer such cases from one body to another.

The Linden Manufacturing Company was also the source of the beautiful marquetry paneling, which

Interior of 1925 Isotta-Fraschini Town Brougham by Fleetwood, purchased by Rudolph Valentino, showing marquetry panelling by Linden. One view shows folding seats opened, and on the other they are concealed in the panelling.

was a feature of many town cars. I know they supplied such panels to Fleetwood and Rollston as well as LeBaron. A great deal of slow and intricate hand work went into these panels, with carefully matched veneers and often elaborate scrollwork. They added

Interior of 1927 Minerva Sedan-Limousine by Hibbard & Darrin, exhibited at 1927 Chicago Salon.

some $400 to $500 to the cost of a body.

Linden once did a panel for Walter Chrysler's yacht, a mural of New York harbor, for which they even found wood with a blue cast to portray the water and sky. Whether anyone else has reached this stage of perfection today, I am unable to answer.

The most usual arrangement was for such a panel to cover the entire back of the partition, facing the rear seat. Sometimes a smaller matching panel was used across the tops of the rear doors, and rarely—mostly on European bodies—the entire door was paneled.

Since auxiliary seats were usual on town cars, the panels were often intricately made to form the bottoms of these seats. They then formed an integral part of the panel when folded away. This of course meant that the seats themselves had to be very carefully fitted.

Sometimes elaborate cabinets were built to accommodate traveling bars—complete with folding cocktail tables—or writing desks. I described one such in the Minerva Sport Sedan which LeBaron had at the 1928 Salon. Some of the French and English carrossiers showed particular ingenuity in this respect.

Even where elaborate paneling or cabinet work was not used, interior window moldings (we called them garnish moldings) were of solid walnut or mahogany, carefully finished. Often we extended these down several inches below the window sill. In later years, they sometimes had vanity cases built right into them.

One set of hardware that stands out in my mind is what was probably the first one fitted with plastic knobs. The idea came from Al Pranz, then interior specialist on Ralph Roberts's staff at the LeBaron Studios, sometime in the Spring of 1931. It was to be tried out on a Lincoln Limousine we were building for Mr. Briggs.

I had arranged to go to New York for a few days,

and while there consulted the Catalin Corporation. They supplied me with some one-inch diameter Catalin rod in a deep red shade we wanted, since the car was to be painted maroon. When I returned to Detroit, I took the rod down to our machine shop and asked our most skilled workman there to turn the knobs on his lathe. He asked me what it was made of, and when I told him nitro-cellulose, he refused to work on it for fear it might explode. Finally, I asked him to chuck it in his lathe and I made the first few knobs. After I had turned two or three, without any explosion, he made the rest.

Much of the concealed mechanism, such as window regulators, was not much different from what is being used today. Lever locks were used frequently, operated by a knob protruding up from a carefully cut slot in the garnish molding. Unlike those used

today, they moved back and forth to unlatch the door, with an extra push needed to lock the door from the inside. Since these knobs were not adequate for pulling the door shut, metal loop handles or straps were used for this purpose.

There were some innovations in window regulators from time to time, the most successful being the Rawlings regulator introduced in the mid-twenties. It operated much like the roller on a window shade, and by means of cables wrapped around the roller and running over pulleys, would raise the window by spring power. A locking device was provided, and the whole assembly carefully balanced. When the lock was released, the window would rise slowly, or it could be pushed down gently with one hand. Power operated windows had not even been thought of yet.

Window shades were, of course, de rigeur on any custom body. Usually they were fitted to all windows of the rear compartment, including the partition behind the chauffeur. They were made of silk, which

Interior of 1931 Duesenberg Beverly Sedan by Walter Murphy. Note speedometer among the instruments for rear seat occupants. Photograph courtesy Automotive History Collection, Detroit Public Library.

we purchased from our suppliers of upholstery fabrics, who kept stocks of silk in colors to match.

Toggle straps (or assist straps as they are now called) were also mandatory on any town car. Sometimes these were made of the upholstery material, but more often of coach lace. This was a wide, patterned braid for which the principal source was the Bridgeport Coach Lace Company. They made it in a variety of patterns and colors. Earlier, coach lace had also been used to trim door panels, but by the mid-twenties it had almost gone out of fashion. The name "toggle straps" comes from the toggle fastenings used to attach them to the body.

In the very early thirties, we began to experiment with other arrangements for vanity cases, to make them less conspicuous. One of the first cars to have them recessed in the rear quarters was a town car we built for Mrs. Walter P. Chrysler in 1931. The vanity case doors were covered with the upholstery fabric, surrounded by a narrow wood rim.

Late in the afternoon before the car was to be delivered, I received a call from the final assembly shop. The vanity cases did not fit.

The cases had been made to our specifications by a northern Michigan firm, which specialized in fine woodwork. A metal shell was attached to the body framework, and the case proper was to be slid into this and held by spring catches.

When I went out to the plant to investigate, I discovered that some genius in our engineering department, who made the drawings for the cases, had forgotten how the upholstery was attached at this point. To keep it smooth, it was mounted over heavy fibreboard, and around the opening for the vanity cases it was folded back underneath and glued in place. That meant a triple thickness of material, and the upholstery was a heavy doeskin broadcloth. The holes for the spring catches were about a quarter of an inch too far back.

Enlarging the holes would not be satisfactory, lest the cases be too loosely held and begin to rattle. With the help of our most expert upholsterer, I finally solved the problem by pulling loose the fabric, cutting away a half-inch strip of the fibreboard, and regluing the fabric to itself. Normally, such gluing was done outside the body, but at this stage we had no choice but to work in cramped quarters and pray we would not soil the material. We managed, but it was near midnight before the job was done. However, Mrs. Chrysler did get her car the next day.

I was pleasantly surprised after writing about this incident to learn that Mrs. Chrysler's town car had been purchased from her estate just recently by Mr. Phil Wichard, who lives only a mile or two from me. When I went to see it, it appeared almost as it had when it left our plant, having been stored for some twenty years. I could even feel the rough edge of the fibreboard under the upholstery, where I had cut it with a knife.

47
Top Materials

SINCE a large proportion of the classics which have been preserved and restored are open cars or convertibles, there seems to be considerable interest in the top materials used on them originally.

Our own favorite at LeBaron was Burbank, an English fabric imported by Laidlaw & Company. It was treated to make it waterproof, but was very light and flexible. One of its greatest advantages was that it permitted the tops to fold very thin and low. Wire-on moldings and bindings were usually made of the same material, but sometimes of leather.

In this connection, I should mention that we always designed our open cars to look their best with the top folded. Often we arranged the mechanism so that the upper bow, when folded, would be level with the belt-line rather than above it. I have suggested to a number of my friends that their open classics be shown or photographed with the tops down, which is the way they were planned to be used except in inclement weather.

The Burbank did have one drawback. It was likely to stretch somewhat. This produced a tendency for the top, when up, to balloon a bit. I remember getting a rather nasty letter from one of the Litchfield family in Akron, who controlled Goodyear, and who recently had taken delivery of a Pierce-Arrow Convertible Sedan with a Burbank top. He complained that all his friends were saying "Here comes the Akron," whenever he drove up to their homes. Goodyear had then just completed the dirigible *Akron,* which had a rather bulbous shape.

One alternative to Burbank was Haartz Double-Textured Duck, made by the J. C. Haartz Company in Watertown, Mass. After Laidlaw went out of business during the depression, Haartz was almost the only source of such material and many convertibles of the thirties used it. The Haartz fabric was laminated, duck on the outside and sateen on the inside, with a layer of rubber between.

This fabric was also used extensively on production cars, and from time to time duPont made a similar one. When I was in the textile business during the thirties and forties, we made some of the sateen duPont used for this purpose. The business was rather sporadic, and I once asked a duPont representative about this. He explained that duPont only made the top material when General Motors could not obtain enough from other sources.

I have often wondered why this was not brought out during the lengthy hearings that led to a court order for duPont to divest itself of its General Motors stock. I read the part of the opinion which made much of the fact that duPont supposedly took advantage of their relationship with General Motors to be a preferred source of materials.

On one occasion, Mr. Haartz visited our suite in the Commodore Hotel during a Salon. We showed him a sample of a German top material, which had been offered to us at a lower price than his. Haartz smelled the sample, and said it would not hold up because the bonding layer was almost pure rubber. He said this would oxidize under prolonged exposure to the sun and lose its resiliency. When we asked him what he did to overcome this problem, he said "I adulterate the rubber," but would not tell us what he used to adulterate it. I do know his fabrics stood up quite well.

We also used Burbank, or Haartz D. T. Duck, on the tops of many town cars, especially full-collapsible ones. Sometimes we used it to cover the stationary top of a sedan, because we liked its appearance or because the customer wanted us to simulate the effect of a convertible.

Where these light-colored materials were used for the top, we generally also used them for spare tire covers, trunk covers, etc. I can even remember one or two open cars for which we made Burbank slip covers. It was soft enough to be comfortable, absorbed less heat than leather, and had the advantage of being waterproof should the car be caught in a sudden shower with the top down.

Many closed cars, especially those with blind

1925 Lincoln Full-collapsible Cabriolet by LeBaron, with Burbank top: From *Lincoln Magazine,* Salon issue of 1924.

quarters, and nearly all cabriolet-type town cars or landaulets, had roofs of Landau leather. Our source for this was also the Radel Leather Company, who I believe still make it. Landau leather was made from the thicker middle layer of the hide, and had a grain embossed on it. The most common was called "Long Grain," because the ridges all ran in one direction. It was almost always applied with the grain running vertically.

In the mid-twenties, Radel came up with an idea for a "Cross Grain," which looked more natural. The first hides were done by embossing in the long grain, and then doing a second embossing with the dies turned at right angles. Later they made special dies for this grain. We liked the idea and arranged with Radel to confine this grain exclusively to LeBaron. We even arranged with them to supply a duplicate set of dies to the Textileather Company, from whom we were buying the artificial leather used for chauffeur's canopies and the center of non-folding roofs.

Then as now, Textileather was a pyroxylin-coated fabric, which had much the same appearance as leather, but was more flexible and less expensive. Pantasote made a similar material, and I believe the parent Textileather Company in Germany later bought out Pantasote. Pantasote also made a fabric

similar to Haartz's Double-Textured Duck. All of these were used for tops of production open cars, but were not favored by custom builders for this purpose.

Both Radel and Textileather would finish their material in almost any color we wanted. They collaborated closely, so that their respective materials would match quite well when used together. For convenience, the wire-on moldings were usually made of Textileather.

Early town cars had chauffeur's canopies and side curtains of this material. We developed the All-Weather type of town car about 1926, with windows in the front doors, and this type of construction soon became general. About the same time, we devised a new method of attaching the canopy. These had previously been put on with snap or Lift-the-Dot fasteners. These were spaced several inches apart, and allowed some seepage of water under the edge of the canopy. Some of this would drip down the chauffeur's neck, and since chauffeurs were very important people to us, we gave it quite a bit of thought.

We finally came up with a scheme using a special extruded aluminum molding we had made up, with a groove running through it, which could be attached to the front edge of the roof of the main portion of the car. A section of cable cord was sewn into the rear edge of the canopy, which could then be threaded through the molding to give a watertight seal. It also made the attaching of the canopy much easier and quicker. This feature will be found on all LeBaron town cars built from 1927 on, and I know it was still in use on those built into the late thirties.

On bodies with metal roof edges, we also used Textileather for the center section of the roof. During the early twenties we had done some experimenting with all-metal roofs, and so had Lincoln. We found them unsatisfactory as we could not eliminate drumming noises. Much work had to be done on insulating materials and on stressed metal before these could be eliminated.

The Textileather was applied over chicken-wire covered with light padding. When radios began to be available for cars in the late twenties (the first ones were in the rear compartments of town cars and limousines, so they would not distract the driver), it became obvious that the chicken-wire would make a good aerial. We began to make it standard practice to attach a lead-in wire, even where we did not install the radio ourselves. Usually this was concealed behind the upholstery on the center pillar.

The chicken-wire was attached to the body with heavy staples, and if these touched the metal panels, that ended the usefulness of the wire as an aerial. We devised a method of avoiding this by hooking up a battery, a buzzer and two long wires that could be clamped one to the chicken-wire and one to a body panel. If a short developed while the wire was being fastened, the buzzer would sound and the problem could immediately be corrected.

The outside bows to lock the top when up we called Prop Joints. This came from their function of "propping up" the top. Other body builders called them Landau Bows, Landau Joints or other names. Even when we used them as a decorative treatment on a non-folding top, the joints were still functional. It gave them some flexibility and so they were easier to mount.

They were always designed with the lower half slightly longer than the top half, and with a larger radius. We felt they looked better that way, but it also allowed them to fold more compactly. Generally they were cast in manganese bronze by Rostand who made other similar items. Sometimes we painted them to blend with the color scheme, but more often they were plated.

48
Paint and Color

WHEN I entered the body business in 1923, varnish was the accepted finish for automobiles. This had been carried over from the coach-building days of earlier centuries with very few changes.

Normally, several priming coats were applied, rather thick and heavy, and rubbed down by hand to a smooth surface. This helped to cover such minor problems as small scratches or irregularities in the metal. The prime coats were thick enough to hide these.

Then, on a custom body, twelve to fourteen coats of color varnish were flowed on. A master painter could do this so the brush marks scarcely showed, but for top quality it was considered good practice to apply each coat at right angles to the previous one. Each coat was "wet sanded" with progressively finer grit and a soft flow of water over the section being worked on, both to act as a lubricant and to carry away small bits of grit and resin from the varnish.

It was at this stage that the color of the body was created. In most cases, the color had been selected by the customer (or our own staff) from chips supplied by the leading paint manufacturers. The pigment to be mixed with the varnish was then ordered, and mixed according to the manufacturer's instructions. Due to variations in the formulas of the basic varnish, we usually used the same brand as that of the pigment.

When the last coat of color varnish had been rubbed to proper smoothness, several coats of clear varnish were carefully applied so that a minimum of rubbing was needed. The last buffing was done with jeweler's rouge, an abrasive even finer than the finest sandpaper.

Since each coat of varnish had to be allowed to dry thoroughly before it was sanded, this was a lengthy process. It took four to six weeks to do a paint job, and almost as long for repainting when this was necessary.

Not only did this delay the completion of the body, but it took up quite a bit of space. The painting and drying took place in rooms as nearly dustproof as possible. They had sliding doors through which the bodies were moved on dollies, and smaller sliding doors gave access for the workmen. Sliding doors were less apt to stir up any latent dust than hinged ones.

Great care was also taken to keep insects out of the paint rooms, but since doors did have to be opened from time to time, this was virtually impossible. If the bugs landed on tacky varnish they could cause quite a mess. The dead bugs would have to be removed and their trails obliterated. This was not too big a problem in the early stages of a paint job, but if it happened in the final coat it could cause havoc. To remove the marks meant sanding off all of the last coat and doing it over again.

Many times I received a call from our plant a day or two before a certain body was to be delivered. A fly had crawled in the varnish, and this meant a delay of at least two or three days. The first few times I told our customers just what had happened, but after hearing the hoots of derision I found it much simpler to make up some other excuse for the delay.

While I have been speaking of bodies, we of course painted the chassis too, most of the work being done before the body was finally mounted. The same materials were used, but the finish was not as carefully handled on unseen parts. Fenders, hoods, and other exposed sections were, however, given the same careful attention as the body.

Normally stock fenders for any American chassis were available in either prime coat or black enamel. If they were to be black on the finished car, we always specified the enamel. Not only did this save work, but the baked finish was much more durable than varnish.

Another step that preceded the final coat of clear varnish was striping. To some extent, in most body shops, this was left somewhat to the judgment of the striper, one of the most highly skilled and presumably intelligent men in the plant.

Since LeBaron's sales and design office was located in New York, some sixty miles from the plant, we carefully included in our paint specifications full and exact details of the striping we wanted. Mostly we used a 3/32" stripe near the edge of each molding or raised panel. Sometimes we used a wider stripe, perhaps a 3/16" one of one color, with a narrow stripe, say 1/16", of a contrasting color at each edge.

On wood or disc wheels, striping was used to harmonize with the body. Often the wheels were painted a different color, and much thought had to be given to selecting a striping color that would look well in both places. Occasionally the wheels might be painted in the color used for striping the body, and the body color then was used to stripe the wheels.

In preparing paint specifications for the plant, we would specify the exact areas to be done in each color. No matter how carefully we tried to follow the nomenclature used by the workmen at the plant, there were sometimes mistakes in interpretation. I made it a point to check on all bodies in the paint shop when I visited the plant, to make sure there were no problems. Sometimes I found one almost completed but with the wrong color in one area. It might take a couple of weeks to sand it down and build the varnish up again, layer by layer.

There were some special finishes used in those days. I have mentioned the Brewster Oil Finish. We used a similar one on some cars, but never duplicated theirs. The Farman for Jay Barnum used such a finish, with the sand mixed in as mentioned. It looked surprisingly more attractive than it sounds, and gave the car the hairy appearance that he wanted.

One more problem in those days, when the Florida boom was under way, was the sun there. It could really play havoc with varnish, and the best finish would not last more than a few months. There were many disgruntled people who took delivery of a new car late in the year, shipped it to Palm Beach, and had to have it repainted when they returned in the Spring. I don't know whether Florida dealers warned their customers to park in the shade, but we did have less complaints about cars delivered there. We grew accustomed to a rash of complaints in March or April, and learned to ask immediately "Did you take the car to Florida?"

When lacquer was introduced in 1925, it was used on production cars for some time before being adopted by custom builders. The early lacquers did not have the color range or the gloss we felt imperative. Its main advantage, as far as we could see, was speed. Not only could it be applied more quickly, with a spray gun, but it dried very rapidly. It cut down painting time by several weeks. When we learned it was also more durable, the change was soon made.

Somewhat the same procedure was followed in custom shops that had been used with varnish, but now two or three thin coats of lacquer were applied in a continuous process, the painter walking around the body as he sprayed. Since lacquer was inherently smoother, less rubbing between coats was needed, but since it was also thinner, more coats were used.

We also learned that the thinner paint layer did not hide the minor imperfections in the metal as well as varnish had. We found it necessary to spend more time burnishing the metal to almost a mirror finish before starting to paint. At least in the custom body industry, lacquer did not save money, although it did permit us to complete a car a few weeks sooner.

At first, no final clear coats were applied with lacquer, but we soon found this did not produce the deep glow we liked. Soon we began to apply several coats of clear lacquer for the final finish, and got almost as fine an appearance as we had with varnish. For some reason, those clear coats of lacquer did not hold up so well as the pigmented ones, but they still lasted longer than varnish.

Lacquer also had some effect on the color schemes used. Certain pigments combined chemically with the lacquer, and were quite durable. Others could not be achieved in this manner, and the pigment remained in suspension in the lacquer. Such colors might look quite well when new, but did not hold up nearly so long.

Maroon and Ultramarine blues were in this category. They had been quite popular, but when people discovered that they did not last and needed repainting almost every year, they fell into disfavor. Anyone who owned a car in the late twenties or thirties finished in these shades will recall that they began to oxidize and look shabby before the first year was out.

On the other hand, most colors in lacquer were more durable and we did not have so many complaints from Florida, at least as long as we were careful in selecting the colors we suggested, The first Florida boom collapsed about then, so this may have been a factor, too.

For both lacquer and varnish, our main sources

were Ditzler and Valentine. I also recall T. J. Ronan and Egyptian Lacquer, and there were others as well.

Much of our sandpaper came from the Minnesota Mining & Manufacturing Company. With the substitution of lacquer, the demand for sandpaper in the automobile industry dropped sharply. Other abrasive manufacturers looked for new markets, but the 3-M Company set out to develop new products for their old customers. Since lacquer was sprayed instead of brushed, masking tape became a big item, and they soon made a better tape than had been generally available.

One day during 1931, I was in the paint shop of the LeBaron-Detroit Company with one of the 3-M representatives. We used wrapping paper for masking large panels, sealed with tape around the edges. Our paint foreman had found that this paper could easily be transferred from one body to another of the same design and used over again. He demonstrated this procedure and commented, "It must have been some Scotchman who invented this." The comment did not go unheeded.

Actually, the wet sanding had not been eliminated completely, and it took a delicate hand to do this without leaving perceptible scratches. One side benefit was that it was easier to correct mistakes. If a wrong color had been applied in one area, it was relatively simple to mask around it and respray in the correct shade.

Later on, considerable strides were made in developing a wider range of colors in lacquer, which would stand up under continued exposure. Most of those now available seem to be quite durable. The enamel finishes now prevalent did not make their appearance until the thirties. Even then, most custom bodies were finished in lacquer because of its greater sheen and smoother surface.

49
Brightwork

IN the earliest days of the automobile, most of the exterior brightwork was brass, as most antique car fanciers are aware. Sometimes I think they feel that the more brass there is, the better the car. Actually, brass was used because it was durable and attractive. Many parts were made of solid brass, which would stand polishing almost indefinitely. They did need a lot of attention, as the surviving ones still do.

Even before World War I, nickel had come into vogue. Many of the pieces of brightwork were still made of brass, but nickel-plated. On custom bodies, the same finish was used on bronze castings. Soon it was found practical to plate pieces made of stamped steel, and these were usually brass-plated first, with a layer of nickel over this. While this procedure was used extensively on chassis parts and on production bodies, because it was less expensive, not many such plated steel parts will be found on custom bodies.

On more expensive cars and for some parts of custom bodies, nickel-silver was used. It had earlier been called German silver, but this name went out of style in England in 1914, and soon after in this country. The entire radiator shells of the Rolls-Royce and Hispano-Suiza were made of solid nickel-silver, as were the exposed piano hinges of their hoods. The alloy was relatively free from corrosion and needed a minimum of polishing. Since it was solid metal, there was no problem of rubbing through the plating.

Monel metal had many of the properties of nickel-silver, but was stronger although more difficult to form. I have mentioned that Lincoln specified monel metal for hinge screws and other body parts. Once we adopted these for Lincoln, we also used them on other bodies where we expected severe exposure to the weather.

Even during the nickel era, some people preferred brass. Most chassis used for custom bodies, such as Lincoln, could be had on special order with brass radiator shells and trim. Where a customer specified

this, or when we felt it to be especially appropriate, we then used brass for all outside body hardware. Occasionally, where this finish was not optionally available on a particular chassis, but someone wanted it, we even had new brass chassis parts made to replace the nickel ones.

Then as now, there were various levels of quality. The nickel-plating on chassis parts of a high-priced car or a custom body was extra heavy, and applied either over solid brass or bronze, or over heavy brass plating, which adhered better to steel than nickel.

In the late twenties, chrome-plating was developed. It was first used on production models, because of its easier care. The owner of a custom body usually had a chauffeur to do the polishing, and the blue tinge of the chrome was considered less desirable than nickel. There was also another problem, on some cars, since the chrome did not match the color of the nickel-silver, which was quite prominent on a Rolls or a Hispano. When we finally did use chrome, we sometimes had a completely new radiator shell made of brass, fitting snugly over the nickel-silver one, and this was then nickel- and finally chrome-plated. Chrome would not adhere well to nickel-silver.

Here again there were differences in quality. We used just as heavy a layer of nickel-plate as we had done previously. This had to be carefully cleaned and buffed to a perfectly smooth finish. Chrome did not adhere closely to nickel, but formed a sort of skin over it. If it were damaged, it would peel off.

This in turn led to experiments with stainless steel, whose color was close to that of chrome. The first stainless steel radiator shell in production, as far as I recall, was on the 1930 Model A Ford. About the same time, we began to use stainless steel moldings for trim.

One of the first places there were used was as a strip along the bottom edge of the window openings. Many drivers, and some passengers, found it comfortable to rest an elbow on the window sill, and this was often one of the first places to show wear in the paint. Adding a stainless steel strip here was not only decorative, but also practical.

As the technique of chrome plating improved, stainless steel was less frequently used. It had presented great problems in forming, and it would discolor if heated to simplify the forming process. However, it continued to be used as a material for exterior parts subject to a great deal of wear.

On very rare occasions, gold-plated outside hardware was used. This was generally for Indian Maharajahs or on cars like the Brunn Pierce-Arrow for the Shah. This was sometimes combined with gold-plated or even solid gold interior hardware. Needless to say, it added thousands of dollars to the cost of the car.

Sterling Silver interior hardware, and sometimes gold-plated or even solid gold parts, were used a bit oftener. One reason was that the car could be locked, making these expensive items difficult to reach. Probably only Heads of State used gold-plated exterior hardware because no one could even imagine their cars being tampered with.

50
Chassis Modifications

WHILE I have mentioned earlier that we often had a chassis modified to suit the particular design we had in mind, I realize from talking to some of my friends interested in this era that this is somewhat of a mystery to them.

One of the simplest modifications in those days was to create a new radiator and hood design. Brass honeycomb radiators were normal to all the better cars, and the Jellinek Auto Radiator Company in New York City would make these up for us in any size or shape. Generally we made them higher than standard, but sometimes when we were building a new body on an old chassis, as with the Crane-Simplexes for Mrs. Riddle, we redesigned the radiator completely. A new shell was then hand-formed to this design, generally of brass, which would be plated or painted according to choice.

These radiators were made from small sections of fluted brass tubing, soldered together at the ends which had been swaged to a hexagonal shape. Air passed through the tubes, and water filled the spaces between them. The tubes themselves, before assembly, always reminded me of rifle cartridges. We left the technical details to Jellinek, merely giving them the outline of the shape we wanted. They usually designed the core to hold the same amount of water as the original, or slightly more. Sometimes they could add onto the existing core to give the new shape.

Naturally a special hood would be required in these cases, but that was no problem to us. It would be formed of aluminum just like our body panels, but of a slightly heavier gauge. Sometimes we used exposed piano hinges like our favorite Hispano-Suiza, and generally doors in the side panels rather than louvres. This latter idea spread to Packard and some other cars in the late twenties.

More complicated were changes in the chassis wheelbase. This meant cutting the frame and adding a section. We usually had this done by the Van Cura Machine Works, whom I have mentioned in my chapter on Rolls-Royce. All we did was tell Emil Van Cura the wheelbase we wanted, and the rest was up to him.

Since we had more Lincoln chassis lengthened than any others, and these had a torque-tube drive, this was an intricate operation. First the frame was cut through, ahead of the cross-member to which the torque-tube was attached. A channel section some eighteen inches longer than the amount the chassis was to be lengthened, and just big enough to fit snugly inside the rails of the original frame, was spliced in. It was usually riveted to the frame, and enough overlap had to be provided to maintain strength.

Then a small section of drive-shaft had to be made up to reach from the back of the transmission to the new location of the torque-tube. Brake rods and other controls had to be lengthened. Lincoln used mechanical brakes in those days. Before the altered chassis was delivered to us, it was carefully road tested. Van Cura's standards were, and still are, high.

While raising or lowering chassis is a favorite pastime of hot-rod enthusiasts today, we never undertook a change of this sort. It would have created too many problems, and besides any car less than six feet tall was considered low in those days. We could achieve this by proper design. Of course, where we were consulted by a manufacturer, which happened often, we always stressed the importance of a long wheelbase and a low chassis. How they achieved this goal was up to their engineers.

Actually, there was some lowering of chassis even then, but this was usually done by individuals too young and poor to afford a custom body. I can remember many Model T Fords with the spring hangers moved below the axles. Some even had custom bodies of a sort, often home made.

Similarly, very little was done on engine modifications. The better chassis were assumed to be the last word in engineering. While a chauffeur might employ a few tricks of tuning on a sport model, most custom-bodied cars were of a type where smoothness and quietness were considered more important than performance.

I have already covered to some extent the use of special fenders and running boards. Side-mounted spare wheels in fender wells were another innovation that started on custom bodied cars. In the early days, we would make up the brackets and cut the fenders to fit hand-made wells.

By 1925 or so, most of the better American chassis were available with side mounts as a factory option. The only time we became involved was where we wanted to alter the position of these spares to fit in with our body design. Usually we could modify the standard brackets and fenders to suit our purpose.

Folding trunk racks were generally included with the side mount option. Earlier we had often made these up, but there were also several sources from which they could be purchased to fit various chassis. Often we would add wood slats to cover the gasoline tank. Where wooden running boards were used, these were carefully matched to them. By the late twenties, most American chassis had neat sheet-metal splash guards covering the gas tank, and the wood slat treatment was sometimes applied over this. European chassis were still generally leaving the tanks exposed, and the slats were more often used on them.

Cowl strips, heavy nickel-plated bands, often with integral brackets to hold the cowl lamps, also were first made up specially, but later came to be standard equipment on good American chassis. Since they were mounted just back of the hood, and had to conform to its shape regardless of the body design, it was both cheaper and simpler to mass produce them.

Special lamps were often fitted. While we liked the Marchal lamps both for their design and their power, there were others made both here and abroad that sometimes suited a particular design better. Often the full set of lamps on a car would be replaced, in order to have them match properly.

One area where LeBaron was a bit unusual was the special searchlight we designed. We had them made up by Perkins, a leading boat light manufacturer in Brooklyn. It was styled somewhat like the earlier acetylene lamps, with a raised duct at the top. They were especially liked for sport cars, and we used them on many phaetons and roadsters. Often they were mounted on stanchions rising from the running boards, but we sometimes used a bracket attached to the body frame. Usually there was just one on the driver's side, but occasionally we balanced this with

another on the right. Other body builders sometimes would order one of these special searchlights from us.

Searchlights were also available from most of the headlamp manufacturers in styles to match the lights that they were making for various chassis. There were also special fog or driving lamps, designed to match or harmonize with standard equipment.

One feature of some classic cars—especially sport models—which many people admire is the huge, shiny outside exhaust. Actually, such arrangements had been used on racing and sports-racing cars since the early days of the automobile. Mercedes used them extensively even on their regular passenger cars, especially those fitted with a supercharger. The principal American exponents of this idea were Auburn and Duesenberg, and since they also used them on supercharged models, they came to be identified with this type of engine. However, some non-supercharged European cars also had them.

I have seen some more recent cars fitted with dummy outside exhausts, but in the twenties I do not recall any such frauds. If an outside exhaust was fitted to the chassis in normal production, it was used. Rarely, someone would have one built for an individual car, but if so it was completely functional.

One other change involved wheels. When balloon tires came into use around 1924, they were found to be much easier riding. It was not feasible to mount larger tires on the existing wheels, since the clearance in the wheelhousings would not accommodate them, although I know this was tried in a few cases. 23-inch wheels were then common with high-pressure tires, and balloons on 20-inch wheels had about the same outside diameter.

While it was not long before nearly every new car was available with balloon tires, quite a few earlier ones had their wheels modified. With wood or wire wheels, we would send these over to Wheels, Inc., who would cut down the spokes and refit them to 20-inch rims. Disc wheels could be replaced more economically than they could be altered. While they were used extensively on production models at this time, most custom builders preferred the appearance of wood or wire wheels.

On the other hand, some cars fitted with wire wheels had Ace wheel covers mounted over them. They were often left in polished aluminum, with just the trim moldings formed into them painted in the body or striping color. The covers were made in England, but were distributed on the Continent by

1925 Isotta-Fraschini Phaeton by LeBaron, with special LeBaron spotlight. Photograph courtesy Automotive History Collection, Detroit Public Library.

1929 Hispano-Suiza Boulogne Coupe by Hooper, with Ace Wheel Discs. From Hispano-Suiza catalog, Floyd Marshall Collection.

Hibbard & Darrin. Because of our earlier association, LeBaron always purchased them from Hibbard.

One point worth mentioning is that it was not altogether unusual for a custom builder to disguise a chassis, at the customer's request, with a radiator and hood from another, usually more expensive, make. This was generally the customer's idea rather than the body builder's. Where someone wanted a different appearance, most of us preferred to design a completely new radiator and hood.

PART VI

51
The Clientele

FREQUENTLY the question comes up: "Who were the famous customers of LeBaron and the other custom body builders?" In many cases, the question has been asked by the present owners of cars who are trying to trace their history back to their origins.

In the latter case, much depends on the individuality of the car. We built a number of bodies of individual design at LeBaron (we never used the term "one off"), and in many instances I can recall the car and the person for whom it was built. Actual records, unfortunately, are few and incomplete.

All the old records of LeBaron from its beginning through the late thirties were disposed of as scrap at the start of World War II, as I have mentioned earlier. Similar procedures were followed at other firms, either then or as they went out of business during the depression.

I have preserved some catalogs of the time, a few production records, and a list of customers to whom we mailed Salon invitations in 1930. Some material in this book is reproduced from the pages of *Autobody*, a trade magazine published from 1921 until the early thirties. The New York Public Library has buried in its archives a fairly complete file of this magazine. Some of the pictures used to illustrate its articles on custom bodies are identified with the names of the people for whom these bodies were built.

In those days, we kept in our office a copy of the current Social Register. Most of our customers were listed in it, and many of the other names are those of people who bought custom bodied cars from other sources.

One of the places that stands out in my mind as being well populated with LeBaron bodies is the Kings Point area of Great Neck, where the United States Merchant Marine Academy now stands. The idea of donating his estate to form the nucleus of the Academy grounds originated with Walter Chrysler. There were some tax advantages which accrued with

this gift, and he persuaded some of his neighbors to follow suit. From 1930 on, Mr. Chrysler's garage had housed several LeBaron Chryslers, including his personal Phaeton and Mrs. Chrysler's Town Car.

Kings Point Park at that time had a high brick wall separating it from the public roads, with access through one guarded gate. Beyond the gate, driveways branched off to each of the dozen estates. Next to Chrysler's was the Thomas Meighan place. Tommy Meighan had been my mother's favorite movie actor, and it was a particular pleasure for me to meet him when we built a Packard Town Brougham for him and his wife, Blanche Ring. Miss Ring was a distinguished actress in her own right, having established her reputation in her native Boston before moving to Broadway.

Somewhat to the left was the Nicholas Schenck property. Here you would find not only his Rolls-Royce, but at least one of his brother's cars. Joseph P. Schenck made his headquarters in Hollywood, but always kept a car at his brother's place for use when he came to New York. The last time I was there it was a LeBaron Packard Town Car.

Farther in along the shore of Great Neck was Saddle Rock, the estate of Miss Louise N. Grace, for whom we built a very attractive Lincoln Town Brougham, similar to the one we had showed at the Salon with the needlepoint upholstery. This entire property was made into a high-grade housing development later, but was still called Saddle Rock Estates.

Farther east along the North Shore of Long Island, then known as the Gold Coast, there was the Guggenheim family in Sands Point. We built a Hispano-Suiza sedan-limousine for Harry F. Guggenheim. I can recall seeing him get into it one day with Charles A. Lindbergh not long after the latter's epoch-making flight. It was around lunchtime at Madison Avenue and 57th Street, and no one paid any attention to the young man they had cheered wildly only a few days before.

Mr. and Mrs. William B. Leeds had a summer home at Oyster Bay, as did several others of our customers. Mrs. Leeds was Princess Xenia of Greece. While their Rolls-Royce Town Car was being built, I made several trips out to their estate to consult with the Princess on various details. Invariably I would take the train to Syosset, where their chauffeur would pick me up for the drive to their beautiful place right on the water.

Not far away were Arthur A. Ballantine, for whom we built a Minerva Sedan; J. G. Cavanagh with a Lincoln Sedan-limousine; Mrs. Robert L. Clarkson with a Pierce-Arrow Town Car; and Nelson Doubleday of the publishing firm, for whom we also built a Lincoln Sedan-limousine. On Center Island in Oyster Bay lived Sherman Fairchild. In addition to the Packard Sedan we built for him in 1924, he had several other cars with LeBaron bodies.

Harvey D. Gibson's Locomobile, E. F. Hutton's Rolls-Royce, and G. Maurice Heckscher's Hispano-Suiza Phaeton would also be seen in that area. It was Mr. Heckscher's chassis that I had helped to measure back in 1924, one of the first Boulogne models to reach this country.

C. F. Mathiessen of the chemical family kept his Isotta-Fraschini at Locust Valley. Perhaps he bought it because the Isotta showroom was practically next door to his town house in New York, where the Sherry-Netherland now stands. Others in Oyster Bay included Van Sanford Merle-Smith of Wall Street, for whom we designed a very racy Lincoln Phaeton, and Mrs. C. Oliver O'Donnell, whose Rolls-Royce Sedan-limousine was quite striking.

H. Nelson Slater is a descendant of Samuel Slater, who built the first textile mill in this country. Besides being an executive of J. P. Stevens & Company, he was also a director of the Chrysler Corporation for some time. He owned one of the first LeBaron bodies built on a Chrysler chassis, and Mrs. Slater later bought a duplicate of Mrs. Chrysler's Town Car.

Another resident of this area was Herbert Bayard Swope. A few months after his Lincoln Sedan-limousine was delivered, it was involved in an accident on the Saw Mill River Parkway. It was my impression that his chauffeur was not at fault, but a suit was filed against Mr. Swope, who immediately filed a counterclaim. I was subpoenaed as an expert witness to testify to the cost of repairs.

I never did get to testify, but I did sit through several days of the trial. Heywood Broun had been riding with the Swopes, and injured his nose when he was thrown against the partition window. While he was testifying, it became so apparent that the judge was a fan of Broun's that soon afterwards the case was settled out of court. Since I was an avid reader of Broun's column in the *New York World,* I had also been quite delighted to meet him.

Obviously all the people I have mentioned were quite well off. Some had made their money in Wall Street, among them Ben Smith, a partner in W. E. Hutton & Co., who made a fortune as well as a reputation as a shrewd trader by forecasting the 1929 crash. Earlier he had been a Duesenberg salesman when their first passenger cars were introduced in 1921. He was also instrumental in negotiating the sale of LeBaron to Briggs.

Smith had many friends on Wall Street, and brought some of them to LeBaron when they were in the market for a custom-built car. The first time he did so, he startled me by asking, just after I had quoted a price, "Now, how much would it cost me?" He conveyed the impression quite clearly that his friend was to be given special consideration. That time I was able to shave off a few hundred dollars, but any time thereafter that Ben Smith brought or sent one of his friends, I simply added $1,000 to the price I had in mind, and then knocked it off as a concession to Mr. Smith.

Since probably the most famous of all Wall Street figures of the period was J. P. Morgan, I regret to say that he was never a customer of LeBaron. His taste was extremely conservative and he leaned to Brewster, but often bought standard limousines of various makes which he felt were less conspicuous than custom-built ones.

However, many other financial titans were among our customers, including Joseph A. Bower of the United States Trust Company, for whom we replaced the Castagna body of an Isotta he had just bought. Another was Arthur de Cordova, whom I once visited at his apartment to discuss some detail. During our conversation he received a telephone call, and when he hung up said, "That call just paid for the car." Later I learned that it confirmed the sale of some R.C.A. shares at a profit of several times the cost of the car.

Others from Wall Street included Hugh Chisholm, Andre deCoppet, Francis V. duPont, H. K. Hochschild, W. F. Ladd, Hunter Marston, Malcolm Meacham, S. W. Straus, E. R. Tinker, Harrison Williams, and Edmund C. Lynch, whose brokerage firm grew to have the longest name in Wall Street history.

Many people prominent in banking not only in

1928 Rolls-Royce Phantom I All-Weather Cabriolet by LeBaron, built for Mr. Sam Katz of Paramount Pictures. Photograph from George Moffitt Collection.

New York but elsewhere in the country also ordered bodies from us. William A. M. Burden, Jr., then quite a young man, had us build two Mercedes for him. Frank A. Vanderlip was another client, with a Lincoln Town Car, and J. F. Talcott had a Lincoln Limousine specially designed. Mrs. Richard B. Mellon had us build her a Hispano-Suiza Town Car, and Mrs. William H. Crocker of San Francisco had several LeBaron Lincolns.

Mrs. H. E. Manville, mother of the oft-married Tommy, ordered a Mercedes Convertible Sedan. Frank H. Goodyear had a Rolls-Royce and a Pierce-Arrow that we built for him, and P. K. Wrigley had several Packards with LeBaron bodies.

Naturally a number of people in the automobile industry were also customers of ours for their personal cars. Edsel Ford had several Lincolns with LeBaron bodies, the first one the Phaeton with disappearing top illustrated herein. I do not recall that we ever built a car for Henry Ford, although he did for a time use one of the Model A Town Cars built by Briggs to LeBaron design. His personal car in New York was usually a Brunn Town Brougham.

I have already mentioned Walter Chrysler and several of the directors of his company for whom we built bodies. In addition, his two right-hand men, K. T. Keller and Fred Zeder, each had a specially-built Imperial Limousine.

Alvan Macaulay of Packard had one or more LeBaron-bodied Packards. When his son took over Packard styling in the thirties, several of the experimental designs he used as his personal cars were built at the LeBaron plant.

There seems to be a special aura about any car that was originally owned by some famous show business personality. I have mentioned a few for whom we built cars. Actually in the late twenties it was the studio heads and owners of theatre chains who had the money, rather than the actors. The Schenck brothers were among these, and we also built cars for Sam Katz of Paramount and Robert Kane of First National, both Rolls-Royces. All of these people spent considerable time in New York, so we could consult directly with them while designing their cars.

We had no direct representation in Hollywood, and while I have been told of various LeBaron bodies owned by movie stars there, many had been sold through local dealers. Most of them were not individually designed, but rather one of the various small series of bodies we built on different chassis. Phil Hill has a Packard LeBaron Convertible Roadster that originally belonged to Harold Lloyd, and there are a number of other Packards as well as Lincolns, Stutzes and Pierce-Arrows in this category.

While these were often completed, as far as paint and upholstery are concerned, to the purchaser's specifications, we rarely knew to whom the car would be delivered unless it was going to a customer of one of the East Coast dealers with whom we worked closely. Those going to the West Coast were normally handled through the chassis manufacturer, who passed the details on to us.

Another point that has been raised by various old-car buffs is whether we gave a discount to famous movie stars. The answer is a very definite no. In the first place, we did not have a sufficient margin of profit to do this, and in the second place our major clientele were not impressed by movie stars but only by fellow members of the "400."

52
Photography

DURING the late twenties and early thirties, the outstanding photographer of automobiles in New York was John Adams Davis. He had a studio on Eighth Avenue near Columbus Circle, but his favorite spot for photographing was one of the roadways in Central Park connecting the East and West Drives.

There was very little traffic there then, and a small knoll by the side of the road enabled him to set up his camera a couple of feet higher than the pavement. He had done considerable experimenting, and found that the best results were achieved by having the camera about at the level of the roof of the car. This made the car seem lower, since in looking at a photograph one tends to assume that the camera is at normal eye level.

Adams did the photography not only for LeBaron, but for Brewster, Fleetwood and other custom builders, as well as for the New York dealers of the cars we worked on. He kept all the negatives, carefully filed, and we would merely order prints from him as needed. Unfortunately, over the years Davis seems to have vanished completely, and his files with him. A few prints survive in various collections and some of them are the source of illustrations in this book.

Earlier, Nathan Lazarnick had done much of the photography for the New York segment of the industry, including the official pictures of the New York Salon. At his death, he left his entire collection of prints and negatives to the Automobile Manufacturers Association, which in turn gave most of it to the Automotive History Collection of the Detroit Public Library. Some of these pictures also grace these pages. Here, too, a good proportion of his pictures seem to have vanished over the years.

A few of the illustrations herein are photographs which I took myself, following the rules which I learned from John Adams Davis, the main points being:

1. Keep the camera high, about the level of the roof of the car. With most classics, this means about six feet above the ground where the car is standing. Use a box to stand on, if no convenient higher ground is available.

2. Study the background, and wherever possible keep it neutral. A few vertical lines such as tree trunks will make the car seem lower. Unfortunately, many nicely restored cars are available only at meets, where the background is apt to be a forest of other cars.

3. By all means, photograph any open car with the top down. This also applies to Convertible Roadsters. These models were designed to look their best that way. On the other hand, most Convertible Sedans and Convertible Victorias look their best with the tops up. The mechanisms were usually bulkier and the tops themselves well padded, so they do not fold as compactly as those of Phaetons.

Many pictures I have seen of various classic cars were obviously taken with the camera well below normal eye level. Presumably the intention was to show how huge and massive the car is. Our efforts as designers were aimed at making a huge and massive car look smaller and lower, and the suggestions on camera angles I have made are intended to enhance this effect.

The most attractive photographs I have seen were usually taken from a point just ahead of the car and, of course, somewhat to one side, so that the lines of the radiator and hood were emphasized. Where there is some special feature at the other end of the car, such as a boat-tail, a three-quarter rear view becomes desirable. One thing we tried to avoid was a straight side view from opposite the middle of the car. This sometimes leads to distortion of the design. Even with the camera twenty or thirty feet away, you can get some odd effects when the car itself is twenty feet long.

One more thought, since the purpose of photographing a classic is presumably to have the car stand out, is to be careful in selecting the color of the background. A dark car will stand out against a light background, and vice-versa. Davis had found that the trees and grass of Central Park were a good background for the darker, conservative colors most often used on custom bodies.

53
Restoration

IT has been suggested to me that I include some comments on restoration. Much can be gleaned from the chapters on construction, but I shall add a few more specific suggestions.

I do not consider myself an expert on mechanical restoration, although I have had some experience in keeping my own cars in condition over the years. During the depression, time was more available than money, and I did most of the work on the succession of second-hand Model As I owned in those days.

I have noticed at various "Swap Meets" and "Flea Markets" that there are considerable quantities of various parts available about the country. Anyone re-building a basket case should of course familiarize himself with the interchangeability of such parts.

During the twenties, the annual model change was not nearly so extensive, especially among expensive cars, and often the change was merely minor face-lifting. The bottom fell out of the market for such cars in October 1929, and quite a few makes continued with the same engines and many other parts for several years, until hopefully the supply of such parts was exhausted. Some did not last long enough to use them all up.

Also at this time, and in fact since about 1925, the production body building firms had largely consolidated as the result of a series of mergers. Fisher was the source of all General Motors bodies and at times some others, and Briggs, Murray, Wilson, and Hayes supplied nearly all other makes.

If you know who built the body on a production model, old issues of *Motor* or other trade magazines will often tell which other makes had bodies from the same source. Quite a few body parts will be found to be interchangeable between different makes of cars, as long as the bodies came from the same factory. During the early thirties, in fact, there were rumors that several medium-priced cars were made in part from Ford rejects. I don't know the truth of this rumor, but there are places where Ford parts will fit.

In 1949, Packard offered as an accessory translucent plastic panels which cemented to the upper part of the windshield, giving much the same effect as tinted glass. I got a pair of these to put on my 1949 Ford, knowing that both bodies had been built by Briggs with windshield frames made by the Motor Products Company. The Packard dealer from whom I bought them was most skeptical, and insisted that I could not return them if they did not fit. The fit was perfect.

Before the mid-twenties, such items as bumpers were not standard equipment. While some cars had factory-supplied options, many were fitted with such addenda by the dealers, and customers often had personal preferences. Even after that time, such items were not included on imported chassis, and were usually fitted by the body builder. The spring type bumper, such as those made by C.G., was the most popular. By modifying the brackets, these can often be adapted from one chassis to another.

Most imports and some domestic chassis were fitted with special fenders, but most domestic ones had standard fenders when fitted with a custom body. The rear fenders would be adapted to the particular body, using the standard type on which the least alteration would be needed. Often a fender from another body can be made to fit, bearing in mind that it is easier to cut away unwanted metal than to add some.

Special running boards, such as the much-admired wooden ones, can be hand-made much as they were originally. Cast aluminum step plates were often used in the early twenties, and at the time these could be purchased from several sources. Cars of that period might have either steps supplied as original equipment by the manufacturer, or similar ones installed by the dealer. Some had small splash shields, like miniature fenders, and these could be readily duplicated.

When side-mounted spares first became popular, they were sometimes used with bicycle-type front fenders and a splash shield at the front of the run-

U.S.E. Bumper, from their advertisement in 1925 New
York Salon Catalog.

ning board. These too could be easily duplicated, bearing in mind that aluminum can be worked more easily than steel.

Often special lights, shock absorbers and other accessories were specified by our customers. These were usually installed by the body builder since special brackets would have to be made, and we always had a blacksmith shop in our plant. Good blacksmiths are not easily found since horses went out of style, but there are a few left and many welding shops can do this kind of work.

Spotlights of various types were a popular accessory. Most headlamp manufacturers made them to match the style of their other lights. I have mentioned that the Perkins Lamp & Hardware Company in Brooklyn made our special spotlights, and they were still in business quite recently. Some of the marine spotlights in their catalog are quite similar to the automobile spotlights used in the twenties.

In discussing interior hardware, I have pointed out that much of this came from a few sources, so that parts might be interchanged between different custom bodies even though they were not built by the same firm. Some custom bodies built in series, such as those for Lincoln, used the same body hardware as their standard models.

Painting is of course an important part of any restoration. There are quite a few quality shops in various parts of the country. As we did some repainting at LeBaron for our customers, I can make a few suggestions on this.

Not many pre-1927 cars have their original varnish finish. Many of them were repainted while still in the hands of their original owners, and this was generally done in lacquer after 1927. I have seen a few with the original, or at least fairly ancient varnish, badly checked. Most of these are antiques rather than classics, and their present owners often seem to prefer this cracked finish. With enough time and money, such cars could still be refinished in varnish.

If an old varnish job is to be redone in lacquer, however, it is necessary to remove all the old paint— right down to the bare metal. The metal itself should then be gone over until it has almost a mirror finish. We found that in such repainting this was the only way to get a really good lacquer job. The metal had to be smoother than if it was to be painted with varnish.

The paint should then be built up just as we used to do it, with several coats of primer and a completely scratchless finish on the last one. After applying the desired number of coats of lacquer, with hand rubbing between about every third and fourth coat, the final one should be completely smooth, finished by buffing rather than sanding. Finally should be added a couple of coats of clear lacquer for the proper high gloss, very carefully applied and buffed lightly. Striping should be done before these last clear coats are applied. It can even be done successfully by an amateur with the striping tape made by the 3-M Company.

Quite a good range of colors is now available in lacquer. One thing to keep in mind is that colors used on custom bodies were generally conservative. Bright colors might be used for trim or striping, but rarely for an entire car. Some of the illustrations herein reproduce color schemes that we actually used.

One of our favorites was all black with vermillion wheels and silver striping, sometimes edged with the same vermillion. Others we liked were a soft grey-green with trim in Ditzler's Desert Sand. This latter color was very close to that of Burbank top material and we often used it for trim and striping. We also used the Desert Sand with a rich maroon in the same manner.

I mention this since I have seen a number of classics, especially open ones, painted a fairly bright red. Offhand, I cannot recall that we ever painted a car solid red, or even red with black moldings. We did sometimes suggest yellow and black, a combination we did admire. Of course, our customers were the ones who had the final decision, and some of them did come up with combinations that we did not really approve of. Usually we were able to convince them that something less shocking would be preferable.

A fact that we discovered quite early was that a light superstructure with a darker lower body made the car look lower, and we used this trick quite often. For the same reason, we invariably painted the sill and wheelhouse moldings in the same color as the fenders.

3-M Company's Striping Tape. Photograph courtesy of 3-M Company.

54
Interior Restoration

AS for the interiors, they might be as flamboyant as the exteriors were conservative. They were considered to be as private as the owner's bedrooms. Mostly, the flamboyance was in paneling and other decoration. As I have said, the upholstery materials themselves were usually neutral.

Broadcloth, Bedford Cord and leather were the most widely used, and reasonable facsimiles of these are available today. Radel supplied much of our upholstery leather, and they are still in business as mentioned in Bob Turnquist's *The Packard Story.* Much imagination went into devising combinations of materials, even to combining fabric and leather in various proportions in the upholstering.

In most cases I have seen, the original seat springs are still usable. Padding, often horsehair, might have deteriorated but can easily be replaced. Foam rubber makes a good substitute, but padding like the original can be supplied by any good upholstery shop. Down-filled loose pillows could be duplicated, but I do not know anyone today using shaped containers of the type we developed at LeBaron. Here again foam rubber might be a good replacement.

Often where Bedford Cord was used for seats, a matching broadcloth was used for the headlining. A reasonably close match was generally used, and this should not be an insurmountable problem. If it was not feasible, a slightly lighter shade was used for headlining, never darker.

If marquetry paneling was originally fitted, it is likely to be still nearly intact, and could be restored by the normal methods known to any expert on antique furniture.

A good furniture man could even replace missing bits of inlay. In the simpler interiors, solid walnut or mahogany was used for moldings and panels, and it should be feasible to replace this where necessary with new wood of the same type.

Probably one of the greatest problems lies in locating suitable replacements for missing bits of interior hardware. For the really ambitious, it would be possible to have new ones cast, using one remaining piece as a pattern. However, as I have mentioned, there are many items here which are interchangeable among different bodies.

Many body parts, such as windshield stanchions, landau joints, etc., were manganese bronze castings. If one needs to be replaced but its mate is in good condition, a good pattern maker can use this as a guide for its mirror image. A firm making custom marine hardware should be able to handle this work. Of course, here too there is the possibility of finding a suitable part from another body. Except where the body was one of a series, this is somewhat like finding a needle in a haystack.

One firm from whom we bought a variety of items is still in business. The Abeles-Lewit Company are wholesalers of body supplies. While I doubt that they have duplicates of items they sold thirty or forty years ago, they might be able to suggest suitable replacements. Window regulators, for instance, have not changed much in basic design, although the more exotic types like the Rawlings regulator are no longer available.

Carpeting was usually a regular automotive type; much of it came from Magee, who are still in business. Sometimes we used a household-type velvet broadloom to get the color we wanted, or even had carpet dyed to the shade needed.

Most custom bodies were fitted with a robe-rail or robe-cord. Laprobes were not standard equipment, but were often ordered as an accessory. The usual type was of the upholstery fabric on one side and a deep-piled plush on the back, with the main fabric folded back to form a two- or three-inch border around the plush. Sometimes they were double-faced, with the upholstery material on both sides, and these were often interlined. Generally they were monogrammed, with the owner's initials cut from a contrasting color broadcloth and appliquéd.

Fur was sometimes used as a lining, and the fashions in this changed with the years. If milady had just bought a new sealskin coat, she might order a matching robe. Often this would be made up by her furrier. Some department stores, notably Altman's, also did quite a business on making up robes to order. If you find the remains of a moth-eaten robe in your car, it should be no great problem to have a new one made following the same style.

Loose pillows were another frequent accessory, usually 14 to 16 inches square, and down-filled. Mostly these were covered in the same fabric used on the seats. Many had silk cords attached which could be slipped over small hooks behind the top of the seat-back. These pillows were also often monogrammed. If the hooks are there, it would be appropriate to have similar pillows made up.

I have noticed that auxiliary seats have sometimes vanished from a body over the years. If they were the forward-facing type, these did not vary much from one body-builder to another in their basic structure. Those from a recent Fleetwood Cadillac would be similar and could possibly be adapted.

On the other hand, the opera type, which was very popular during the classic period, has virtually gone out of use. Since the side-facing seat was usually left exposed, it would be possible to mount one from another body, if it can be located. On the other hand, the jump seat often folded flush into the partition, but even here it would be fairly simple to build a new one or adapt one from another body.

Since front seats were not usually adjustable in custom bodies, especially those intended to be chauffeur-driven, I would suggest that this point be given careful attention in reupholstering. More or less padding can be used to get the seating position most comfortable for the person usually driving the car. The original seat was probably built to suit the chauffeur of the moment, and they did come in a variety of sizes. Sometimes we even had to reupholster the front seat when for some reason a new chauffeur was hired. Fortunately, in those days, the leading families often kept the same chauffeur for years.

While working on the interior, it would be a good idea to check the body number. Most custom builders stamped this into the right front seat frame or the support for the right front toeboard, sometimes both. It is questionable whether records exist against which this could be checked, but I do have a list of some Le-Baron body numbers from 1926 to mid-1927, and another set running from late 1928 into 1929.

Finally we come to the question of accessories, most of which were readily removable and quite pos-

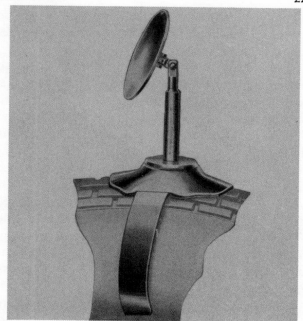

See-Rite spare-tire mounted rear-view mirror, from their advertisement in 1927 Salon Catalog.

sibly have disappeared. Vanity cases are in this category, but as mentioned many of these came from the same two sources, MacFarland or Linden, and if a proper color can be found would be easily interchangeable.

On individual bodies, we sometimes made up special instrument panels of wood to match the interior trim. They were still called dashboards then. Often there were special instruments fitted to the taste of the purchaser. Frequently these came from Jaeger, although Waltham was another highly regarded source. Usually these instruments were of better quality than the standard equipment of the chassis, and sometimes extra instruments were added.

With side-mounted spares, it was usual to have rear view mirrors on them. Most of these came from See-Rite and were strapped to the spare wheels. The same types were used on both custom and production models, but on custom bodies mirrors on both sides were general, more for balance of design than for practical reasons.

Special radiator ornaments were often supplied. The ones from Lalique were particularly attractive, and as I have mentioned one or two patterns are still available from France. Rarely we had special ornaments cast in bronze to blend with the design or to suit some idiosyncrasy of the purchaser. These would be quite expensive to duplicate. A few people had their own made up—perhaps a statue of a horse or dog of which they were particularly fond—and these were often transferred from car to car as new ones were purchased.

Trunks were usually made up specially for each custom body, where they were used. In the twenties, these were generally leather-covered and carried matching fitted luggage. Two or three suitcases and a hatbox were normal. There are still luggage makers who can do this type of work, for a price. It was normal to cover the trunk with a dust cover to match the top.

By 1930, we had begun to use metal-covered trunks to blend with the design of the body and painted the same color. These usually had moldings around the edges, and these should be painted the same color as the moldings on the bodies. At least, that was our usual practice.

Since many American chassis came with standard folding trunk racks when side-mounted spares were used, stock trunks were available to fit these racks and were sometimes used on custom bodied cars.

Air conditioning and defrosters were unknown, and it was sometimes thought desirable to mount a small fan at one side of the windshield to blow across it and keep it clear. These were run off the car battery, and I have seen similar small fans recently. If none can be found, it should not be difficult to replace the motor in an old one.

I know that windshield wings on open cars are highly thought of today. We considered them suitable for a Kissel or an Auburn, but not generally for a Lincoln or a Pierce-Arrow with a custom body. Sometimes they were added later in a car's career.

On the other hand, tonneau windshields were frequently used. LeBaron designed a number of double-cowl Phaetons. The windshields on these rear cowls were always of the folding type, and the cowl itself carefully counterbalanced to make it easy to raise and lower. Around 1928, we and some others experimented with rear windshields operated by regulators.

The J-H Tonneau Windshield was a regularly available accessory often fitted where a double-cowl was not wanted. It had hinged side-wings, and the entire windshield could be folded down out of sight. Some styles had folding arms so they could be pulled back close to the rear passengers. The same types were used on custom and production bodies, and at most the brackets would need to be altered to transfer them from one body to another.

I have seen a few open cars of the classic period on which the tops are nonexistent. One such is the Le-Baron Chrysler Phaeton restored by Bob Gottlieb, which seems to have given rise to the rumor that the car was so designed, since this particular one has been widely photographed. This is definitely not true since no Phaeton was built in the 1920s or later without some form of folding top. Any custom-built one had a carefully fitted top boot to match. On the other hand, many speedster type roadsters built before 1921 did not have tops, the assumption being that they simply would not be driven in inclement weather.

Finally, I shall repeat my comment that just about anything might be authentic in a custom body. The people who purchased them were highly individualistic, and while most of them had good taste, there were some with a definite leaning toward the unconventional. Some of the more unusual items I have seen recently were, however, obviously added by someone other than the original owner. Where specific information is lacking, I would suggest that the guidelines of good conservative taste be followed during restoration.

55
Finis

SEVERAL times I have been asked why I did not continue my career as an automobile designer. I did make some unsuccessful attempts to return to the field, but I could never quite picture myself as a member of a staff whose duties would be confined to, say, drawing all possible variations on the styling of a hubcap. Essentially, in recent years, no individual has designed a whole car, merely a section of it.

Had I stayed in Detroit when my services were terminated by LeBaron at the end of 1931, I should probably have wound up on one of these staffs. However, at the time I had no interest in remaining in Detroit. My family lived on Long Island, and the young lady I would marry as soon as I could afford it was in New York.

When I returned home, I found that Harvey H'Lavac, who had been assistant to George Robertson at the eastern Lincoln headquarters in New York, had set himself up as a Ford dealer a few miles from my home. I went to work for him as a salesman and continued for several years. In the early thirties, there was not much money to be made in the automobile business at any level, and I spent part of my time seeking other employment.

Soon I became associated with a textile firm—Parker, Wilder & Company—where I worked myself up into an executive position. I still toyed with designs in my spare time, but made no strenuous effort to return to this career.

At one point in 1936, I did send some sketches to General Motors with an application for employment in their Art & Color Section. The sketches were returned with a letter stating my application was not accepted. When some of the ideas in my designs appeared on Cadillacs a couple of years later, I was rather disillusioned about this method of approach.

Late in 1944, I heard that Tom Hibbard, who had been running a war production plant for Ford, had returned to Detroit to set up the nucleus of a styling section, to be ready for postwar operation. I made a trip to Detroit sometime in 1945, and he suggested that I submit some sketches and a resume. At the time, my duties in New York were quite strenuous, as we were working almost entirely for the Navy. I did not have time to make up new sketches, and merely submitted those I had sent to General Motors in 1936, and a few even earlier ones. They did not impress Hibbard's superiors.

I realized something new and different was needed, and set to work—whenever I could find time—on more advanced ideas. I felt that a color rendering would be more impressive, but was not satisfied with the first ones I made. By the time I had one I considered to be of suitable quality, it was already early 1948.

I sent my new attempts to Tom Hibbard with a letter, and was somewhat surprised to receive, a few weeks later, a form letter of the type Ford would send to anyone submitting an unsolicited idea. I concluded that their own styling was well along, and probably close to the ideas I had submitted. I immediately placed an order for one of the new Fords, for delivery when available. It turned out I had guessed right, and I was quite pleased with the appearance of my new car. At the time, I did not know that George Walker and his independent design firm had been engaged to style the new Ford, nor that Hibbard and his associates were about to leave the company to make room for younger blood.

When Walter Briggs died, and arrangements were being made to dispose of most of his holdings, the entire body business was sold to the Chrysler Corporation. I wrote to the Controller of Briggs, whom I had known quite well when I was with LeBaron, to inquire about the disposition of the original LeBaron corporation. I was told this had been dissolved some years earlier.

Feeling that we had some claim to the name, Stickney and I set up a new New York corporation under the old name, with the intention of reengaging in the design and building of custom bodies. There seemed to be some demand for such a facility at the time, around 1952. We were a bit discouraged when Alan Buchanan told us he had not had much success in selling custom-bodied Lincolns, as mentioned in an earlier chapter. Costs had risen too much to make it possible to compete with European body builders.

The crowning blow, however, came when we sent out some announcements to a few old customers and the automobile manufacturers. We got an immediate reply from Chrysler's attorneys that they would file suit if we did not discontinue use of the name LeBaron. It seems that Briggs had been issued a trademark registration on the name in the 1930s, and this trademark was among the assets Chrysler bought.

So I continued until recently with my business as a manufacturer's representative in the knitting field, which I had started in the early fifties. While working on this manuscript, I retired from that to resume the education I interrupted back in 1925 to work for LeBaron. At the time of this writing I am in my second year of college, as the oldest sophomore at the State University of New York at Stony Brook.

In my spare time, I conduct an extensive correspondence with the owners of cars I had a hand in. I also explain to all who ask why I have not reentered the custom body business. Of course, if anyone wishes to put up the capital, say a million or so, with no hope of any return, I should be glad to run the business for them.

Index